REGIMES OF IGNORANCE

Methodology and History in Anthropology

General Editors: David Parkin, Fellow of All Souls College, University of Oxford
David Gellner, Fellow of All Souls College, University of Oxford

Just as anthropology has had a significant influence on many other disciplines in recent years, so too have its methods been challenged by new intellectual and technical developments. This series is designed to offer a forum for debate on the interrelationship between anthropology and other academic fields but also on the challenge to anthropological methods of new intellectual and technological developments, and the role of anthropological thought in a general history of concepts.

For a full series listing, please see end matter.

REGIMES OF IGNORANCE

Anthropological Perspectives on
the Production and Reproduction
of Non-Knowledge

Edited by
Roy Dilley and Thomas G. Kirsch

berghahn
NEW YORK · OXFORD
www.berghahnbooks.com

First published in 2015 by
Berghahn Books
www.berghahnbooks.com

© 2015, 2017 Roy Dilley and Thomas G. Kirsch
First paperback edition published in 2017

Library of Congress Cataloging-in-Publication Data
Regimes of ignorance: anthropological perspectives on the
production and reproduction of non-knowledge / edited by Roy Dilley
and Thomas G. Kirsch.
pages cm. -- (Methodology and history in anthropology; 29)
Includes bibliographical references and index.
ISBN 978-1-78238-838-8 (hardback) – ISBN 978-1-78533-746-8
(paperback) – ISBN 978-1-78238-839-5 (ebook)
1. Ethnology--Philosophy. 2. Ignorance (Theory of knowledge)-
-Social aspects. 3. Ethnopsychology. I. Dilley, Roy, 1954- II. Kirsch,
Thomas G.
GN345.R44 2015
301.01--dc23

2015002052

British Library Cataloguing in Publication Data
A catalogue record for this book is available from the British Library

ISBN 978-1-78238-838-8 (hardback)
ISBN 978-1-78533-746-8 (paperback)
ISBN 978-1-78238-839-5 (ebook)

CONTENTS

REGIMES OF IGNORANCE

AN INTRODUCTION

Thomas G. Kirsch and Roy Dilley

The chapters that appear in this volume are based on a set of com-
missioned essays that were initially written by, and then discussed
among, a group of invited scholars. A number of those scholars met
at the Institute for Advanced Studies at the University of Konstanz
in August 2012 to begin a conversation about how to tackle from
an anthropological perspective the production and reproduction of
non-knowledge, glossed as ignorance.[1] A series of areas were outlined
for intellectual reflection, and contributors to this volume were invited
to approach the problem of ignorance from at least two points of view.
They were asked to consider first how to present ethnographic examples of social contexts in which ignorance (both actors' and analysts')
features as a significant element. The second consideration was how to
provide material that would lend itself to theoretical elaboration about
the significance of ignorance within a broader field of social analysis.
From this conversation, the concept of ignorance came to stand as
a portmanteau term that embraced various forms of not-knowing
(intentional and unintentional), unknowing and secrecy. These types
of concern are approached from the perspective of how they each
constitute an absence, an epistemological gap, a lacuna, the presence
of which has social consequences.

The problem of ignorance addresses as much the subject of our
own conceptions of non-knowledge as it does any attempt to try to
plot the variety of uses and abuses of ignorance in the cultural institutions, social relations and political dynamics among other peoples
(see also Dilley 2010). In this volume, we wish to go beyond a limited 'ethnographic' treatment of ignorance as a series of case studies
and instead tackle questions about the production and reproduction

of ignorance within specific socio-cultural regimes of non-knowledge and power. Part of the aim of this Introduction is, therefore, to provide some background to the constructions of ignorance we encounter in our analyses. It also attempts to plot out a brief genealogy of ignorance that might provide us with the grounds for defining ignorance as being part of a regime – that is, a constellation of discursive practices and power relations giving rise to epistemological gaps and forms of un-knowing that have generative social effects and consequences.

Looking out on Ignorance

To conceptualize the reproduction of non-knowledge requires a consideration of the ontological status attributed to 'non-knowledge' in specific socio-cultural settings. This is not to say that this Introduction seeks to provide an exhaustive classification of the diverse manifestations of non-knowledge in all social worlds we know of, past and present, distant and near. They are simply too numerous. Instead, reflecting on empirical examples of how non-knowledge forms part and parcel of historically situated 'social ontologies' (Searle 1995, 2010) can help to underline a main proposition of this volume, namely that non-knowledge, even if it is defined in negative terms, should be treated not as a residual category but as though it has a social life.

For the latter case, take the example of a canonical text by the Bahá'í Faith, which was founded in the nineteenth century by the Persian prophet Bahá'u'lláh and nowadays has an estimated membership of five to six million worldwide. This scripture states:

> Evil does not exist. Death is only the lack of life; therefore death does not exist. Darkness is only the lack of light. Evil is only the lack of good. *Ignorance is only the lack of knowledge.* Poverty is the lack of wealth. Misleading is the lack of guidance. ... All these things are non-existent. (Holley 1923: 440; italics added)

In terms of its history and theology, the Bahá'í Faith draws inspiration from Buddhism, Christianity, Islam and other religious traditions and claims to fulfil the end-time promises of previous sacred scriptures. At the same time, as is evident in the quotation above, some teachings of the Bahá'í Faith differ from ontological assumptions in previous scriptures. For example, Bahá'ís do not believe that evil in the form of a demonic entity exists. In other words, from their perspective, 'the devil' has neither agency nor ontological meaning. This might be compared to Christianity, whose history is replete with attempts to counter what are felt to be real effects of the malicious workings of the non-human actant called Satan. And the Bahá'í statement referred to above, which says that 'ignorance is only the lack of knowledge', denies 'non-knowledge' an existence in its own right.

Contrast this with another form of non-knowledge that is commonly not only said to exist but also, depending on the perspective, either treasured or feared – the secret. Generally speaking, the notion of 'the secret' describes the unequal distribution of knowledge in a social field, with some people sharing a certain stock of knowledge and others being ignorant of its contents. At the same time, this ignorance of the contents of a secret is usually more than just a residual category of 'knowledge' and is instead something that actively contributes to the social construction of reality, for example in the form of conspiracy theories. The social construction of reality through secrecy can, moreover, take two different forms. On the one hand, as Beryl Bellman has pointed out, secrecy follows certain linguistic conventions, for example when certain acts of communication become labelled as 'secrets', meaning that the 'informant who is telling a secret either directly or tacitly makes the claim that the information he or she speaks is not to be spoken' (Bellman 1981: 10). On the other hand, secrecy contributes to the social construction of reality when those who are not participating in a given stock of secret knowledge communicate among themselves about other actors who have secrets, of whose contents the non-participants are ignorant (see also Kirsch, this volume). The conspiracy theories mentioned above are thus a good example of an ontology of non-knowledge that attributes ignorance a catalytic role in social life.

However, examples are also found of situations where non-knowledge is not just felt to be a troublesome thorn in the flesh but considered an agent in its own right that actively works against the strategies of other social actors. In Mexico there is a board game, very similar to the English-speaking world's Trivial Pursuit, in which players have to answer questions on history, geography, politics, sport and so on. Called *Maratón* (Marathon), the game pits players one against the other; but the unusual feature of the game is that it also pits them against 'Ignorance'. Every time a player gives a wrong answer, Ignorance moves forward in the race. Players are thus competing individually against each other, but also collectively against the progress of Ignorance. An online version of the game was available that carried the strap-line 'defeat ignorance in cyberspace'.[2]

The role of ignorance in this game resonates with a recurring image of ignorance in European art and literature. For example, Andrea Mantegna's Renaissance painting in the British Museum

entitled the 'Allegory of the Fall of Ignorant Humanity' (also known
as the 'Allegory of Vice and Virtue') illustrates the idea of the hold of
Ignorance over humanity. Ignorance is represented by the figure of a
nude woman without eyes, and she is led by Error, a man with ass's
ears, towards the edge of a pit. He is encouraged in this by a satyr,
a half-man/half-goat with bat's wings and bird's feet, playing a pipe,
and is accompanied by a man with a sack over his head, leading a dog.
Here ignorance is again reified, but this time represented as a being in
female form.

In this example and that of the board game *Maratón*, knowledge
and ignorance are thrown together in antagonistic relationships: in a
battle over the fate of humanity or in competition with players to win
a board-game marathon. This speaks of a very particular conception
of the relationship between knowledge and ignorance: knowledge has
the potential to eradicate ignorance in the progress of humankind,
who will be all the better for the triumph.

Another example of the idea of a strained relationship between
knowledge and ignorance is provided by Plato's well-known allegory
of the cave, in which prisoners are chained since childhood, condemned to see only the reflected shadows on the cave wall. This invokes the image of a world unknown directly to those set in chains.
Ignorance and knowledge are here located in different spatial positions, quite separate from each other, and each one is exclusive to one
sort of being or another. The mutual relationship between knowing
and not-knowing is again antagonistic, and it defines opposed categories of living and being: either those who know and live in the truth or
those who lack a full knowledge of the world and live in the shadows.

In terms of the ontologies of non-knowledge expressed in them,
the latter examples have in common, first, that they set ignorance and
knowledge in a mutually antagonistic relationship, and second, that
they tend to reify ignorance as a thing or as a being. In combination,
this type of perspective runs deep through the way we think about
knowing and not-knowing; it is a powerful trope that underlies areas as diverse as educational policy, systems of restorative justice, the
spread of global democracy or the onward march of science.

The contributors to the present volume are aware of the challenges
involved in the attempt to steer clear of the conventions and preconceptions implied in these sorts of perspective. They seek to develop
an analytical angle on ignorance that takes account of the fact that
'non-knowledge' is thought and experienced by people throughout
the world to be more than just a residual category of 'knowledge' but
something that has palpable effects in the world. For instance, in the

English-speaking world, proverbial sayings have it that ignorance is 'bliss' and 'the mother of superstition'. At the same time, while acknowledging the positivity of non-knowledge, an appraisal of the significance of ignorance within the broader field of social analysis also needs to avoid its reification. As will be elaborated in the closing paragraphs of this Introduction, a balance between these notions can conceptually be reached by showing consideration for the fact that every 'regime of knowledge' simultaneously is a 'regime of non-knowledge' that is socially produced and reproduced through time.

Studying Ignorance

Many years ago Mark Hobart pointed to the 'growth of ignorance'. It would seem that in the intervening years since the publication of Hobart's edited collection in 1993, ignorance has burgeoned; there is simply a lot of it about nowadays. But the shape of the configuration of knowledge and ignorance has started to shift too. A concern with ignorance and not-knowing has been the subject of numerous seemingly unconnected enquiries by researchers from diverse fields including not only anthropology but also sociology, political science, history of science and information technology studies, among others.[3] By pushing at the boundaries of our knowledge of knowledge, researchers have increasingly become aware of the flipside to ways of knowing: the place of ignorance, not-knowing and nescience in their own academic disciplines and in their daily social life. Specifically, anthropologists, in their intense desire to discover knowledge about the native Other, have increasingly become aware of how often they have overlooked informants' own accounts of ignorance: those points where the people themselves recognize the limits of local knowledge.[4] These concerns are developed and addressed in this volume.

Moreover, it has lately become much harder to overlook the fact that a form of ignorance sits at the very core of anthropological method. It is built into the very method of social anthropological fieldwork, whereby an anthropologist goes to the field in order to learn and perfect skills in another language and to adopt the habits, dispositions and appropriate bodily responses that make up what passes as a competent cultural performance. Fieldwork allows the anthropologist to turn his or her ignorance into a positive strategy for learning, assimilation and insight; it allows for culturally specific knowledge to fill the gaps left by broad-brush anthropological training in the academy. Indeed, we suspend the seeming certainty of our own knowing (which comes through training) when we enter the field, and our ignorance opens up for us areas for comparative reflection and contemplation. Ignorance is productive, therefore, in highlighting the nature of the taken-for-granted worlds in which others (including ourselves) live, and to which we adapt over the course of our fieldwork. Indeed, our conscious recognition of other people's taken-for-granted understandings of the world opens up for us another dimension of ignorance within anthropological methodologies.

The recent increase in scholarly attention given to questions of ignorance, unknowing and non-knowledge is striking. What might be the reasons for this recent efflorescence in the topic? Why has ignorance become a topic of research at this particular historical juncture? While the U.S. Secretary of Defence Donald Rumsfeld's observations in 2002 on 'known knowns', 'known unknowns' etc, in answer to a question about the relationship between the Iraqi regime and weapons of mass destruction, may have brought the issue of non-knowledge to the forefront of popular consciousness, it is unlikely that his contribution was anything more than an amusing distraction from an otherwise serious debate of critical importance on the situation in the Middle East.

More importantly perhaps is the idea that there is a general crisis of confidence in contemporary society about what knowledge is, what it is for and what its impact on others might be. The debate going on at the heart of education in the U.K. and elsewhere at present is stimulated by the policies of governments aimed at making teaching and research more accountable, more relevant to tax payers and the labour market. These concerns act as triggers of epistemological doubt, and they raise our awareness of how not only knowledge, but also ignorance, is produced.

In addition, that we live in an age of information, in a so-called 'knowledge economy', has no doubt also stimulated a critique of the worst excesses and the contradictory tensions of our current situation. Democratic access to information, so the story goes, will help eradicate ignorance, the scourge of oppressive political regimes and of faulty market mechanisms in economies across the globe. As Christos Lynteris has argued, however, 'the dominant doctrine of information capitalism is that everyone can know everything, that ignorance is a thing of the past, and that this is a desirable state of equality and freedom' (personal communication). Our sense of scepticism, however, is triggered by the alternative forms of knowledge and practices of learning that are being nurtured by politicians and educationalists, by governmental controls on the flow of information and debates about access to state knowledge; furthermore, our sense of unease is heightened by the way in which lives can be manipulated through information technologies and by the sheer superabundance of things to know. All these considerations render us critical about what is being left out, what is absent – namely, non-knowledge and ignorance.

This is not the first time that ignorance has caught the imagination – if only temporarily – of scholars, who appear to be both attracted by the topic and then equally prone to ignore it after a while. It is a subject that pops its head above the academic parapet from time to time, only to disappear again for long periods. The term 'agnoiology', the 'theory of ignorance', was first coined in the nineteenth century by the philosopher James Ferrier (1854), who also proposed the concept of 'epistemology'. His project came to nought, and it no doubt died a quick death on the swords of those philosophers who would have pointed out that the production of knowledge of ignorance dissolves the object of study at the outset.

There is, therefore, a paradox in the idea of examining ignorance in the hope of coming to know it. Linsey McGoey (2012b: 3) echoes this view: 'Ironically, once ignorance is identified, it loses its own definition'. Also, once ignorance is claimed to have a degree of concreteness, once it is reified, then its very conception is undermined. This paradox should not necessarily mean that once grasped, ignorance loses its significance, potentiality or positivity. But it does present the task of determining how to represent a field of ignorance and how to capture the positivity of ignorance. The following excursion into the poetics and politics of anonymization can provide some insights into this issue.

Representing (Non-)Knowledge: An Excursion into the Ethics of Ethnography

Writing about the distinction between 'risk' and 'danger', Niklas Luhmann once asked: 'Is the common shared assumption still justified that more communication, more reflection, more knowledge, more learning, more participation – that more of all of this would have positive, or at least no negative, impact?' (Luhmann 1991: 90; cited in Japp 2000: 235). Reading present-day primers on ethnographic methods and ethics in anthropology, one gets the impression that this question would nowadays be answered in the positive by most anthropologists. This stands in contrast to earlier generations of ethnographers who entered into long conversations with 'native interlocutors' about the latter's specific ways of knowing, yet mostly left their interlocutors in a state of ignorance when it came to communicating the possible risks these conversations could have for them once they were made public.

Partly due to the geopolitical transformations following political independence of former colonies in the global South, this situation started to change in the 1960s. Consequently, the unequal structural relationship between 'research subject' and 'research object' was problematized and checked for potentially adverse ethical and political implications. Since then, anthropologists have been called not only to take responsibility for the poetics and politics of ethnographic representation (Clifford and Marcus 1986) but also to be accountable to people in their research sites as well as to the wider public in their respective countries of origin (see, for example, Strathern 2000). On the one hand, this process brought about a multiplication of the audiences with which anthropologists were expected to engage actively. On the other hand, it influenced what and how ethnographers communicated in fieldwork encounters. Most importantly for this volume on the topic of ignorance, the researcher now has to procure people's 'informed consent' (Fluehr-Lobban 2003; Kelly 2003) which, in turn, entails the expectation that a negotiated balance will be achieved within a knowledge/'ignorance economy' of research.[5]

For example, the Committee on Ethics of the American Anthropological Association (AAA) in 2010 listed ten characteristics of how valid and informed consent can be attained. Included in the list were the following: to 'engage in an ongoing and dynamic discussion with collaborators ... about the nature of study participation, its risks and potential benefits' and to 'demonstrate, in the appropriate language, all research equipment and documentation techniques prior to obtaining consent so that research collaborators, or participants, may be said to be adequately informed about the research process' (Clark and Kingsolver 2010). Anthropologists are here called to fend off potentially adverse effects of scientific knowledge production by selectively reversing the flow of knowledge between themselves and (nescient) people in their fieldsites.

Yet, most notably, one of the items listed in the AAA *Briefing Paper on Informed Consent* is also indicative of the difficulties anthropologists face when trying to draw a conceptual boundary between knowledge production and ignorance production: 'Inform potential subjects of the anonymity, confidentiality, and security measures taken for all types of study data, including digitised, visual, and material data' (ibid.). Rendering anonymous the names of persons, institutions and places of one's fieldsite certainly represents one of the most common and commonsensical strategies in protecting the interests of the persons being studied. Yet, we suggest that the anonymization of ethnographic data produces a peculiar ambiguity within the heart of the anthropological method. While imparting knowledge about a particular 'epistemic object' (Knorr Cetina 2001), the method casts a veil at the same time over basic aspects of the identity of this object, thus amalgamating the production of knowledge with an intended production of ignorance.

Vincent Crapanzano's controversial book *Waiting: The Whites of South Africa*, published in 1985, may be taken as an example. In the acknowledgements of this book, Crapanzano writes: 'There are a great many people in the United States, Europe and South Africa whom I should like to thank. To protect the identity of the people with whom I worked in South Africa, I have chosen not to name them' (Crapanzano 1985: ix).[6] For the most part, the book consists of descriptions of encounters between the ethnographer and 'white' South Africans, in which the latter give fine-grained and self-reflexive accounts of their biographies and of how they position themselves in the wider context of apartheid South Africa. There is a lot one can learn from these descriptions, which are among the first of their kind, making not 'black' but 'white' South Africans the topic of ethnographic research (for an overview, see Niehaus 2013). At the same time, however, the reader of this book is – apart from a rough indication of the region – deliberately kept ignorant with regard to the question of the particular location of the study.

Another, even more extreme example is Richard Rottenburg's *Far-Fetched Facts: A Parable of Development Aid*, which states in the prologue that 'the case depicted in this book has been fictionalized' (Rottenburg 2009: xvii) due to the sensitive political and moral issues involved and in order 'to direct attention away from the strengths and weaknesses of specific real actors and toward the significance of general structural principles and the contingencies of the mundane practices of the development world' (ibid.). Presenting his book as an example of experimental ethnographic writing on the basis of field research and professional engagement in development aid in 'Ruretania', a fictional country in sub-Saharan Africa, Rottenburg professes that 'characters in the present text have been given fictional names and are literally figures in a play. They do not depict any real, existing people but are constructed from the cumulative characteristics originally belonging to the various people I met during my tenure in the field of development cooperation' (ibid.).

We are not simply concerned here with the questions of the moral justification or political adequacy of anonymizing ethnographic data to such an extreme extent. Instead, what these two examples make clear is that anonymization introduces an ambiguous epistemic logic to ethnographic representation in which readers are simultaneously equipped with a specific type and stock of knowledge (e.g., the fact that something was done by social actors) and left in the dark or ignorant as concerns other types and stocks of knowledge (e.g., who in particular did it).

When seen in the wider semantic context of 'knowledge' and 'ignorance', anonymized ethnographic representations of this kind are neither 'lack of knowledge' nor 'false knowledge' nor an expression of ignorance in the sense of Nicholas Rescher's definition of it as the 'inability to answer meaningful questions in a way that manages to convince people' (Rescher 2009: 2). Instead, anonymization is a deliberate and conventionalized hybridization of abstracted knowledge and ignorance about the particular details of any individual case study. As such, it is an apt – though in part counterintuitive – example not only of the positivity of ignorance, mentioned above, but also of how a specific (in this case: well-meaning) scientific regime of ignorance becomes established and put into effect.

The Shifting Sands of Anthropological Nescience

When seen from the perspective of the history of science, cultural and social anthropology has long been driven by an encyclopaedic desire to identify, document, classify and archive to the greatest possible extent what was previously unknown. This desire is shared with other scientific disciplines with historical roots in the Enlightenment. Confining themselves to the 'savage slot' (Trouillot 1991), anthropologists up to the mid-twentieth century drew up a mythological charter to shed scientific light on what they acknowledged to be areas of ignorance, thus 'supplanting that ignorance with knowledge' (Merton 1951: 417). In turn, associating 'culture' with stocks of knowledge of given groups of people who were assumed to live in spatially separated and bounded territories (Ferguson and Gupta 1997), the world was imagined as a knowledge map with a gradually shrinking number of blanks to be filled in through field research. Thus, by continuously expanding the anthropological horizon and systematically compartmentalizing the knowledge gained this way, such as in the form of the Human Areas Relation Files,[7] there was a sense in which, at that time and for those who believed in this accumulative logic of scientific progress, the end of anthropological nescience was attainable – at least in principle.

In the decades that followed, a well-rehearsed argument was formulated claiming that this epistemological self-confidence was only possible on the grounds of questionable premises concerning the nature of society, such as 'the overemphasis on consensuality as the basis for orderly social interaction' (Smithson 1985: 152). These premises led some anthropologists 'to define culture solely in terms of shared cognitive orientations and symbol systems' (ibid.) and to stress societal equilibrium. By the 1960s (with notable precursors such as Max Gluckman's 'Analysis of a Social Situation in Modern Zululand' (1940)) new theoretical developments in anthropology which highlighted the important heuristic role of historicity, contextuality, 'situativity' and conflict for anthropological analysis (see, for example, Werbner 1984; Evens and Handelman 2006) gained momentum. What has increasingly been taken into account in the wake of these developments is a series of ideas: that knowledge is not just given but socially constructed, debated and negotiated; that knowledge is distributed unequally within any society as well as between societies (Weinstein and Weinstein 1978: 151); that knowledge can be used to establish but also to criticize and subvert power; that the value of a certain type of knowledge depends on the standpoint taken to evaluate it; and that one and the same person can in specific situations take recourse to different – and partly contradictory – stocks of knowledge. In addition, from the mid-twentieth century onwards, anthropologists increasingly started to study 'up' (Nader 1972) and 'sideways' (Hannerz 2006), to shift their fieldsites from societies in the global South to the global North (Jackson 1987) and to focus their attention less on empirical phenomena in the (alleged) 'periphery' (Ardener 1987) than on the 'centres of calculation' (Latour 1987). These developments resulted in a pluralization of what could (and should?) be known by anthropologists as well as, most important for our argument here, a diversification of the other side of knowing; that is, in a diversification of co-produced non-knowledge.[8]

The Shadow of Ignorance in Anthropology

To grasp the nettle of ignorance in the discipline of anthropology is an act of politics. While Bronislaw Malinowski (1974) grappled with questions of native knowledge, practical know-how and the native need for psychologically reassuring practices of magic in stressful and dangerous situations in the Trobriand Islands, Sir James Frazer proposed a conception of magic in terms of 'the bastard sister of science', a native discipline which, although it sought causal connections between events, was nonetheless based on error – that is, it enshrined an ignorance of the 'true' nature of the world. He argued: 'The fatal flaw of magic lies not in its general assumption of a sequence of events determined by law, but in its total misconception of the nature of the particular laws which govern that sequence'. He continues some lines later:

> The principles of association are excellent in themselves, and indeed absolutely essential to the working of the human mind. Legitimately applied they yield science; illegitimately applied they yield magic, the bastard sister of science ... [. A]ll magic is necessarily false and barren; for were it ever to become true and fruitful, it would no longer be magic but science. (Frazer 1976 [1922]: 64–65)

Lucien Lévy-Bruhl (1985) was equally forthright in his assumptions about how natives thought. His idea that non-European peoples lived in a state of mystical participation with the world was predicated on a conception of the inability of such folk to know that things and events might be ontologically separate. His theory also suggested that natives were content to entertain logical contradictions. This attribution of ignorance to other cultures fed debates about the political and ethical stance that anthropologists might adopt with respect to strange and exotic statements such as 'twins are birds' or 'men are storks'. As Godfrey Lienhardt argued, even generous interpretations of Lévy-Bruhl's 'impressionistic accounts of primitive peoples being utterly mystical in the apprehension of reality' are a form of 'old-fashioned literalism' which often made other people 'seem childish and irrational' (Lienhardt 1954: 106). These folk, Lienhardt stated, are no less practical or logical than us, nor do they lack empirical knowledge and skill. The attribution of ignorance to other cultures, even if only implied, carries a heavy postcolonial political loading. Moreover, the political dynamics of the study of knowledge, non-knowledge and of the ethics of anthropological methodologies point to the way in which we might conceive of the idea of regimes of production of ignorance, which lie at the heart of our discipline.

Another perspective on the shadow of ignorance within anthropology can be gained by considering arguments developed by structuralist thinkers and then by those opposed to their perspective. In *The Savage Mind*, Claude Lévi-Strauss draws attention to two important references to motivations for knowledge, both of which relate to affect and/or need rather than pure intellect or rationality. First, he states that 'the thirst for objective knowledge is one of the most neglected aspects of the thought of people we call "primitive"' (Lévi-Strauss 1989: 3. In the French original this begins: '*cet appétit de connaissance objective...*' (Lévi-Strauss 1962: 5)). This thirst/appetite for knowledge comes from an intellectual or theoretical interest to create order in the world, rather than imperatives predicated on biological needs or practical uses. Second, he talks of a 'desire' (*désir*) for knowledge, and how the desires of Western observers and those of natives might be regarded as being 'out of balance' (Lévi-Strauss 1989: 6). Lévi-Strauss gives examples that suggest that the attribution by the native of ignorance to Western observations is as likely as Western attributions of ignorance relating to native practice and classification. Lévi-Strauss addresses by implication a double form of ignorance: there is on the analyst's part a supposed 'ineptitude' – or perhaps a better translation from the French would be the '[mental] incapacity' (*inaptitude*) – of 'primitive people' for abstract thought; there is also the idea that analysts who suggest the opposite thesis are 'ignored' ('*omettait*' in the French text), for these commentators 'make it plain that richness of abstract words is not a monopoly of civilised languages' (ibid.: 1). The other's desire for abstract knowledge is overcome by the analyst's wish not to represent it as knowledge: it is ignored.

But there is another dynamic between knowledge and ignorance in Lévi-Strauss' work, one which he himself creates, that draws into tension the interpretations of analysts and those of natives. It is here that Lévi-Strauss himself ignores, or discounts, those forms of native interpretation that go against the grain of his own favoured analysis. With respect to the logical nature of classification discovered by the analyst, he notes: 'There are cases in which one can make hypotheses with regard to the logical nature of classification, which appear true or can be seen to cut across the natives' interpretation' (1989: 59). That is, native interpretation is something that might either be confirmed as true by the analyst or dismissed by him or her because it is at odds with an anthropological interpretation. Or again, in the chapter 'Do Dual Organisations Exist' in *Structural Anthropology*, he remarks: 'Today, this distinction appears to me naive, because it is still too close to the native's classification' (Lévi-Strauss 1977: 150). And finally, he claims in his *Introduction to the Work of Marcel Mauss* that there are instances in which the ethnologist allows him/herself to be mystified by the native (Lévi-Strauss 2002 [1950]: 45–50). In all these cases, Lévi-Strauss does not seem to hesitate to attribute either ignorance, a lack of clarity or an absence of proper scientific knowledge to the native. Anthropological knowledge trumps native knowledge if the status of the analytical structures envisioned in the anthropologist's own writings about ethnographic material is put in doubt.

The political and ethical implications of this analytical stance were questioned by, among others, Ladislav Holy and Milan Stuchlik (1981, 1983), whose body of work raised a major methodological concern about what warrant the anthropologist possesses to go beyond native knowledge and impose interpretations on a specific people. For them, the problem related to the idea that if anthropological categories of analysis did not coincide with those used by the people under study – more particularly, if the anthropologist's analytical models were at odds with native folk models – then the anthropologist's methods of study were in error. Thus, according to Holy and Stuchlik, we should not be allowed to consign to the rubbish bin of ignorance those native ideas that folk use to interpret and give sense to their own day-to-day lives.

While the pendulum of interpretative power may have begun to swing during this period in the direction of native exegesis, the question of ignorance raised its head yet again but now in a different form. This new concern had less to do with analysts discounting forms of knowledge and instead highlighted the problem of how to deal methodologically with 'protestations of ignorance' by informants in the field. As Richard Fardon points out, anthropological accounts usually paper over protestations of local ignorance and indeed fill in things left unsaid. When anthropologists go beyond what informants say, their accounts 'rest of the shadow side of their [natives'] assertions: the absences, ignorances and unsayabilities which must exist for things to be as they are claimed. Yet systematic attention is rarely given to these ethnographic non-events' (Fardon 1990: 8). Indeed, there is a range of reasons Fardon puts forward as to why things might not be made explicit or articulated by natives, and these include the following: there may be purposeful concealment, folk trying to protect secrets of one form or another; people might alternatively have tacit or implicit knowledge, in that they may know how to do something but not why it is the way it is; knowledge might axiomatically be mysterious and ineffable to them; or it could be the product of unknowable generative schema of the sort proposed by Foucault, Freud or Lévi-Strauss. Fardon argues that in a complex institutional context of Chamba social relations, his informants ran out of interpretations in 'interestingly different ways', and that 'there are reasons for the unknowns and unknowables clustering in Chamba accounts as they do' (1990: 22). In his anthropological account, Fardon not only points to the disciplinary dispositions that attempt either to attribute ignorance to others or to acknowledge forms of native knowledge, but also points out that at a micro-level in the production of ethnography and the writing of analyses different types of knowledge and ignorance are engendered in a range of social relations at various phases during the process of investigation.

In terms of the disciplinary practice within anthropology outlined above, it is apparent that ignorance is not eliminable through a simple widening of knowledge horizons. Ignorance is part of an anthropological regime of knowledge; it is part of a disciplinary practice that constitutes an economy of ignorance. Moreover, anthropological non-knowledge nowadays seems to take a rhizomatic form with endlessly extending ramifications, paralleled by the emergence of new disciplinary subfields and thematic specializations devised to keep track of what is found to be not known within and in relation to heterogeneous research sites. Moreover, in contrast to earlier periods, present-day anthropology has shifted its main focus of attention from wondrous unknowns in exotic places – regarding, for example, witchcraft (Evans-Pritchard 1937), notions of 'virgin birth' (Leach 1966) or spirit possession (Boddy 1994) – to manifestations and modalities of non-knowledge that are closer to the anthropologists' own life-worlds in terms of spatial proximity as well as in terms of similitude of the respective 'epistemic culture' (Knorr Cetina 1999), meaning the socio-cultural configuration that determines how we know what we know. In this process, non-knowledge is less and less defined with a view to modernity's Other, but increasingly found to be located in the disquieted heart of (post)modernity itself.

Contributing to Ignorance

All the chapters in this volume subscribe to the idea in one way or another that ignorance and knowledge are mutually constitutive, and that ignorance is not simply the absence of, or a gap in, knowledge. Ignorance is a social fact. Indeed, all contributors point towards the positivity of ignorance, that it has generative social effects, that it is produced in specific socio-cultural contexts and that there are political consequences that flow from its production and reproduction.[9]

Carlo Caduff's analysis, based on fieldwork among U.S.-American microbiologists, focuses on 'the regulation and appropriation of ignorance in the context of ... the discourse of emerging infectious diseases'. He explores scientists' understanding of viruses, which constitute 'a heterogeneous population of mutant strains in constant flux'; and he points out how the scientists' awareness of their own ignorance has been normalized. Caduff shows that the unpredictability of their object of knowledge has given rise to an institutionalized approach to what microbiologists anticipate they will be ignorant of in the future. What is more, awareness of the scientists' ignorance in these matters has even been made productive by incorporating a conception of the unknown into new experimental research designs that expressly take account of the 'eventfulness' of viruses. Caduff concludes that ignorance is a discursive object; that it is a 'stratified' not a 'flat' object; and moreover, as a stratified object, ignorance has a political history and a geopolitics.

Christos Lynteris' chapter examines another example of biopolitical practice, but his focus is on interpretations by early Russian ethnographers, Chinese scientists and others of a highly contagious, airborne form of plague in Inner Asia in the late nineteenth and early twentieth centuries. He examines the so-called 'native knowledge hypothesis' – that is, 'the contention that Mongols and Buryats knew plague as a zoonotic disease, being thus able to prevent the perilous bacterial species-jump leading to human outbreaks of plague'. At the turn of the twentieth century this hypothesis had many adherents in popular and professional science in both China and Russia, and Lynteris traces the history of this hypothesis, which is replete with misunderstandings and mistranslations. Lynteris' analysis exposes the persistent reproduction of a scientific epistemological practice that, paradoxically, did not allow 'natives' to be ignorant of their own physical environment. Furthermore, while native populations were burdened with an epidemiological knowledge they did not have, they were simultaneously deprived by scientists of a mythical and ritual knowledge, which formed a central part of a precarious social autonomy that they had developed at the borders of powerful centralized polities. It is evident here how the denial that others can not-know led to all manner of social and political consequences.

In the chapter by Trevor Marchand, where he reflects on his own experiences during his training as a fine woodworker in a college in London, ignorance appears in a variety of forms. For example, ignorance is used actively to structure social relationships within the class as well as between trainers and trainees because '"not knowing" where to find the information or "not knowing" where to begin a task were the premise for asking others to show and lend a hand'. Furthermore, the trainees' utopian ideas of autonomy about becoming an independent bespoke artisan suggested a wider significance of not-knowing. As 'authors of utopias', trainees 'wilfully suspend[ed] for a temporary period their knowledge of the fuller spectrum of forces at play in daily life'. Ignorance was therefore a central defining feature of the artisans' attempts to create and maintain a utopian vision. Within the broader institutional set-up of the college, ignorance of marketing, an area concerned with 'the critical importance of basic business and marketing skills to succeed, as well as the reality of the U.K.'s narrow and highly competitive marketplace for makers and sellers of bespoke furniture', slowly became apparent to a number of trainees. Marchand's analysis thus makes clear that the productivity of ignorance within specific contexts is at once something that is sought and something that creates feelings of unease. Indeed, when utopian visions could no longer be maintained in the face of the realities of marketing and business promotion outside the college, the strategic concealments of individual social projects became visible and their exposure had serious personal consequences, fracturing utopian visions of budding bespoke artisans.

Casey High's chapter on Waorani people in Ecuadorian Amazon discusses how anthropologists can deal with ethnographic contexts 'in which the people we study insist on ignorance as a social value'. The examples he chooses to illustrate this idea are set within local debates about shamanism and are concerned with intergenerational conflicts in relation to educational issues, more particularly the allegation by older generations that young people lack a particular type of bodily knowledge. Concerning the shamanism, High argues that 'Waorani people are "wilfully ignorant" of shamanism in part because its practice is associated with assault sorcery'. In both instances, the claim to ignorance – whether evaluated negatively (as in the intergenerational conflict) or evaluated positively (as in the case of shamanism specifically) – is embedded in specific relations of power and social morality, which define what should and what should not be known. Not knowing about shamanism is, therefore, not only a strategic claim in a particular context, but also a statement about a 'desired state of being that confers a person's moral position' within a wider set of social and political relations. Furthermore, the strategic claims of ignorance about shamanism and the laments about the ignorance of young people give a lie to the disciplinary predisposition by which anthropologists claim that other people cannot not-know. Ignorance, High concludes, is 'produced and conceived and acquires meanings in ways that depart significantly from economies of knowledge familiar to the West'.

John Borneman's chapter deals with the therapeutic treatment of child sex offenders in Berlin. In the context of these therapies, the

offender's ignorance is perceived to be a problem that needs to be overcome through introspection and empathy. Offenders adopt strategies
to protect themselves from accusations, for it becomes self-incriminating for them to attempt to assimilate their experiences as the perpe-
trators of sexual abuse. As Borneman shows, the accusation of 'sex
abuse' not only requires the accused men to organize the details of
their past experiences according to certain schemata, but also presupposes that these men are not ignorant of their deeds but rather
'motivated to ignorance', a view held by the therapists involved. The
problem thus focuses 'not on what the victims of sex abuse experience
or know but on how the offenders come to know, and what they then
in fact do know, in light of what we know about the intersubjective
experience of the child' at the centre of the accusation. Borneman argues that more 'information' cannot overcome the issue of motivated
ignorance; nor can the intersubjective experience of the child be revealed straightforwardly. Indeed, since child molestation and sexual
abuse are taboos, Borneman concludes that 'they are structured in
part by silences that one might characterize as integral to a regime of
ignorance'. This chapter is an example of a powerful institutionalized
approach to ignorance, taboo and the uneven distribution of knowledge.

While Borneman critiques the notion of 'the uncovering of the
truth of sex' and the power of the confessional in Foucault's work,
Leo Coleman takes us beyond the same author's ideas of power-
knowledge, especially with respect to the way spectacular ceremonial and disciplinary ritual practices can be read through them.
Instead, he offers a Freudian reading of 'the metaphysics of the
British Crown, as they were personified and substantialized in the
Imperial Durbar, and as they contributed to the making of an imperial state'. The Foucauldian conception of power-knowledge is inadequate to deal with a situation in which governmental knowledge in
colonial India was unstable and insecure. Indeed, 'individuals and
institutions within the colonial state worked to constitute ... absences
in the fabric of governmental knowledge'. Rather than systematic
knowledge being the outcome, it was systematic ignorance that was
promoted and produced in rituals of display. Coleman constructs
a powerful argument to unpick the ritual and political logic of the
Coronation Durbar by recourse to Freud's theory of the fetish, an
account of which is used to understand the dynamics of power-ignorance within the operation of colonial government. Coleman argues
that the Crown played a special role as fetish, since it obscured real
governmental knowledge about the needs and interests among the

Indian population, and operated by means of secrecy and through processes of concealment.

The production and reproduction of ignorance within parts of the French colonial apparatus and within networks of social relations among colonial officers in West Africa are examined in Roy Dilley's chapter. Two problematic areas for the colonial regime are considered here: the offspring of colonial officers and indigenous women; and slavery within West Africa, especially how individual officers reacted towards it in specific local contexts. The analysis focuses on how non-knowledge was created through contradictory pressures operating within the colonial regime and through intimate social interactions in colonial outposts. The production and reproduction of non-knowledge is conceived as an artefact of colonial relations – a function of a regime of governmentality – and of the effort expended by social actors in creating 'holes', 'positive absences' or zones of non-knowledge. Dilley shows, for example, how a desire for secrecy around the issue of slavery resulted in forms of social practice being obscured from the view of metropolitan France; how individual officers, caught within the contradictory currents of colonialism, chose to ignore or conceal certain unpalatable issues; and how as a system of relations, French colonialism created, sustained and reproduced not-knowing. Both institutions and individuals worked to produce and reproduce zones of ignorance, positive absences in the fabric of colonial understanding. Knowledge and ignorance were not simply the result of abstract epistemological relations, but they were created and recreated simultaneously within a regime of colonial political control and in relation to human emotions and desires.

Thomas G. Kirsch's chapter explores secretiveness as a specific form of asymmetrical (non-)knowledge that has generative social effects. Questioning the widely held assumption that 'human beings are epistemophilics; that is, that they have "a natural desire to know"', he takes African Christianity in Zambia as the example to show that use of the category of 'the secret' presupposes the existence of (real or imagined) Others who are interested in the disclosure of what is concealed from them. In other words, contrary to Simmel's definition of secrecy as 'consciously willed concealment', Kirsch suggests that the fact of concealment is not enough to account for the form of sociality constituted through secrecy. An example to illustrate this point pertains to controversies with regard to the herbal substances used in prophet-healing churches: while some people classify them as 'curative medicine', others categorize them as 'witchcraft items'. Yet, in both cases, the covert storage of these substances does not mean that

'epistemophilic Others are ... already out there prior to acts of secretiveness'; instead, Kirsch argues, they 'are performatively constituted
and thus brought into existence through acts that are classified in that
way', for example by healers who, in an act of self-aggrandisement,
insinuate the existence of epistemophilic Others in relation to the
'secret lore' of their own religious expertise. The positivity and social
productivity of secrecy thus lies in the insinuation that people have a
desire to know what they are kept ignorant of.

In Lieu of a Conclusion

Those who have travelled on French motorways will have seen sign-
posts at the roadside that pose an intriguing ambiguity about holes:
'*trous en formation*', the signs say – 'holes in the making'. This statement does not, without doubt, refer to spontaneous, self-generated
events, but implies that there are agents responsible for making the
holes. As all good road-workers who dig holes in the ground are aware,
the production of absences is a strenuous and tiring business. And
this is where the '*trous en formation*' dovetail with our concerns in this
present volume: it is the social, cultural and political processes that go
into the production and reproduction of the absences of knowledge
that is of empirical and theoretical interest in the chapters to follow.
More particularly, we contend that the anthropological study of the
significance of ignorance within the broader field of social analysis
should pay regard to three overarching conceptual commitments, all
of which are shared by the chapters in this volume.

Conceptualizing Ignorance as Positivity

As elaborated above, recent work on ignorance suggests different ways
of conceptualizing the relationship between knowing and not-knowing, and these provide fruitful areas for further research. Rather than
knowledge and ignorance being seen as the negation of each other,
they are instead construed as intimately related, each one deriving
its character and meaning from a mutual interaction. As Giorgio
Agamben states: 'The ways in which we do not know things are just
as important (and perhaps even more important) as the ways in which
we know them' (2011: 113); and he points out that 'the articulation
of a zone of non-knowledge is the condition ... of all our knowledge'
(ibid.). Agamben goes on to observe that 'we lack even the elementary principles of an art of ignorance', and that 'there is no recipe for

articulating a zone of non-knowledge' (ibid.: 114). The relationship, therefore, between knowledge and ignorance appears to be less antagonistic and more complimentary and mutually reinforcing than one might have initially imagined. But there is more to it than this. As we have tried to demonstrate in this Introduction, there is a positivity to ignorance, a potentiality that provides the grounds for action, thought and the production of social relations.

Specifically, Agamben argues that: 'The art of living is ... the capacity to keep ourselves in harmonious relationship with that which escapes us' (2011: 114). This is one sort of ignorance at the core of existence, an existential ignorance as it were. Luhmann points to a similar conclusion in his discussions of an ecology of ignorance, a kind of systemic ignorance, in his book *Observations on Modernity*. He quotes from one of Socrates' dialogues: 'Man is capable of taking actions only because he is capable of being ignorant, and of contenting himself with a portion of the consciousness that is his singular oddity' (Luhmann 1998: 94). In other words, at the heart of human choosing and doing is a form of ignorance that makes possible future courses of action.

This positivity of ignorance can be seen too in the acknowledgement of the fact of ignorance as a central idea to sociological theories of action (for example of the type proposed by Robert Merton, 1951). If action is employed to bring about conditions that would otherwise not exist, then the foreseen and unforeseen consequences of that action hang on the potentiality of ignorance. To know all the consequences of an action, anticipated and unanticipated, is to become incapable of action. Luhmann suggests that the relationship between knowing and ignorance reaches a point at which 'ignorance becomes the most important resource of action', lest we be frozen in inaction due to the burden of contemplating all possible outcomes of an act (1998: 94).[10]

Building on these insights, the chapters in this volume highlight the idea of the positivity of ignorance in order to underscore the relationship of ignorance to power, ethics and social practice.

The Reproduction of Non-Knowledge

A major challenge in studying 'non-knowledge' that needs to be taken into account is the question of the reproduction of that non-knowledge. In different ways and to different degrees, the issue of reproduction certainly lies at the heart of the social sciences and humanities, for example when dealing with the reproductive dynamics of power relationships, practices of cultural transmission between generations, and the reproduction of ignorance rather than just knowledge alone. We suggest, therefore, that the focus of anthropological study should be on the production and reproduction of ignorance or non-knowledge, rather than on the illusory qualities of ignorance as a (reified) thing in itself. In doing so, we need to keep 'the right relationship with ignorance, allowing an absence of knowledge to guide and accompany our gestures', as Agamben (2011: 114) says. He goes on to observe that 'it is possible that the zone of non-knowledge does not really contain anything special at all. Perhaps ... [it] does not exist at all; perhaps only its gestures exist' (ibid.).

Turning Agamben's observation into a question, we ask: How can we come to a conceptualization of what is addressed in the subtitle of this volume – the reproduction of non-knowledge? Conceptualizing this notion poses difficulties because it requires developing an analytical approach that allows us to grasp the reproduction of an absence – of knowledge that is lacking, non-existent. Metaphorically speaking, the puzzling question is how a 'void' can be reproduced through time if the 'void', characterized by emptiness, does not have content or substance in and of itself?

At first sight, the answer to this question seems clear: A 'void' is reproduced by establishing a frame; that is, through the reproduction of those characteristics that demarcate and define the void's categorical opposite – that is, the 'frame'. When seen from this rather obscured vantage point, the reproduction of non-knowledge through time is simply a by-product of the reproduction of knowledge through time because, in a manner of speaking, non-knowledge is here located at the lee side of knowledge and conceptualized as residual negativity if positive knowledge is lacking. By contrast, we would emphasize the social and cultural labour that goes into the production of frames and the evacuation of their contents; that is, the production and reproduction of voids and absences.

Regimes of Ignorance

It is noteworthy that much anthropological and sociological work has for a long time almost exclusively addressed genealogies of knowledge; that is, the historical processes of how one field of knowledge is transformed into or replaced by another field of knowledge. However, as Andrew Mathews (2005) has recently pointed out, Michel Foucault's analyses of the reorganization of knowledge in its interconnectedness with the emergence of new forms of power neglects the idea that these processes are not just about 'knowledge' but also about 'non-knowledge'. In other words, there needs to be an acknowledgement of the fact that the emergence of new forms of power is linked to the momentous transformation of one field of non-knowledge into another field of non-knowledge. Following from the above, we argue that every 'regime of knowledge' simultaneously is a 'regime of ignorance': by determining legitimate types, modes and objects of knowing, parallel forms of non-knowing with their respective modes and objects are (more or less implicitly) determined too.

To explicate what we mean by this, it is worthwhile remembering that Foucault has time and again stressed the productivity and positivity of power: 'We must cease once and for all to describe the effects of power in negative terms ... [. P]ower produces; it produces reality; it produces domains of objects and rituals of truth' (Foucault 1977: 194). In combination with our argument above with regard to the positivity of ignorance as well as concerning the interlinkage of power and non-knowledge, we might therefore come to an appreciation of the powerful productiveness of non-knowledge; that is, to an appreciation of the fact that the phrase 'knowledge is power' represents just one aspect of study and that the productiveness of power can also be constituted through what is ignored or not known by subaltern others or by those holding dominant positions. The Foucauldian conceptual pair power/knowledge must consequently be broadened to include those aspects of power relations that are associated with people's unknowing, non-knowledge, nescience and ignorance.[11]

In other words, our analyses should be mindful of the cultural specificities of how 'knowledge' and 'non-knowledge' are configured, first, towards each other and second, in relation to socio-political asymmetries and to processes of power, domination and hegemony. It is with this in mind that, in this Introduction, we speak of a 'regime of ignorance' in order to acknowledge the wider social and political field in which the production of ignorance is set. We take a regime of ignorance to be the total set of relations that unite, in a given period or cultural context, the discursive practices and power relations that give rise to epistemological gaps and forms of unknowing that have generative social effects and consequences.

Notes

1. We would like to thank the Centre of Excellence at the University of Konstanz for providing us with the funds and the facilities to enable us to

bring this group of scholars together for discussion of this set of anthropological concerns.

2. Our thanks go to Professor Will Fowler, Department of Spanish, University of St Andrews, who provided us with the details of this example.

3. See for some notable examples of recent publications: Gershon and Sarhadi Raj (2000); Littlewood (2007); Proctor and Schiebinger (2008); Roberts and Armitage (2008); Gross (2010); High, Kelly and Mair (2012); Beck and Wehling (2012); Firestein (2012); and McGoey (2012a).

4. See for accounts of a growing anthropological awareness of ignorance, Fardon (1990) and Last, who points out 'the importance of knowing about not-knowing', of the understandable 'reluctance in ethnography to record what people do not know ...; [for] it is hard enough to record what they do know' (1992: 393). This Introduction will return later to the debate of which this sort of work forms a part.

5. See Roberts and Armitage (2008), who first coined the phrase 'ignorance economy', and also High (2012: 120–23).

6. That *Waiting* is a controversial book is also reflected in the fact that Crapanzano has even opted 'not to name the Europeans and Americans who have also helped me with my research. They will all understand, I am sure' (Crapanzano 1985: ix).

7. Based at Yale University, the Human Relations Area File organization aims to encourage and record comparative studies of human culture across the globe.

8. This statement reflects one of the most momentous insights gained in studies on non-knowledge, namely that the scientific endeavour to increase the available knowledge about the world does not automatically lead to a concomitant decrease in non-knowledge. Almost to the contrary, there are several ways in which scientists intentionally or unintentionally contribute to the growth of ignorance. First, as Wilbert Moore and Melvin Tumin pointed out as early as 1949, ignorance is used to preserve 'social differentials' (Moore and Tumin 1949: 788) either between scientific competitors or in attempts to maintain knowledge-based positions of authority vis-à-vis non-scientists. Second, instead of eliminating ignorance, knowledge production can be said to co-produce non-knowledge in systematic ways. This is because, conceived of as 'the other side of knowing' (Luhmann 1998: 81), what is not known is always and necessarily specified in relation to existing knowledge. Moreover, as Robert Merton has noted, 'As new contributions to knowledge bring about a new awareness of something else not yet known, the sum of manifest human ignorance increases along with the sum of manifest human knowledge' (Merton 1987: 10). It therefore becomes clear that – despite claims to the contrary by scientific modernists – there can never be an end to ignorance: the more we know, the more we do not know.

9. Raj (2000: 31) captures an important point when he states: 'Ignorance is *the presence of an absence*' [italics in the original]. We develop this particular idea by trying to grasp how the presence of an absence can be produced and reproduced in different social and cultural contexts.

10. A kind of positivity of ignorance also runs through in a number of other social theories. One example is Georg Simmel's study of the social functions of ignorance in his 1908 book entitled in English *Sociology: Investigations on the Forms of Sociation*, in which he argued that there were positive social functions resulting from not-knowing, and benefits for the conduct of social relations and for interactions between individuals in the practice of reciprocal concealment (see for further commentary on Simmel's work, Gross 2003, 2007, 2012). This line of sociological analysis, later developed by Merton, was specifically taken up by Wilbert Moore and Melvin Tumin, two Princeton sociologists, who published in 1949 an article in *American Sociological Review* entitled 'Some Social Functions of Ignorance'.

11. In a similar vein, Paul Rabinow (2004) has argued, in an address to an audience of biological scientists on the topic of ethics within an ecology of ignorance, that we have a certain responsibility to ignorance in that we must acknowledge that ignorance is part of a social and political field that implies relations of power and ethical concerns.

References

Agamben, G. 2011. *Nudities*. Stanford, CA: Stanford University Press.

Ardener, E. 1987. '"Remote Areas": Some Theoretical Considerations'. In *Anthropology at Home*, ed. A. Jackson. London: Tavistock, 38–54.

Beck, U. and P. Wehling 2012. 'The Politics of Non-Knowing: An Emerging Area of Social and Political Conflict in Reflexive Modernity'. In *The Politics of Knowledge*, ed. F.D. Rubio and P. Baert. New York: Routledge, 33–57.

Bellman, B.L. 1981. 'The Paradox of Secrecy'. *Human Studies* 4, 1–24.

Boddy, J. 1994. 'Spirit Possession Revisited: Beyond Instrumentality'. *Annual Review of Anthropology* 23, 407–34.

Clark, L. and A. Kingsolver 2010. *Briefing Paper on Informed Consent by the AAA Committee on Ethics*. Available at http://www.aaanet.org/committees/ethics/bp5.htm/. Accessed 16 August 2013.

Clifford, J. and G. Marcus (eds) 1986. *Writing Culture: The Poetics and Politics of Ethnography*. Berkeley: University of California Press.

Crapanzano, V. 1985. *Waiting: The Whites of South Africa*. New York: Random House.

Dilley, R.M. 2010. 'Reflections on Knowledge Practices and the Problem of Ignorance'. *Journal of the Royal Anthropological Institute* 16, 176–92.

Evans-Pritchard, E.E. 1937. *Witchcraft, Oracles and Magic among the Azande*. Oxford: Oxford University Press.

Evens, T.M.S. and D. Handelman (eds) 2006. *The Manchester School: Practice and Ethnographic Praxis in Anthropology*. Oxford: Berghahn Books.

Fardon, R. 1990. *Between God, the Dead and the Wild: Chamba Interpretations of Religion and Ritual*. Edinburgh: Edinburgh University Press for the International African Institute, London.

Ferguson, J. and A. Gupta (eds) 1997. *Anthropological Locations: Boundaries and Grounds of a Field Science*. Berkeley: University of California Press.

Ferrier, J.F. 1854. *Institutes of Metaphysic: The Theory of Knowing and Being*. Edinburgh: Blackwell.

Firestein, S. 2012. *Ignorance: How it Drives Science*. New York: Oxford University Press.

Fluehr-Lobban, C. 2003. 'Informed Consent in Anthropological Research: We Are Not Exempt'. In *Ethics and the Profession of Anthropology: Dialogue for Ethically Conscious Practice*, ed. C. Fluehr-Lobban. Walnut Creek, CA: AltaMira Press, 159–77.

Foucault, M. 1977. *Discipline and Punish*. New York: Pantheon Books.

Frazer, J. 1976 (1922). *The Golden Bough: A Study in Magic and Religion*. London: Macmillan.

Gershon, I. and D. Sarhadi Raj 2000. 'Introduction: The Symbolic Capital of Ignorance'. *Social Analysis* 44, 3–13.

Gluckman, M. 1940. 'Analysis of a Social Situation in Modern Zululand'. *Bantu Studies* 14, 1–30, 147–74.

Gross, M. 2003. 'Sociologists of the Unexpected: Edward A. Ross and Georg Simmel on the Unintended Consequences of Modernity'. *The American Sociologist* 34, 40–58.

———. 2007. 'The Unknown in Process: Dynamic Connections of Ignorance, Non-Knowledge and Related Concepts'. *Current Sociology* 55, 742–59.

———. 2010. *Ignorance and Surprise: Science, Society and Ecological Design*. Cambridge, MA: MIT Press.

———. 2012. '"Objective Culture" and the Development of Nonknowledge: Georg Simmel and the Reverse Side of Knowing'. *Cultural Sociology* 6, 422–37.

Hannerz, U. 2006. 'Studying Down, Up, Sideways, Through, Backwards, Forwards, Away and at Home: Reflections on the Field Worries of an Expansive Discipline'. In *Locating the Field: Space, Place and Context in Anthropology*, ed. S. Coleman and C. Peter. Oxford: Berg, 23–42.

High, C. 2012. 'Between Knowing and Being: Ignorance in Anthropology and Amazonian Shamanism'. In *The Anthropology of Ignorance: Ethnographic Perspectives*, ed. C. High, A. Kelly and J. Mair. New York: Palgrave Macmillan, 119–35.

High, C., A. Kelly and J. Mair (eds) 2012. *The Anthropology of Ignorance: Ethnographic Perspectives*. New York: Palgrave Macmillan.

Hobart, M. (ed.) 1993. *An Anthropological Critique of Development: The Growth of Ignorance*. London: Routledge.

Holley, H. (ed.) 1923. *Bahá'í Scriptures: Selections from the Utterances of Bahá'u'lláh and 'Abdu'l-Bahá'*. New York: Brentano's Publishers.

Holy, L. and M. Stuchlik (eds) 1981. *The Structure of Folk Models*. London: Academic Press.

———. 1983. *Actions, Norms and Representations*. Cambridge: Cambridge University Press.

Jackson, A. (ed.) 1987. *Anthropology at Home*. London: Tavistock.

Japp, K.P. 2000. 'Distinguishing Non-Knowledge'. *The Canadian Journal of Sociology* 25, 225–38.

Kelly, A. 2003. 'Research and the Subject: The Practice of Informed Consent'. *PoLar* 26, 182–95.

Knorr Cetina, K. 1999. *Epistemic Cultures: How the Sciences Make Knowledge*. Cambridge, MA: Harvard University Press.

———. 2001. 'Objectual Practice'. In *The Practice Turn in Contemporary Theory*, ed. T.R. Schatzki, K. Knorr Cetina and E. Von Savigny. New York: Routledge, 175–88.

Last, M. 1992. 'The Importance of Knowing about Not-Knowing: Observations from Hausaland'. In *The Social Basis of Health and Healing in Africa*, ed. S. Feierman and J. Jansen. Berkeley: University of California Press, 393–406.

Latour, B. 1987. *Science in Action: How to Follow Scientists and Engineers through Society*. Cambridge, MA: Harvard University Press.

Leach, E.R. 1966. 'Virgin Birth'. *Proceedings of the Royal Anthropological Institute of Great Britain and Ireland*, 1966, 39–49.

Lévi-Strauss, C. 1962. *La Pensée sauvage*. Paris: Librairie Plon.

———. 1977. *Structural Anthropology*. Harmondsworth: Penguin.

———. 1989. *The Savage Mind*. London: Weidenfeld and Nicolson.

———. 2002 [1950]. *Introduction to the Work of Marcel Mauss*. London: Routledge and Kegan Paul.

Lévy-Bruhl, L. 1985. *How Natives Think (Les fonctions mentales dans les sociétés inférieures, 1910)*. Princeton, NJ: Princeton University Press.

Lienhardt, G. 1954. 'Modes of Thought'. In *The Institutions of Primitive Society: A Series of Broadcast Talks*, ed. E.E. Evans-Pritchard. Oxford: Basil Blackwell, 95–107.

Littlewood, R. (ed.) 2007. *On Knowing and Not Knowing in the Anthropology of Medicine*. Walnut Creek, CA: Left Coast Press.

Luhmann, N. 1998. *Observations on Modernity*. Stanford, CA: Stanford University.

Malinowski, B. 1974. *Magic, Science and Religion and other Essays*. London: Souvenir Press.

Mathews, A.S. 2005. 'Power/Knowledge, Power/Ignorance: Forest Fires and the State in Mexico'. *Human Ecology* 33, 795–820.

McGoey, L. 2012a. 'Special Issue: "Strategic Unknowns: Towards a Sociology of Ignorance"'. *Economy and Society* 41, 1–16.

———. 2012b. 'Making a Buck in a Blind Man's World'. *Charisma: Consumer and Market Studies*, 19 February. Available at http://www.charisma-net-work.net/markets/making-a-buck-in-a-blind-mans-world/. Accessed 15 March 2014.

Merton, R.K. 1951. *Social Theory and Social Structure: Toward the Codification of Theory and Research*. Glencoe, Ill.: The Free Press.

———. 1987. 'Three Fragments from a Sociologist's Notebook. Establishing the Phenomenon, Specified Ignorance, and Strategic Research Materials'. *Annual Review of Sociology* 13, 1–18.

Moore, W. and M. Tumin 1949. 'Some Social Functions of Ignorance'. *American Sociological Review* 14, 787–96.

Nader, L. 1972. 'Up the Anthropologist: Perspectives Gained from Studying Up'. In *Reinventing Anthropology*, ed. D.H. Hymes. New York: Pantheon Books, 284–311.

Niehaus, I. 2013. 'Anthropology and Whites in South Africa: Response to an Unreasonable Critique'. *Africa Spectrum* 48, 117–27.

Proctor, R. and L. Schiebinger (eds) 2008. *Agnotology: The Making and Unmaking of Ignorance*. Stanford, CA: Stanford University Press.

Rabinow, P. 2004. *Assembling Ethics in an Ecology of Ignorance*. The closing plenary lecture of the First Conference on Synthetic Biology at MIT, 10–12 June. Available at http://openwetware.org/images/7/7a/SB1.0_Rabinow.pdf/. Accessed 9 November 2011.

Raj, D.S. 2000. 'Ignorance, Forgetting and Family Nostalgia: Partition, the Nation-State, and Refugees in Dehli'. *Social Analysis* 44, 30–55.

Rescher, N. 2009. *Ignorance: On the Wider Implications of Deficient Knowledge*. Pittsburgh, PA: University of Pittsburgh Press.

Roberts, J. and J. Armitage 2008. 'The Ignorance Economy'. *Prometheus* 26, 335–54.

Rottenburg, R. 2009. *Far-Fetched Facts: A Parable of Development Aid*. Cambridge, MA: MIT Press.

Searle, J. 1995. *The Construction of Social Reality*. London: Penguin.

———. 2010. *Making the Social World: The Structure of Human Civilization*. Oxford: Oxford University Press.

Simmel, G. 1908. *Soziologie [Sociology: Investigations on the Forms of Sociation]*. Leipzig: Duncker and Humblot.

Smithson, M. 1985. 'Toward a Social Theory of Ignorance'. *Journal of the Theory of Social Behaviour* 15, 151–72.

Strathern, M. (ed.) 2000. *Audit Cultures: Anthropological Studies in Accountability, Ethics, and the Academy*. London: Routledge.

Trouillot, M.-R. 1991. 'Anthropology and the Savage Slot: The Poetics and Politics of Otherness'. In *Recapturing Anthropology: Working in the Present*, ed. R.G. Fox. Santa Fe, NM: SAR Press, 17–44.

Weinstein, D. and M. Weinstein 1978. 'The Sociology of Nonknowledge: A Paradigm'. In *Research in Sociology of Knowledge, Sciences and Art*, ed. R.A. Jones. Greenwich, CT: JAI Press, 151–66.

Werbner, R. 1984. 'The Manchester School in South-Central Africa'. *Annual Review of Anthropology* 13, 157–85.

Thomas G. Kirsch is Professor of Social and Cultural Anthropology at the University of Konstanz. He has published two books on African Christianity – one of them entitled *Spirits and Letters: Reading, Writing and Charisma in African Christianity* (2008) – and articles in some of the major refereed journals for anthropology and sociology in Germany. Other articles have been published in the journals *American Anthropologist, Visual Anthropology* and *American Ethnologist*. Since 2003, he has also conducted fieldwork on issues of violence, security and crime prevention in South Africa; he is co-editor of *Domesticating Vigilantism in Africa* (2010).

Roy Dilley, D. Phil. (Oxon) 1984, is Professor of Social Anthropology at the University of St Andrews. Having completed over thirty years of field research in Senegal, West Africa, he now works in French colonial archives on historical ethnography, biography and photography. He was a visiting Professorial Research Fellow at the Institute for Advanced Studies, University of Konstanz, 2011–2012. His books include *Islamic and Caste Knowledge Practices among Haalpulaaren* (2004), *Nearly Native, Barely Civilized: Henri Gaden's Journey across Colonial French West Africa* (2014) and the edited volumes *Contesting Markets* (1992) and *The Problem of Context* (1999).

Chapter 1

MIND THE GAP
ON THE OTHER SIDE OF KNOWING

Carlo Caduff

Over the past few years, anthropologists, sociologists, philosophers and historians have drawn attention to the significance and relevance of 'ignorance' for our social, cultural and political existence.[1] Peter Galison has termed this growing interest in contexts where knowledge is missing a concern with 'antiepistemology', by which he means a scholarly investigation of the systematic ways in which knowledge is covered and obscured intentionally (Galison 2004: 237). Yet, conceived in the spirit of the Enlightenment, Galison's approach puts knowledge and ignorance in opposition, and in doing so, perpetuates a problematic binary. Exploring the expanding universe of classified information in the United States, Galison illuminates the bureaucratic apparatus of state secrecy, but he also restricts the problem of ignorance to a question of actors and institutions involved in the business of removing knowledge from the public domain. Ignorance, however, is not always the result of deliberate concealment and institutional suppression.

Expanding infrastructures of digitalization have made knowledge instantly available for some people, but even for those people who seem to have it at their fingertips, there continues to be knowledge that is not immediately accessible. Political contestations are increasingly struggles for access to knowledge, struggles that are structured by social conditions of place, class, education, race, gender and generation. Today's knowledge economy has produced new inequalities, which have inspired new social and political movements to fight for open access to the world of digital information. But for people in privileged places with almost unlimited access to this world, living in a time of digitalization has increasingly meant dwelling in the light of too much information. Not surprisingly, such people are now inclined to consider the shade of ignorance as bliss, and they can do so because they can afford it.

Whether bliss or not, ignorance operates as 'the other side of ... knowing', as Niklas Luhmann underscores (Luhmann 1998: 81). Strictly speaking, ignorance is not an absence of knowledge. On the contrary, ignorance always depends on knowledge. Ignorance and knowledge are not opposed to each other; they are linked with each other; they depend on each other; they are made for each other. Ignorance and knowledge allow each other to become appealing and attractive, making each other valuable and desirable. Ignorance always takes a specific shape in relation to already existing knowledge and thus constitutes the other side of this knowledge.[2] Ignorance, moreover, interacts with knowledge, and interrupts and intensifies it. In today's world of digital globalization, people are encouraged to be creative. And to be creative increasingly means to produce knowledge and control access to it. Paradoxically, this production of more knowledge has simultaneously resulted in a production of more ignorance.

The other side of knowing may not yet require a subscription, but it is not necessarily easily accessible. Ignorance is addressed through discourse, and discourse is always organized and regulated in particular ways. There are things that can and that cannot be said about ignorance at a particular time in a particular place. Only certain fields of ignorance are open for public debate and political contestation. Culturally distinctive and historically specific rules govern these debates and contestations, establishing the limits of what can be known about the unknown and what can be said about the unsaid. Ignorance, therefore, is a discursive object, but it is not a flat object; it is a stratified object with multiple levels and layers. As a stratified object, ignorance has a political history and a geopolitics.

How, then, are subjects of knowledge engaging the other side of knowing? How is ignorance experienced, encountered and embodied? Which kinds of ignorance are capacitated and which kinds are incapacitated discursively? What allows particular forms of ignorance to gain traction in the world? These questions are at the heart of this chapter, which begins with the assumption that ignorance is envisioned, endured, engaged, opposed, embraced, arranged, evaluated and incorporated in many ways. Some kinds of ignorance are kept hidden as public secrets, while others are relentlessly exposed with the greatest possible media coverage. Given the historical variation in the social, cultural, and political appropriation of ignorance, it seems important, both analytically and politically, to explore the rise and fall of particular engagements of the other side of knowing.

The focus in this chapter is on a group of American scientists, exploring in detail how these scientists relate to the other side of knowing. The broader aim here is to illuminate the regulation and appropriation of ignorance in the context of a particular discourse: the discourse of emerging infectious diseases. At issue in this regulation and appropriation of ignorance is a more general ontology, which foregrounds the volatility of viruses. Drawing on my work with microbiologists in the United States, I trace the ascendancy of a scientific understanding of viruses as a heterogeneous population of mutant strains in constant flux. I argue that this ontological account has fundamental implications for the practice of microbiology and its goal of epidemic control. Confronted with viruses that are constantly evolving in unpredictable ways, microbiologists are caught in a condition of ignorance. This condition reflects the temporal disjuncture of a natural evolution that is believed to be ahead and a scientific understanding that is believed to be behind. The notion of emerging infectious diseases has naturalized and normalized this gap.

In the second part of the chapter, I examine how microbiologists have become mindful of this kind of ignorance grounded in the natural evolution of viruses. As we shall see, scientists have designed experiments of concern for the anticipation of nature's eventfulness. These experiments have taken advantage of the gap that has opened up between the object and its knowledge. Ignorance is temporalized, and this temporalization has made it possible for science to maintain its promise of prediction and project a sense of progress. The localization of ignorance in time has allowed science to appear energetic, dynamic and future-oriented. In the third and last part of this chapter, I suggest that the attempt of microbiologists to be faster than nature's evolution and leap over the gap between the object and its knowledge entails another form of ignorance that might be called the public secret.

The argument is based on empirical materials drawn from anthropological fieldwork that I conducted in New York City, where I worked with Dr Peter Palese, a prominent microbiologist and influenza researcher at Mount Sinai School of Medicine. With Palese and his team of researchers I discussed developments in the world of experimental science and learned about the challenges and

opportunities of contemporary infectious disease research in the
United States. Palese invited me to spend time in his lab and I was
able to learn and familiarize myself with some of the basic microbiological techniques deployed in the experimental investigation of
influenza viruses. Concomitantly to my work with this group of scientists, I observed meetings, attended lectures, visited workshops,
travelled to conferences, read scientific papers, interviewed microbiologists and participated in preparedness exercises and public health
emergency training in the United States. The following analysis is
based on this fieldwork, but it also includes relevant materials drawn
from scientific literature and public debates.

The Gap

In his contribution to a landmark volume on the nature of viruses, the
microbiologist Edwin D. Kilbourne offers a series of reflections on the
kind of entity that a virus might be. According to Kilbourne, a virus
sample is commonly thought of as something homogeneous, but it
actually represents a rather heterogeneous population of micro-organisms. It really is, Kilbourne suggests, 'a statistical consensus of a
genetically heterogeneous population ... in constant flux' (Kilbourne
1993: 294). What microbiologists use for their experimental investigations in the laboratory is, in Kilbourne's terms, a swarm of diverse
creatures caught in a process of constant change. As I learned from
the microbiologists with whom I worked, a virus sample inevitably
consists of multiple variants that are relentlessly replicating, mutating and recombining, even in the test tube. Microbiologists, in other
words, are working with an ephemeral entity lacking the necessary
means to maintain a stable biological form.

'Viruses', Manfred Eigen notes, 'have the ability to mystify laypeo-
ple and experts alike'. He explains: 'Early in their studies of viruses, in-
vestigators became puzzled by the high mutation rates they observed:
the magnitudes indicated that viruses must evolve more than a million times faster than cellular micro-organisms. If that were true, how
could viruses maintain their identities as pathogenic species over any
evolutionarily significant period?' (Eigen 1993: 42) Viruses are indeed
mystifying. They are caught in a process of permanent change. This
change, moreover, is random and totally unpredictable. Of course,
microbiologists are studying the modalities by which microbes mutate, but these studies have been unable to provide certainty about the
probability of a change in a virus. Celia Lowe puts it nicely when she

observes that viruses exist in a 'state of indeterminacy' with respect to the future forms that they generate (Lowe 2010: 627). The episte-mological endeavour to produce objective knowledge about such an entity has thus become almost impossible because the endlessly pro-liferating and rapidly mutating microbial creature is lacking a proper end point (see Landecker 2007: 20).

Today, the conception of the microbe as a moving target is com-mon sense among influenza researchers. It has developed over the past decades, solidifying into a powerful discourse that has funda-mentally reshaped the way a growing number of biomedical scien-tists and public health professionals approach infectious diseases worldwide. In the late 1980s and early 1990s a group of influential American scientists and public health specialists argued that new in-fectious diseases were likely to surface in the future. Coined by epide-miologist Stephen S. Morse, the seminal concept of 'emerging viruses' was officially launched in early May 1989 at a high-profile confer-ence in Washington, D.C., sponsored by Rockefeller University, the National Institute of Allergy and Infectious Diseases, and the Fogarty International Center (Altman 1989). Morse and his colleague, the Nobel Prize-winning virologist Joshua Lederberg, convened more than two hundred participants to the scientific meeting in order to discuss their concerns about the relentless evolution of microbes that seemed to account for the growing number of unexpected eruptions of infectious disease observed around the world, including, most im-portantly, the rapid spread of HIV/AIDS.[3] These concerns, as it turned out, were shared by many a scientist and, over the next decades, were frequently repeated by journalists.

The historian of medicine Nicholas King has underscored that the tremendous success and popularity of the concept of 'emerging viruses' was largely due to two American journalists, Laurie Garrett and Richard Preston (King 2001). Garrett, a former National Public Radio and Newsday correspondent, conducted extensive research for a book project on the appearance of a set of known and un-known infectious diseases while she was a fellow at the Harvard School of Public Health in the early 1990s. Upon learning that her colleague, Richard Preston, was working on a similar manuscript, Garrett intensified work on her rapidly growing publication in order to release it at the same time. In 1994, Garrett's *The Coming Plague* and Preston's *The Hot Zone* were published almost simultaneously to great public acclaim (Garrett 1994; Preston 1994). Both books instantly became bestsellers, effectively establishing the crisis im-aginary of a vulnerable nation threatened by an obscure mix of pathogenic agents lurking in the rain forests of far-away countries. As King points out, the discourse of emerging infectious diseases has been so powerful in the past few years because it is 'tremendously flexible, allowing a wide variety of actors to adopt it, moulding small parts or emphasizing particular elements and downplaying others to suit their own purposes' (King 2002: 768). The discourse furnishes actors

> with a consistent, self-contained ontology of epidemic disease: its causes and consequences, its patterns and prospects, the constellation of risks that it presents, and the most appropriate methods of preventing and managing those risks. It comes equipped with a moral economy and historical narrative, explaining how and why we find ourselves in the situation that we do now, identifying villains and heroes, ascribing blame for failures and credit for triumphs. (King 2002: 768)

Significantly, the discourse of emerging infectious diseases is animated not only by a biological understanding of the relentless evolution of microbial organisms, but also by a moral perception of the harmful consequences of modern progress.

Biomedical scientists, public health experts and journalists underscore that many factors are responsible for the rapid spread of contagious germs and the emergence of unknown diseases across the world.[4] An influential report, *Microbial Threats to Health in the United States*, published by the U.S. Institute of Medicine in 1992, foregrounds changes in human demographics and behaviour, technology and industry, economic development and land use, and international travel and commerce as crucial elements that have contributed to the emergence of new infectious diseases (see Lederberg, Shope and Oaks 1992). With a focus on the unpredictable interactions of social, biological, political and economic factors, the textual productions and technical interventions around emerging infectious diseases provide a critical account of modernity, which resonates with more general concerns about the critical condition of the environment. The discourse of emerging infectious diseases thus intersects with a broad range of other discourses, practices and affects, providing symbolic means to draw attention to and mobilize social and political action.

Not surprisingly, the concern with emerging viruses also resonates powerfully with the world-historical narrative of 'globalization'. Indeed, the troubling notion of a relentless traffic of microbial organisms falls on fertile ground in a world that increasingly finds itself in the grip of global 'flows' and their 'unintended consequences' for the health of populations and the wealth of nations. Anxieties about emerging viruses thus represent a version of what Anna Tsing terms 'globalism', by which she means the explicit endorsement 'of the importance of the global' (Tsing 2000: 330). Today, the 'global village' is considered a dangerous 'breeding ground' for deadly diseases. In the world of modern trade and travel, national borders have become permeable and the next pandemic is 'no more than a plane ride away' (Specter 2005: 50).[5] Viruses circle the planet in the shadow of the growing traffic of people, goods and things. Jean Comaroff underscores that emerging infectious diseases have come to symbolize 'biopolitical insecurities: unrecognizable aliens capable of disrupting existing immunities, penetrating once-secure boundaries at a time of deregulated exchange' (Comaroff 2007: 198).

At the heart of this understanding of the human condition in an age of globalization and deregulation is a distinctive ontology of mutant strains. What this ontology highlights is the ever-changing, ever-evolving nature of viruses. There is no end to the mutation of these viruses, and the future of their evolution remains unknown. Emerging viruses are able to trigger epidemics that end quietly, or that return with a vengeance. They are constantly reinventing themselves in response to the antiviral treatments that have been developed over decades. The microbes strike back, 'and yet we can never be sure when and how it will happen', as Melinda Cooper (2006: 117) phrased it. New agents emerge that challenge the scientific knowledge on which today's most effective treatments are based. The mutant strains are constantly evolving and adapting, and they will therefore always appear to be one step ahead. They change rapidly, spread instantly and become ever-more dangerous. Yet who is most at risk is unknown.

Thus, this historically specific ontology of mutant strains has naturalized the expert's ignorance. 'Often, for newly recognized diseases, the causative agent is unknown, making vaccine and drug development essentially impossible', the Institute of Medicine's 1992 report bluntly stated (quoted in Lederberg, Shope and Oaks 1992: 167f). In this ontology of mutant strains, disease has become unpredictable, understanding improbable and treatment unavailable. Experts are destined to be ignorant, at least in part, because nature is believed to be one step ahead, cooking up a new virus that does not even have a name.[6] And once it has been given a proper name and a proper place in an expanding genealogy of microbial descent, the virus mutates and recombines, making itself different from itself again. The next new virus and the next new disease are already in the offing.

At the heart of this ontology of mutant strains is thus a particular temporality. Nature is assumed to have advanced and to be already one step ahead. Microbiologists, by contrast, are behind and always respond belatedly. The rapid spread of SARS in 2003 is an example, demonstrating how today's 'microbe hunters' are struggling to keep up with nature's inventiveness. This ontology of mutant strains has forced microbiologists to accept a certain kind of temporal incongruity at the heart of their profession, making it impossible for them to accomplish the daunting task of 'achieving simultaneity with the present moment', to borrow Hirokazu Miyazaki's apposite phrase (Miyazaki 2003: 255). It comes as no surprise, then, that the temporal incongruity, which has taken shape between the object and its knowledge, has created a certain anxiety.

Tracking the circulation of mutant strains, microbiologists have increasingly accepted their tragic fate. But they have not only accepted it; they have also created a powerful place for themselves in the ontology of mutant strains, transforming the temporal incongruity into a pragmatic opportunity for intervention. Microbiologists have embraced the condition of ignorance and have extended their perspective beyond the narrow domain of science, urging people to protect themselves against the unknown. 'If humans are to survive the inevitable "counter-strike" from microbial life ... we need to prepare for the unexpected; learn to counter the unknowable, the virtual, the emergent', writes Cooper (2006). In today's ontology of mutant strains, ignorance is accepted as the normal and natural result of an inevitable temporal dissonance. For the microbiologists I worked with, this temporalized notion of ignorance has become a self-evident fact, reflecting the disjuncture of a natural evolution that is already ahead and a scientific understanding that is limping behind. The emergence of viruses, which are unknown at the time when they emerge, cannot be predicted in advance. Ignorance, therefore, is not only temporalized; it is also naturalized. And what this temporalization and naturalization of ignorance have enabled are new experiments, experiments of concern, designed to prepare for the unexpected. Such preparation reflects the growing desire of microbiologists to leap across the gap that has opened up between the object and its knowledge.

And so, the condition of ignorance has not undermined the possibility of microbiological research. On the contrary, ignorance has become an important resource for a certain kind of scientific practice, which leads us from the construction of the gap to the leap across the gap. How exactly have microbiologists appropriated this temporalized and naturalized condition of ignorance and turned the temporal incongruity into a pragmatic opportunity? What are the consequences that are specific to this kind of ignorance?

The Leap

In October 2011, the journals *Science* and *Nature* each received a research paper for peer review. The paper submitted to *Science* had been written by a team of microbiologists headed by Dr Ron Fouchier at Erasmus Medical Centre in Rotterdam. Fouchier's colleague, Dr Yoshihiro Kawaoka, of the University of Wisconsin, had submitted a similar paper to *Nature*. In the papers, the scientists and their teams of researchers independently reported results of a series of experiments conducted with H5N1 avian influenza viruses that had been modified in the laboratory. Using the ferret as an animal model, the viruses had been manipulated to make them more transmissible between humans. The purpose of the research was to determine the pandemic potential of the highly pathogenic H5N1 avian influenza virus. Would this virus be able to mutate and change? Would it be able to adapt to humans and cause a deadly pandemic?

In an ABC News report broadcasted on U.S. television in February 2012, a journalist declared that 'all sides agree that the mutated bird flu virus created by scientists ... could kill millions if it gets out'. Fouchier, who was introduced as a 'respected microbiologist', told journalists that his team had crafted in the laboratory 'probably one of the most dangerous viruses you can make' (quoted in Enserink 2011: 1192). The researchers nevertheless insisted that they were far from being 'mad scientists'. They considered themselves 'responsible researchers', enabling a better understanding of pandemic influenza. To know more about the potential of the virus seemed important for preparedness efforts. As Fouchier and his colleagues remarked in their paper: 'Whether this virus may acquire the ability to be transmitted via aerosols or respiratory droplets among mammals, including humans, to trigger a future pandemic is a key question for pandemic preparedness' (see Herfst et al. 2012: 1535). And Kawaoka and his team suggested that their 'findings emphasize[d] the need to prepare for potential pandemics ... and [would] help individuals conducting surveillance' (Imai et al. 2012: 420). Exploring the potential of the pathogenic agent in the laboratory, the scientists claimed to contribute to preparedness efforts and surveillance activities. They were trying to create a virus that nature had not yet been able to create. They were trying to overcome the condition of ignorance, be faster than nature's evolution and prevent a potentially catastrophic future from occurring. They were trying to prevail over the temporal disjuncture of a natural evolution that is ahead and a scientific understanding that is behind.

But what if the scientific information about the mutated virus inadvertently falls into the wrong hands, or the virus escapes by accident? The science journalist Laurie Garrett, of the U.S. Council on Foreign Relations, was interviewed for the ABC report.[7] 'My first reaction was "Oh, my God, why did they do this?"' She then added, 'I'm not real comfortable with having this virus exist – anywhere!' Security experts, the ABC journalist noted, 'say it's crazy to let these secrets get into the hands of terrorists'.

The research papers submitted by Fouchier and Kawaoka sparked a controversial debate about infectious disease research and its contribution to the effort of preparing for the coming plague – the 'species-threatening event forecast by scientists and journalists and dramatized in fiction and film in the closing decades of the twentieth century' (Wald 2008: 1). In an editorial, the *New York Times* called the germ a 'doomsday virus' that 'could kill tens or hundreds of millions of people if it escaped confinement or was stolen by terrorists'.[8] Hundreds of journal articles, opinion pieces, newspaper reports and blog entries were published, offering a broad range of suggestions on what should or should not be done with the research. Commentators underscored that there are limits to scientific freedom and that these limits had been transgressed in this case. This contribution to the prevention of pandemics had not delivered on its promise, making the world safer; on the contrary, it had manufactured a new threat, turning anxieties about an apocalyptic disease into a self-fulfilling prophecy. Richard Elbright, a biologist at Rutgers University, was shocked by this attempt to produce such a virus in the test tube, noting that 'it should never have been done' (quoted in Enserink 2011: 1192).

In an unprecedented move, a prominent U.S. science and security advisory board, the National Science Advisory Board for Biosecurity, or NSABB, recommended that the journals *Science* and *Nature* withdraw key details of the studies which would allow bioterrorists to replicate the experiments and generate the 'deadly virus'. 'It's the first time I'm aware of in the life sciences that this kind of recommendation has been made', commented the public health professional Michael Osterholm, a member of the NSABB.[9] The moment seemed portentous; the world of infectious disease research was in great turmoil. The U.S. Department of Health and Human Services contacted the journals, requesting that the editors postpone the publication and redact the papers. The Department also suggested that the full information should be released only to 'responsible scientists'. In January 2012, influenza researchers announced a pause of sixty days in transmission experiments with the mutated strain. For the time being, it seemed better to remain on the other side of knowing. In the face of potentially dangerous knowledge, ignorance was valuable and desirable.

In February 2012 the journal *Nature* joined the controversial debate, announcing that more discussion was needed, but that the papers should be published eventually. In a sudden and completely unexpected turnabout, the National Science Advisory Board for Biosecurity reversed its original decision in March and recommended that both papers be published in full. No straightforward explanation was given as to why the board suddenly revised its recommendation.

At a forum, organized by the Harvard School of Public Health, the epidemiologist Marc Lipsitch had suggested 'it's good that the research was done'.[10] He had continued:

> I think it helps us to remember that the H5N1 pandemic threat is a real one. Every year that a pandemic didn't occur, people began to think we were crying wolf and there was some reason to think this threat was diminished. And I think psychologically with the 2009 pandemic, which was not H5N1[,] ... a lot of people found it hard to maintain the same level of preparedness. But the threat continues, and I think this is a scientific piece of evidence that it continues. So in that regard, I think it's important.[11]

According to Lipsitch, Fouchier's and Kawaoka's controversial research was important because it allowed experts to keep attention strong, struggle against 'pandemic fatigue' and prevent the threat from settling into oblivion. Scandalous publicity seemed better than no publicity.[12] Bruce Alberts, the Editor-in-Chief of *Science*, concurred, underlining that 'people worldwide are now much more aware of the potential threat that this virus ... poses to humanity' (Alberts 2012: 1521).

At a conference, organized by the American Society of Microbiology in March, Fouchier admitted that his research actually demonstrated that the mutated strain was less lethal and contagious for ferrets than those found in nature. A few months earlier, the same scientist had claimed to have 'created one of the most dangerous viruses you can make'. Contrary to what he had suggested earlier, the 'doomsday virus', extensively discussed and debated in the public sphere, actually turned out to transmit very poorly in the laboratory. In fact, the 'deadly strain' did not kill any of the ferrets. This important information was released by Fouchier only several months into the controversy. The 'killer virus', fabricated in the laboratory, turned out to be all hype and no substance. Fouchier nevertheless affirmed that he would stick by his original comment. 'Maybe I'd put it slightly differently next time', he explained at a meeting of the Royal Society in London in April, 'but it is the truth. Flu viruses are scary and if they acquire the ability to go airborne in humans, they cause pandemics'.[13]

Dr Peter Palese, Chairman of the Microbiology Department at Mount Sinai School of Medicine in New York, was outraged and upset about his colleagues Fouchier and Kawaoka. He could hardly contain himself. 'Fouchier and Kawaoka should have gone to the press', he told me. 'They should have gone to the press and said: Look, we want to make a statement that these viruses that we have produced in the laboratory have lost any virulence in ferrets' (personal communication). The hype about the 'doomsday virus' was unnecessary and unwarranted in Palese's view:

> It is absolutely fraudulent, and I think Fouchier and Kawaoka should lose their National Institutes of Health grant, as far as I'm concerned. I feel very strongly about it. Because it is dishonest and scientifically fraudulent. It's fraudulent when the virus is now completely, completely a-virulent, a-pathogenic, in ferrets ... and not [to] say anything for more than half a year! Not to admit it, not to say it, after everyone is up in arms ... it's criminal! (Peter Palese, personal communication)

Tracing mutant strains and designing experiments of concern, microbiologists were increasingly drawn into contentious debates about the security implications of their work. Officials, journalists and policy-makers were alarmed; they emphasized that scientists must prevent dangerous knowledge getting into the wrong hands.

The Faith

The highly pathogenic H5N1 avian influenza virus that has caused so much concern among experts, journalists and the wider public was originally detected in 1997 in Hong Kong, where it infected twelve people, eight of whom died. To prevent the spread of the germ, authorities ordered the culling of Hong Kong's entire poultry population. As a result of this massive intervention, the virus vanished for a while, but then it reappeared in 2003, infecting animals on a regular basis, but killing humans only sporadically. Tracking the spread of the germ from Asia to Africa, scientists suggested that the virus was evolving rapidly, that it was adapting to humans, and that it might cause a catastrophic pandemic (see Lowe 2010). Exploring the potential of the virus in the laboratory, microbiologists sought to determine whether the microbe might be able to mutate and transmit more efficiently between humans. This part of the chapter will explore how experts, journalists and the public responded to the publication of the contested research.

In June 2012, a CNN report announced that Fouchier's and Kawaoka's 'deadly bird flu research' had finally been published after a long and controversial debate. As the CNN journalist stressed, 'the story could affect people all over the world'. Referring to the notorious papers that had just been released, the news report suggested that 'now you and I can go online and basically read how you can make a super-deadly version of the bird flu virus'. But the journalist wondered how many people had actually died from this virus: 'It's an important question because people talk about bird flu and sort of flip out. So let's get some numbers behind the actual flipping'. According to the World Health Organization, the H5N1 avian influenza virus has affected 602 people, 355 of whom have died. 'So it doesn't take a mathematician to figure out that this is more than a 50 per cent mortality rate', the journalist remarked. She continued:

> That is not good. That's the bad news. The good news is that this virus does not spread easily person to person, and that's what the super-bug would do. If you could create a super-bug version of this that spreads easily from person to person then you've got a 50 per cent mortality rate virus spreading [from] person to person easily. And that's the thing we're talking about, which is why this makes it so concerning.

As a result of the publication of Fouchier's and Kawaoka's articles, a 'blueprint' for a 'biological weapon of mass destruction' was now online. The fact that the scientists had exaggerated the lethality of the agent crafted in the laboratory was not even mentioned by the journalist.

What has made the H5N1 avian influenza virus generally so scary for many people in the first place is its staggering mortality rate. If a virus with such a high mortality rate evolves and begins to circulate more efficiently from person to person, it might turn into a 'super-bug', suddenly killing people by the million. As the CNN report demonstrates, the terrible mortality rate of more than 50 per cent was simply taken for granted in the frantic debate about the looming threat. The figure is an official one; it is based on the accumulated number of cases and deaths confirmed by the WHO in Geneva. Given these numbers, no expert is necessary to calculate the fatality rate and explain its significance for public health.

Peter Palese, the Mount Sinai microbiologist with whom I worked, was troubled. He was troubled by the simplicity of this mathematics of disaster. As he explained to me: 'They say we have a 50 per cent fatality. But the 50 per cent fatality in H5N1 infections in humans is based on a definition by the WHO'. The health organization actually underscores, Palese pointed out, that 'we don't know who gets infected, so we can only count those people where samples have been sent to London or Atlanta. And this is a legitimate definition'. He continued, 'But that is not the real number, because only the people who are dead or half-dead in Vietnam or Indonesia are counted' (Peter Palese, personal communication). Officials at the WHO recognize the great difficulty of identifying cases in remote areas of rural Asia and thus include only infections that have been verified and certified. As a result of this strong emphasis on confirmation, fatal cases are more likely to be counted simply because they are much more visible than other, less dramatic cases. The result of this focus on fatalities is a very low number of statistically documented infections and, as a consequence, a very high rate of mortality. According to Palese, the WHO's case definition is extremely rigid. It does not allow for asymptomatic infections and essentially requires that a sick person in a remote village in Vietnam seeks expert medical help at a hospital with sufficient resources to identify the illness and draw a sample. These samples must be collected and shipped to London or Atlanta for additional laboratory confirmation. They must be sent on dry ice, which is not easily available in many countries. Additionally, commercial couriers are reluctant to ship contagious samples across the world owing to safety concerns and liability issues. All these practical factors make statistical documentation difficult and contribute to a considerable overrepresentation of fatal cases in the numbers that are reported by the WHO. The deep desire to be as 'rigid' and 'objective' as possible has reduced the total number of infections to a few cases of severe disease that are observed in the hospital and verified in the laboratory.

In an article, Palese and his Mount Sinai colleague Taia T. Wang argue that only a 'small fraction of the total number of infected cases has been accounted for under the WHO surveillance system' (Palese and Wang 2012: 2212). As Palese explained to me, 'If 1 million or 10 million people have been infected, namely a-clinically or sub-clinically, then this 50 per cent fatality rate is completely idiotic. There are now studies by Chinese researchers where they observed that 3 per cent of the rural population has antibodies [against the H5N1 avian influenza virus]' (personal communication). According to Palese, these studies show that millions of people have been exposed to the virus. Most of these infections have been mild or asymptomatic. For the calculation of the fatality rate it makes a huge difference if the denominator, the number of actual cases of infection, is 602, or 1 million, or 10 million. In fact, the denominator is completely unknown today. What the ominous 50 per cent fatality rate of the H5N1 virus reveals, therefore, is a misplaced faith in confirmed numbers. 'The frequency and certainty with which the staggering fatality rate is reported is troubling when one considers how the numbers are generated', Palese and Wang (2012: 2212) point out. At the heart of these numbers is thus an ignorance, and this ignorance is itself ignored. Today, no effort is made to gain more insight about the actual extent of a-clinical or sub-clinical H5N1 infections in Asia. The fact that no effort is made is stunning, given the number of resources that have become available over the past decade for influenza research. The focus of the WHO continues to be on the conditions of hospitalized patients. No large-scale, standardized epidemiological studies are conducted to detect asymptomatic infections. Thus, the actual scope of the epidemic is unknown. We might call this ignorance a 'public secret', in Michael Taussig's sense of the term (Taussig 1999). It is the result of actors and institutions having learned to know what not to know. This ignorance of ignorance is essential for the publicity of the pandemic threat. It allows actors and institutions to highlight the threat, reveal the vulnerability of the population and authorize the message of preparedness. Faith in the lethality of the virus draws attention, spurs action and motivates people to remain alert and watch out for signs of an impending pandemic.

Conclusion

Linsey McGoey underscores that attention to the work of ignorance calls for 'a subtle shift in the epistemological gaze that seeks to offer non-knowledge its full due as a social fact, not as a precursor or an impediment to more knowledge, but as a productive force in itself, as the twin and not the opposite of knowledge' (McGoey 2012a: 3).[14] In today's world of pandemic preparedness, ignorance indeed operates as a productive force. Scientists, journalists and officials emphasize that under conditions of uncertainty people need information about what is known and what is not known. However, while some kinds of ignorance are highlighted, other ones are systematically ignored. From an anthropological perspective it is thus essential to examine whether forms of ignorance are considered an opportunity or an obstacle for

particular formations of agency and their uneven distribution across
the social world. As we have seen, the temporalization and naturalization of ignorance, its localization in the gap between the present
and the future shape of viruses, has become an important source of
agency for microbiology. It makes the science significant and relevant
as well as exciting and challenging. Typically, the temporalized and
naturalized kinds of ignorance that are taken up as a source of agency
become hyper-visible in public discourse, and this hyper-visibility in
turn contributes to the constitution of a certain form of experience:
an experience of the present as eventful. The constant invocation of
such temporalized and naturalized ignorance plays a crucial role in
today's normalized understanding of emerging infectious diseases.
Scientists, journalists and officials have selected one type of ignorance
over other types, and they are now referring to the other side of knowing, to *this* other side of knowing, in order to justify interventions into
the conditions of existence.

This chapter has shown how the ontology of mutant strains constitutes and is constituted by ignorance. The sedimentation of a certain
kind of ignorance has allowed actors and institutions to transform an
absence of knowledge into a lack of knowledge, and, as a consequence,
establish a regime of representation and intervention concerned with
this lack. Thus, the authority of science lies not just in the ability to
make knowledge claims, but also in the capacity to designate, demarcate and regulate the other side of knowing. In public performances
scientists foreground certain kinds of ignorance, aiming to convince
others to address *these* gaps rather than other gaps. A focus on such
performances of persuasion, and their contestations, can explain how
and why apocalyptic anxieties about the health of the population and
the wealth of the nation emerge in specific contexts. Such an explanation requires an investigation of how science, medicine, media and
the state interact, and how these forces are reconfiguring perceptions
of the world for certain kinds of ignorance to appear as relevant and
significant, plausible and compelling. Which absence of knowledge
acquires the constitutive function of a lack? What makes a particular absence persuasive? What are the motivations of actors and institutions to engage and perpetuate the ontology of mutant strains?
How are particular designations and demarcations of the other side
of knowing anchored in historically specific discourses and practices?
Ignorance is always an essential part of the scientific endeavour, but
the challenge is to figure out which conception of ignorance becomes
hegemonic, why, when and how. Additionally, scholars can show
how scientists have become mindful of some gaps but less mindful of

others. Such studies will help us to better understand how circumscriptions of ignorance acquire social, cultural and political force.

Acknowledgements

I would like to thank the editors, Thomas Kirsch and Roy Dilley, and the other contributors to this volume. Their comments and suggestions on an earlier version of this chapter were generous and insightful. Thanks as well to my new colleagues at the Department of Social Science, Health & Medicine, King's College London for excellent suggestions. I am very grateful for the careful readings of Orkideh Behrouzan and Hanna Kienzler. Thanks, as always, to Peter Palese, who continues to be an inspiring interlocutor.

Notes

1. See, among others, Dilley (2010); McGoey (2012a); Proctor and Schiebinger (2008).
2. See as well Gross (2007).
3. See Lederberg, Shope and Oaks (1992); Morse (1995); and Krause (1998).
4. See, for example, Culliton (1990); Krause (1992); Morse (1993); Satcher (1995); or Krause (1998).
5. On the scale politics of emerging infectious disease discourse, see King (2004).
6. 'Ignorance' here simply refers to the symbolical constitution of a person, thing or event as unknown.
7. Laurie Garrett's bestsellers are: *The Coming Plague: Newly Emerging Diseases in a World out of Balance* (1994) and *Betrayal of Trust: The Collapse of Global Public Health* (2000).
8. See 'An Engineered Doomsday', *New York Times*, 7 January 2012.
9. See news item 'US Government Urges Journals to Omit Details of Two H5N1 Studies', *CIDRAP News*, 20 December 2011.
10. 'Bird Flu Research: Dangerous Information on a Deadly Virus'. Forum at the Harvard School of Public Health, 15 February 2012.
11. 'Bird Flu Research: Dangerous Information on a Deadly Virus'. Forum at the Harvard School of Public Health, 15 February 2012.
12. 'Scandalous publicity' is Lawrence Cohen's term (see Cohen 1999).
13. This was announced at a meeting entitled 'H5N1 Research: Biosafety, Biosecurity and Bioethics' at The Royal Society, London, 3–4 March 2012.
14. See also McGoey (2012b).

References

Alberts, B. 2012. 'Introduction: H5N1'. *Science* 336, 1521.

Altman, L.K. 1989. 'Fearful of Outbreaks, Doctors Pay New Heed to Emerging Viruses'. *The New York Times*, 9 May 1989.

Cohen, L. 1999. 'Where it Hurts: Indian Material for an Ethics of Organ Transplantation'. *Daedalus* 128, 135–65.

Comaroff, J. 2007. 'Beyond Bare Life: AIDS, (Bio)Politics, and the Neoliberal Order'. *Public Culture* 19, 197–219.

Cooper, M. 2006. 'Pre-Empting Emergence: The Biological Turn in the War on Terror'. *Theory, Culture & Society* 23, 113–35.

Culliton, B.J. 1990. 'Emerging Viruses, Emerging Threat'. *Science* 247, 279–80.

Dilley, R.M. 2010. 'Reflections on Knowledge Practices and the Problem of Ignorance'. *Journal of the Royal Anthropological Institute* 16, 167–92.

Eigen, M. 1993. 'Viral Quasispecies'. *Scientific American* 269, 42–49.

Enserink, M. 2011. 'Controversial Studies Give a Deadly Flu Virus Wings'. *Science* 334, 1192–93.

Galison, P. 2004. 'Removing Knowledge'. *Critical Inquiry* 31, 229–43.

Garrett, L. 1994. *The Coming Plague: Newly Emerging Diseases in a World out of Balance*. New York: Penguin Books.

———. 2000. *Betrayal of Trust: The Collapse of Global Public Health*. New York: Hyperion.

Gross, M. 2007. 'The Unknown Process: Dynamic Connections of Ignorance, Non-Knowledge and Related Concepts'. *Current Sociology* 55, 742–59.

Herfst, S., et al. 2012. 'Airborne Transmission of Influenza A/H5N1 Virus Between Ferrets'. *Science* 336, 1534–41.

Imai, M., et al. 2012. 'Experimental Adaptation of an Influenza H5 HA Confers Respiratory Droplet Transmission to a Reassortant H5 HA/H1N1 Virus in Ferrets'. *Nature* 486, 420–28.

Kilbourne, E.D. 1993. 'Afterword: A Personal Summary Presented as a Guide for Discussion'. In *Emerging Viruses*, ed. S.S. Morse. Oxford and New York: Oxford University Press.

King, N.B. 2001. 'Infectious Disease in a World of Goods', Ph.D. Thesis, Harvard University.

———. 2002. 'Security, Disease, Commerce: Ideologies of Postcolonial Global Health'. *Social Studies of Science* 32, 763–89.

———. 2004. 'The Scale Politics of Emerging Diseases'. *OSIRIS* 19, 62–76.

Krause, R.M. 1992. 'The Origin of Plagues: Old and New'. *Science* 257, 1073–78.

———. (ed.) 1998. *Emerging Infections*. San Diego, CA: Academic Press.

Landecker, H. 2007. *Culturing Life: How Cells Became Technologies*. Cambridge, MA: Harvard University Press.

Lederberg, J., R.E. Shope and S.C. Oaks (eds) 1992. *Emerging Infections: Microbial Threats to Health in the United States*. Washington, DC: National Academy Press.

Lowe, C. 2010. 'Viral Clouds: Becoming H5N1 in Indonesia'. *Cultural Anthropology* 25, 625–49.

Luhmann, N. 1998. *Observations on Modernity*. Stanford, CA: Stanford University Press.

McGoey, L. 2012a. 'The Logic of Strategic Ignorance'. *British Journal of Sociology* 63, 533–76.

———. 2012b. 'Strategic Unknowns: Towards a Sociology of Ignorance'. *Economy and Society* 41, 1–16.

Miyazaki, H. 2003. 'The Temporalities of the Market'. *American Anthropologist* 105, 255–65.

Morse, S.S. (ed.) 1993. *Emerging Viruses*. Oxford and New York: Oxford University Press.

———. 1995. 'Factors in the Emergence of Infectious Diseases'. *Emerging Infectious Diseases* 1, 7–15.

Palese, P. and T.T. Wang 2012. 'H5N1 Influenza Viruses: Facts, Not Fear'. *PNAS* 109, 2211–13.

Preston, R. 1994. *The Hot Zone*. New York: Random House.

Proctor, R.N. and L. Schiebinger (eds) 2008. *Agnotology: The Making and Unmaking of Ignorance*. Stanford, CA: Stanford University Press.

Satcher, D. 1995. 'Emerging Infections: Getting Ahead of the Curve'. *Emerging Infectious Diseases* 1, 1–6.

Specter, M. 2005. 'Nature's Bioterrorist: Is There Any Way to Prevent a Deadly Avian-Flu Pandemic?' *The New Yorker*, 28 February 2005, 50–61.

Taussig, M. 1999. *Defacement: Public Secrecy and the Labor of the Negative*. Stanford, CA: Stanford University Press.

Tsing, A. 2000. 'The Global Situation'. *Cultural Anthropology* 15, 327–60.

Wald, P. 2008. *Contagious: Cultures, Carriers, and the Outbreak Narrative*. Durham, NC: Duke University Press.

Carlo Caduff received his Ph.D. in Anthropology from the University of California at Berkeley. Before joining the Department of Social Science, Health & Medicine at King's College London, he was a Lecturer in the Department of Social and Cultural Anthropology at the University of Zurich. Carlo Caduff works on the changing relations between science, medicine, media and the state. His work has appeared in *Anthropological Theory*, *Annual Review of Anthropology*, *Cultural Anthropology* and *Current Anthropology*. He is co-organizer of the Wenner-Gren Symposium 'New Media, New Publics?'

Chapter 2

IGNORING NATIVE IGNORANCE

EPIDEMIOLOGICAL ENCLOSURES OF
NOT-KNOWING PLAGUE IN INNER ASIA

Christos Lynteris

One of the gravest epidemiological crises in twentieth-century East Asia occurred in northeast China in the winter of 1910–1911.[1] The great pneumonic plague epidemic originated in the Sino-Russian border town of Manzhouli and spread rapidly along the tracks of the newly built Manchurian railways, striking Harbin and Mukden by the end of October 1910, reaching Beijing in January 1911 and the Shandong Peninsula in February 1911. Before it finally waned, by the end of March, this contagious, airborne form of plague left approximately sixty thousand dead (Nathan 1967; Gamsa 2006; Summers 2012).

As it unfolded on the contested ground of Manchuria, the epidemic offered itself for geopolitical strife between Russia, China and Japan, the three empires contending for control of the region (Nathan 1967; Summers 2012). Two questions hovered over anti-plague efforts in Manchuria during the winter of 1911: who was to blame and who was capable of arresting the course of the disease? As Nathan and Summers have demonstrated, the answer to this twin problem was a determining factor of a far more important question: who was modern, responsible and civilized enough to rule Manchuria? With the aim of settling the imperial dispute over the origins and containment of the disease, the First International Plague Conference was convened at Mukden in April 1911 just a few days after the plague came to a sudden stop.

During the conference, China's anti-plague mastermind, the Cambridge-educated Wu Liande, supported a radical theory regarding the origins of the epidemic, arguing that the Manchurian outbreak bore no relation to rats (an idea aggressively supported by Japan and its colonial agents in the region) but actually originated in marmots known locally as *tarbagan*. At the same time, Wu defended the position that native Mongol and Buryat hunters of this particular animal were free of plague. This he attributed not to bacteriological immunity but to the indigenous hunters' knowledge of plague and its mode of infection (Lynteris 2013). The latter were hence seen as incorporating a traditional knowledge of what was known as 'harvesting' the animal without contracting the deadly disease. In my previous work I have demonstrated how this discourse was linked to allegations that the cause of the spread of plague was the ignorance and ineptness of migrant Chinese workers employed in harvesting marmot fur for the international market. These so-called coolies from Shandong were constituted as a degenerate and degenerative trait of the Qing Empire, an apt symbol in the hands of scientific-minded reformers who applied themselves to the urgent need to save the Chinese race by reconstituting China on a modern governmental basis (Lynteris 2013).

Rather than revisiting the biopolitical-geopolitical complex leading to this 'skilled native, inept coolie' binary (Lynteris 2013), and its impact on inter-imperial and intra-imperial strife, I would here like to problematize the very basis of what may be called the 'native knowledge hypothesis': the contention that Mongols and Buryats knew plague as a zoonotic disease, being thus able to prevent the perilous bacterial species-jump leading to human outbreaks of plague. Did native hunters really recognize plague as a distinct zoonotic disease or pathogen? Were they aware that marmots were the original source of a distinct disease which was contagious amongst humans? Did they know the mode of infection, and the way to diagnose an ill animal? Did they moreover take measures against the contagious spread of the disease between humans in case a hunter was in fact infected from its marmot prey?

From a methodological perspective, contemporary ethnography offers no solution to this historical problem, as the native knowledge hypothesis became a state doctrine after 1911, and was actively indoctrinated into local populations in China, Russia and Mongolia through medical education campaigns for many decades thereafter. As a result it is impossible to conclude from observations in the field today what Mongol and Buryat hunters knew back at the turn of the twentieth century. As I have often encountered in my fieldwork, traditional knowledge of plague has become a ubiquitous and undisputed object of national pride. The only reliable source hence lies with historical ethnographic records uncontaminated by the question of plague in the region. These, it is safe to say, are composed of original ideas that existed prior to the articulation of the native knowledge hypothesis in 1895. But of equal interest is the examination of medical research propounding the native knowledge hypothesis before this became part of the Chinese and Russian state ideological apparatus (i.e., before 1911). For in such sources is found the raw material of the native knowledge hypothesis, which can then be compared to what is actually known about plague today. Does what native hunters were supposed to know match the biological reality of *Yersinia pestis* and the epidemiology of plague? Or does it simply match misconceptions of turn-of-the-century medical professionals about what was then a newly discovered disease?

This chapter will demonstrate that what Mongols and Buryats were supposed to have known clearly reflected the latter. In other words, medical scientists projected their mistaken scientific theories about plague to indigenous subjects. More than that, however, I would like to argue, this projection did not take place on an empty canvas, but on an actually existing matrix of human–marmot interactions, which was enclosed within a medical-materialist paradigm. The term 'medical materialism' originated with William James, who argued against physiological explanations of religious experience:

> Medical materialism finishes up Saint Paul by calling his vision on the road to Damascus a discharging lesion of the occipital cortex, he being an epileptic. It snuffs out Saint Teresa as an hysteric, Saint Francis of Assisi as an hereditary degenerate... All such mental over-tensions, it says, are, when you come to the bottom of the matter, mere affairs of diathesis (auto-intoxications most probably), due to the perverted action of various glands which physiology will yet discover. (James 2008: 19)

Building on this idea, in her influential book *Purity and Danger* (1993) Mary Douglas famously confronted approaches that portrayed eating taboos as hygienic practices thinly covered by a symbolic or ritual cloak. She argued that even in cases when such practices do have a hygienic effect, as seen from a contemporary biomedical viewpoint, this should not be assumed to be their underlying aim. Similarly, I want to argue, the native knowledge hypothesis had at its heart an operation of medical-materialist reductionism which translated Mongol and Buryat cosmologies, as a matrix of human–animal relations, into metaphors of hygienic precaution and epidemiological prevention.

This chapter will argue that in order to break the spell of medical materialism still dominating understandings of the social ecology of plague in Inner Asia, the actually existing native ignorance of plague must be approached as a condition for other ways of knowing and relating to what is considered to be its local host.

Birth of the *Tarbagan* Hypothesis

The Siberian marmot was first studied by Gustav Radde during the Great Siberian Expedition of the Russian Geographical Society in the 1850s. Radde (1862) identified the animal, noting that it was hunted by natives, yet did not record any particular illness harboured by or related to it. The first observation of an epizootic among *tarbagans* came in 1867 in the memoirs of Aleksandr Cherkassov, a Russian hunter who noted that 'there are years when natives stop eating *tarbagan*, due to rampant disease in the latter; they are dying like flies and many natives, reckless enough to feed on roasted marmots, have paid with their lives' (Cherkassov 2012: 365, my amended translation). Cherkassov did not, however, name the disease or describe the symptoms in animal or man, making any diagnostic identification impossible.

The first medical report of an outbreak of infectious disease of bubonic character in the region came in 1888, from the region south of Lake Baikal known as Transbaikalia (Reshetnikov 1895: 6). Almost annually thereafter small outbreaks would be reported in the early autumn amongst Cossack hunters in the region. In October 1894 after a feldscher named Savateev reported news of an outbreak in the village of Soktui, the senior medical doctor Mikhail Eduardovich Beliavsky was dispatched to investigate. Beliavsky claimed that the disease was *chuma*, the Russian term used at the time to refer to human epidemics characterized by buboes. Rather than it being just any sort of bubonic pestilence, the disease was called by Beliavsky '*tarbagan* plague'. In his six-page article in the April–June 1895 issue of the *Review of Public Hygiene, Forensic and Practical Medicine*, the Russian doctor followed Cherkassov in claiming that Siberian marmots suffered from occasional late-summer epizootics, particularly manifested in animals that would still roam the steppes when other marmots were already in their burrows preparing for hibernation. These, Beliavsky claimed, were 'plague-ridden' marmots, although here the term 'plague' (*chuma*) should be taken in its broader sense, as at the time of observation the bacteriological identity of the disease was just being ascertained (Beliavsky made no mention of bacteria in his report). According to Beliavsky, ill marmots 'do not bark, become sluggish, their walk is shaky, they often develop a reddish hard tumour under the shoulder; and when they go far away from their holes they cannot get back in, and become easy targets for their enemies' (1895: 2). Human infection was believed by Beliavsky to result from hunting and skinning the animal, which was an important source of fat, fur and meat in the region. However, he claimed, native Mongols and Buryats were able to avoid such dangerous prey, as they could readily recognize a plague-infected marmot from its unusual behaviour. As if that was not fortunate enough, he claimed that native knowledge of marmot-plague was not limited to distanced diagnosis. Mongols and Buryats were said to have developed a post-capture haematological test in order to verify the health state of marmots: 'there is also a post-mortem feature by which the Buryats judge if a killed *tarbagan* was ill or healthy. They make a cut on its sole, and if they see gore in the wound, they consider this *tarbagan* plague-ridden and pass it to be eaten by dogs' (Beliavsky 1895: 2). If in spite of all precaution the disease spread to humans, then the family of the patient was said to leave him or her in the yurt, fleeing to further pastures. Upon their return, relatives would bury the patient's corpse and burn the yurt with all its contents (ibid.: 6).

Immediately following Beliavksy's narrative, a second article was authored, by Reshetnikov, a Russian doctor who three years earlier had attended a previous limited outbreak in the area. Reshetnikov (1895: 8) claimed that the plague-stricken marmot 'walks sluggishly, staggers like a drunk'. As it would lie sleeping on top of its mound, the ill marmot was said to become an easy target for predators and shepherds alike. Reshetnikov claimed that whilst animals could eat ill marmots with impunity, according to 'local old-timer residents', humans who ate an infected marmot or made 'use [of it] at home' were contaminated by '*tarbagan* plague'; Reshetnikov stressed that individuals were infected only through direct contact with the animal's body fluids (ibid.: 8).

In the light of what epidemiologists consider to be the third plague pandemic, spreading in the second half of the nineteenth century from the Yunnan highlands via Hong Kong across the globe (Benedict 1996; Echenberg 2007), these otherwise obscure Russian reports acquired unexpected fame and meaning. International fascination with Beliavsky's and Reshetnikov's work lay mainly in the fact that it identified plague as a disease contracted by an animal. Reading the reports in light of Alexandre Yersin's discovery of the plague bacillus in the summer of 1894 must have been a sensation. In fact, Beliavsky's and Reshetnikov's zoonotic theory was articulated three years before Paul-Louis Simond published his authoritative study arguing for the role of the rat in the spread of plague. Thus, it was the *tarbagan* hypothesis that proposed for the first time an animal source of the disease.

It is no wonder then that, unusually for Russian medical research at the time, before a full year had elapsed, note of Beliavsky's and Reshetnikov's evidence was made in *The British Medical Journal* (Anonymous 1895). German authors also showed great interest in the *tarbagan* hypothesis and its ethnographic context, lending credence and a wide scientific audience to the native knowledge hypothesis (Favre 1899; Müller 1900). Most significantly, however, the two interlinked hypotheses found an enthusiastic reader in Franck Clemow (1900), who provided the English-speaking world with a long and authoritative review of the plague situation in Inner Asia in the pages of *The Journal of Tropical Medicine*, where Russian findings were presented approvingly. Clemow's article quickly achieved canonical status with dozens of scientific papers, books and manuals on plague soon mirroring his synopsis of the reports, which fully adopted the native knowledge hypothesis. Clemow would continue to provide readers of *The Lancet* and *The British Medical Journal* with snippets of the continuing Russian plague-research in the region, singling out information that supported the two hypotheses.

Come the Manchurian crisis, Wu Liande, who had no previous experience with plague, was thus in a position to draw upon this literature on plague at the northern edge of the Chinese Empire and systematize its native knowledge hypothesis into an epidemiological regime of knowledge which, while pleasing the Russians, struck a blow at Japanese claims of scientific superiority, by discrediting Tokyo's insistence that the origins of the epidemic lay with rats (Nathan 1967; Summers 2012; Lynteris 2013).

Wu Liande's Scientific Fiction

Although at the time of Wu's address to the First International Plague Conference the existence of *Yersinia pestis* in marmots had not been bacteriologically confirmed, Wu defended the *tarbagan* origins of plague.[2] At the same time, he defended the native knowledge hypothesis. In his opening speech, Wu claimed that 'the local people have long been familiar with this disease, both in men and in animals':

> Nature is very rich in coincidences, and perhaps as scientists more
> than any other class of men you are prepared for such, but who would
> have dreamed that the healthy marmot, basking, as it loves to do, in
> the warm sunshine, utters a cry resembling the sound of '*bu pa, bu pa*'
> which in Chinese language, at any rate, means 'don't be afraid', or 'no
> harm'. Sickness renders it mute, so that in the light of present knowl-
> edge it would seem that when the marmot is not crying 'no harm, no
> harm', there is very real harm indeed. The sickness in the *tarabagan*,
> which we presume is the forerunner of the plague, in this case is char-
> acterised by an unsteady gait, inability to run or to cry when chased,
> and when caught, the physical signs are seen to consist principally of
> enlargement of the glands. When noticing the above signs, the experi-
> enced hunter leaves his quarry severely alone and betakes himself to
> more distant sphere. (Strong 1912: 19–20)

If extant, this linguistic trait would form sufficient basis for some
ravelling debate in both evolutionary and semiotic circles. What
paradoxical process of adaptation could afflict an animal with so in-
advertent an evolutionary trait as advertising its edibility to its hunters? And how should one account for the testimony that this '*bu pa*'
invitation is spoken in human tongue, albeit not the one understood
by its native hunter but by his imperial master instead?

Besides being a wonderful scientific fantasy, Wu's '*bu pa*' testimony led to another link in his epidemiological reasoning: if the
healthy *tarbagan* fatefully speaks out its edible state, on the contrary,
the silence of the marmots signals danger of infection, a fact readily
understood by native hunters, in association with other supposed
traits of ill animals like an unsteady gait. Thus, if perhaps Mongols
and Buryats could not speak Chinese well enough to decipher the
marmot's uncanny invitation to a feast, Wu appeared certain that
they were able to semantically decipher the absence of linguistic
output as signalling danger.

This fantastic complex of zoosemiotics is a good vantage point
from which to ask a crucial question: what was the source of the
data composing the native knowledge hypothesis? At the time of
the conference Wu had not yet ventured to the steppes, hence his
sources were previous writings on plague in the region and the
field notes of his subaltern, Dr Chuan Shaojing, who had visited
Manzhouli in the winter of 1911. However, it is evident from the
conference proceedings (Strong 1912) that Chuan did not actually
venture to the steppes beyond the border town itself. Even if he had,
by the time of his visit marmots would have been hibernating deep
in their burrows. Thus all access to observed behaviour relating the
tarbagan's signalling was effectively barred to Chuan. His data were

gathered, as he himself admitted, from two sources: a Russian rail-
way medical doctor and hunters wintering in Manzhouli. In a short
speech he gave to the conference, Chuan nonetheless claimed that
the local hunters he had approached had denied any knowledge of
plague. Hence his only source affirming the native knowledge hypothesis against the opinion of local hunters themselves was the
Russian medical doctor. It thus becomes pertinent to ask: how did
the Russians know that (or what) the native hunters knew? In fact
neither Beliavsky nor Reshetnikov actually saw these practices for
themselves, nor did they even lay eyes on living marmots, as these
were hibernating at the time of their research. All information in
Beliavsky's and Reshetnikov's reports was based on word of mouth
from inhabitants of Soktui. And yet the crucial ethnomethodologi-
cal distinction between observed facts and recounted facts, as underlined by Holy and Stuchlik (1983), was never made by the Russian
researchers or by Wu.

This then introduces the second and most important set of questions one needs to pose regarding the native knowledge hypothesis.
Based as they were on data conferred by word of mouth and not
observed in the field, are the diagnostic principles described as part
of traditional Mongol and Buryat knowledge actually able to detect
plague in a marmot? In other words, could Mongols and Buryats
know plague as a distinct zoonotic disease without access to bacteriological instruments and methods, based on the alleged empirical
animal-observation practices in the field?

Authors from Beliavsky to Wu claimed that native hunters were
able to recognize a plague-infected marmot from afar. Anyone familiar with marmot ethology should be able to spot two simple but
crucial diagnostic problems here. The first is that only terminally ill
marmots demonstrate any variance in their walking or calling behaviour (Dudchenko-Kolbasenko 1909). This means that if hunters
were in fact able to recognize these symptoms as signs of plague,
they would be able to recognize and avoid only terminally ill animals. Given that in experimentally inoculated marmots plague has
been found to last between seven and eighty-six days before it killed
the stricken animal (Wu 1923), this would leave hunters exposed to
any given vector for considerable time before it demonstrated any
physiological or behavioural symptoms observable by the naked eye.
Hence Mongols and Buryats would continue to hunt and be exposed
to a critical number of plague-infected animals. The second problem
lies with the fact that a great number of diseases harboured by marmots may lead to precisely the same terminal symptoms (morbidity

of marmots has been recorded for eleven distinct zoonoses; Pole 2003). As the Russian plague expert Ivan Stepanovich Dudchenko-Kolbasenko noted as early as 1909 (and subsequently ignored), anthrax in particular is in this respect empirically indistinguishable from plague among marmots. In his 1923 speech to the Far Eastern Congress of Tropical Medicine, during a rare yet overlooked moment of critical reflection, Wu (1924: 126) underlined both diagnostic problems: 'although an unsteady gait on the part of these animals while in the wild state suggests the possibility of plague, we have often seen similar symptoms present in *tarbagans* dying of other diseases. On the other hand, quite frequently plague-infected animals remained strong and fierce up to the last moment of their demise'. The fact that Wu recognized this major diagnostic problem certainly poses the question of why he subsequently chose to ignore it. More importantly, from a historical epidemiological point of view, the combination of the two diagnostic problems can only mean one thing: in the case that native hunters did observe unusual physiological and/or behavioural traits in a given marmot, (a) they had no way of knowing if this was the result of plague, anthrax, another infectious disease or a non-infectious condition of the animal; and (b) they would be able to observe this generic trait of illness, empirically unidentifiable with any distinct disease, only at the terminal stage of that illness. This precludes both distant diagnosis of whether a marmot is harbouring a disease or not (for infected marmots look healthy unless terminally ill), as well as distant diagnosis of an ill-looking marmot as harbouring plague or not. All that natives could possibly see was that a given marmot was terminally ill, not if it was infectious or if it harboured plague. Moreover, the exclusive identification of infectiousness with external signs of illness, if extant, would mean that hunters continued to be readily exposed to a great number of infectious but healthy-looking marmots.

But even this limited ability to diagnose terminally ill marmots as diseased should not appear as self-evident. For the way in which marmots were 'harvested' more often than not disabled even this diagnostic function. As our earliest sources on marmot hunting verify, natives hardly limited their activities to hunting marmots with bow and arrow or rifles – activities that may have permitted the generic and limited distanced diagnosis described above. Instead they actively engaged in both trapping *tarbagans* and digging them out of their burrows during early stages of hibernation, when the soil was still not frozen. The latter method is noted both by Radde and Cherkassov. Trapping and digging techniques, far more productive in terms of marmot harvest, clearly excluded any possibility of detection of the health state of the animal based on its walking or calling behaviour.

What is left then is the contention that native hunters could recognize whether a captured marmot was plague-infected or not by performing an incision on its paw and examining the quality of the blood. The only source on this matter, Beliavsky (who could not have observed it himself), gives no information as to how the blood should look. The trait, if in fact observable at all by the naked eye, would be present only in the rare case of septicaemic plague amongst marmots, and would be equally present in any case of septicaemia, not only one caused by *Yersinia pestis*. Hence even if a marmot's paw was in a condition to be examined in such a way – a fact upon which Dudchenko-Kolbasenko (1909) cast serious doubt, given the usual hunting methods and state of captured marmots – the only possible diagnosis could be of whether the animal suffered from septicaemia, not what disease caused this or if it was infectious.[3]

Should we, given the above evidence, thus be satisfied with stating that the native knowledge hypothesis, which has stood unchallenged to this day, was based on a gross misinformation of the original scientific sources, which were in some cases unreliable (Beliavsky), in some cases duped (Clemow, Müller) and in some manipulative (Wu)? If so, we would have to accept that the hypothesis is ethnographically unfounded and epidemiologically unsustainable. Yet such a reading of the case in hand would miss the point that what is actually in operation here is not simply a chain of misunderstandings but a separation, in Agamben's sense of the term (2011: 113–14); that is, a denial that turn-of-the-century Mongols and Buryat societies possessed the ability to not-know plague and still survive in an area where the disease is endemic.

What I want to argue here is that native ignorance of plague did not constitute simply a lack of knowledge but a capacity for not-knowing. This was an epistemological impotentiality that was dialectically linked to the potentiality to arrive at a different regime of knowledge, which was not merely a different perspective of the self-same fact (plague zoonosis), but a practice that constituted autonomous subjects and agencies vis-à-vis a completely different register of the real, namely myth. Here is where my critique of the native knowledge hypothesis meets Mary Douglas' critique of medical materialism. For the projection of erroneous turn-of-the-century theories of plague onto the register of native tradition necessitated the medical-materialist reduction of actually existing, cosmologically informed human–animal relations in the region to hygienic operations.

Shape-Shifting: Myth into Medicine

This section will begin by reference to a very illuminating, if over-looked, vignette offered by the biographer of the most prominent plague researcher in tsarist Russia, Danilo Kirivolich Zabolotny (Golubev 1962). In the part of the biography describing the professor's celebrated 1898 plague expedition to what today is Inner Mongolia, Zabolotny is said to have wanted to test Beliavsky's hypothesis. He thus asked native hunters to organize a marmot hunt. When the Mongols shot at a *tarbagan* but failed to kill it on the spot, Zabolotny suggested they pull it out of its hole where it had sought refuge. To this the hunters reportedly replied:

> The devil pull it out! You know what we say in our places? If a *tarbagan* is killed on the spot, that's fine. If hit by an arrow it [escapes] into its burrow – too bad. There, underground, an evil spirit revolves/turns inside out/shape-shifts [*oborachivaet'sya*]. You know what? Ten men cannot pull it out. Pull it out and death is revealed. (Golubev 1962: 39)

To the scornful retort about yet another were-marmot (*tarbaganye-ob-orotnye*) legend, Zabolotny reportedly replied that the story makes sense in the light of the disease carried by the animal. Strangely the incident is not related in any of Zabolotny's extensive reports from the expedition, or the rest of his voluminous work. What makes the story even more suspicious is that the words spoken by the hunters seem to be coming out of one of the most famous works on Mongolian ethnography in nineteenth-century Russia: the four-volume *Ocherki Severo-Zapadnoĭ Mongolii* by Grigory Potanin, the fruit of the great Russian ethnologist's 1876 expedition to the region. It is by following this work that we may arrive at a first understanding of the operation of medical materialism as regards human–marmot relations in the region.

Siberian marmots were animals of great significance in Mongolian mythology, with Potanin recording eleven marmot-related mythic variants. Central to nineteenth-century *tarbagan* mythology was the notion that marmots originated from a great mythic archer, Erkhei Mergen, who sought to rid the earth of the seven (or in some vari-ants three or four) suns that were reducing all life to dust. Having shot down six of the suns, the hero aimed at the seventh, the sun that now reigns in the sky. As his mighty arrow shot off, a *tel'gen* bird flew in front of it, so that instead of shooting the sun down, the arrow simply split the bird's tail. Angered and boastful, the archer pledged to bring it down, or else chop his thumbs off and bury himself in the ground. Failing to shoot the elusive bird, Erkhei Mergen fulfilled his pledge and, once buried underground, transformed into the first *tarbagan*. In other variants Erkhei Mergen is punished for killing too many animals, with Potanin noting that 'the main idea is the punishment of the boastful proud hunter' (Potanin 1883: 767).

What is of particular interest here, in relation to the story recounted by Zabolotny's biographer, is what happened to the marmot once it became earthbound. For one of the variants recorded by Potanin involves a stern warning, which immediately recalls Zabolotny's encounter: 'If one has shot down a marmot from the bow it is well; but if he escaped with the arrow into his hole it is evil. He changes himself into a *chetkur* [devil]. Ten men, the whole *gachoun*, will not then dig him out. It will be hard for the whole Aimak to get him' (Potanin 1881: 152; Gardner 1895: 319).

Given Potanin's fame, one may well suspect that Golubev borrowed elements from this entry for Zabolotny's biography. In fact, Golubev's opening sentence is a direct loan from Potanin: 'If a tarbagan is killed on the spot, that's fine. If hit by an arrow it [escapes] into its burrow – too bad'. Yet rather than stopping at that, Golubev added: 'There, underground, an evil spirit revolves/turns inside out/shape-shifts' (Golubev 1962: 39). This polysemic phrase is crucial, as it refers to *oborachivaet'sya*, a property which is then directly linked to a supposedly prolific 'were-marmot' or 'shape-shifting marmot' (*tarbaganye-oborotnye*) belief in the region.

Oboroten is a noun signifying a were-animal (usually werewolf) or a shape-shifter. In this sense, *oborachivaet'sya* should be translated as the reflexive of 'shape-shifts'. What is thus presented here is not just any act of transformation but a self-metamorphosis that turns oneself inside out, thus rendering the marmot a dangerous demon: 'pull it out and death is revealed'. From this point of view, pulling the wounded marmot out of its burrow at the same time pulled its position in the predatory chain inside out, transforming it from prey to predator.

In reducing the shape-shifting capacity of the *tarbagan* to a precaution against plague, Golubev was following a long-standing tradition of medical materialist reductionism as regards the transformative qualities of marmots. Interestingly, the first recorded marmot-transformation myth comes not from Potanin, but from the discoverer of the Siberian marmot, Gustav Radde (1862: 168–69):

An animal which, as we have seen, is important to the nomadic people of the high Gobi as food and clothing, has been connected by these people to those of their animal myths which are most widely known among them and have a certain poetic sway. They say that the bobacs in the dim past were humans, who worked the pastures arrogantly and boasted that they could kill all birds with the first shot. This boasting made the strongest of the evil spirits angry, so that he wanted to take revenge over this. He came among them and spoke to the best of the hunters: I want to see proof of your skill and will recognize it, when you kill a swallow in flight with the first bullet. If you fail, however, I will punish you for your boasting. The brazen hunter loaded his weapon, the swallow flew, he shot. But only the middle of the swallow's tail was torn by the bullet. Since that time, say the steppe Tungus and Mongols, all swallows have a forked tail and the arrogant hunters were transformed by the anger of the evil spirit into marmots, which are animals and therefore edible except for a spot in the armpit. In this spot they show you a usually somewhat lighter, whitish stain (which probably belongs to the hibernation gland), which is supposed to represent the human flesh, and they tear this out with great care before they eat the bobac.[4]

Radde thus provides an Erkhei Mergen mythic variant including an unusual element which did not fail to elicit the attention of epidemiologists in the years to come. The body part referred to by the explorer is none other than what is called *khun* (meaning 'human'), an axillary gland that is usually removed by Mongols before cooking the *tarbagan* to avoid cannibalism. For the *khun* is considered to be the last remaining human trait in the marmot.

Radde's description had a formative effect on Skrzhivan, who in the early 1900s recorded some 'Buryat epics' relating to *tarbagan*: 'a fairy tale where you can probably find a hint of *tarbagan* disease – the risk of ingestion of lymphatic glands' (Skrzhivan 1901: 610). The 'fairy tale' (*skazka*) in question was a variant of Erkhei Mergen's punishment for boasting his archery skills, and repeated the story told by Radde about the axillary lymph being a 'human meat' (*chelovechkoe myaso*) that is avoided by Mongols (ibid.: 611). Whereas both Radde and Skrzhivan gave no medical interpretation of this belief, in his influential treatise *Die Pest*, the influential German medical author Georg Sticker (1908: 404–405) was more creative, providing a bold medical materialist exegesis of the myth at hand:

The myth is childish; but the habit that is accentuated through it has a deeply serious reason. Myths which are kept alive among people, habits which they keep with religious zeal, always hide, even if they appear so strange and unexplainable to those who don't know, an important truth. The *tarbagan* myth has remained until today an unheeded folk fiction. Now we can uncover its meaning.

According to Sticker, Mongols avoided the marmot's axillary gland as an anti-plague precaution. From a medical materialist point of view, this must have looked like a perfect match of legend and hygienic reality. But there are a number of problems with this idea: on the one hand, eating the cooked meat of a plague-infested marmot cannot actually give one the dreaded disease; on the other hand, as Wu (1924: 126) himself was ready to accept, the 'axillary tumours' that were supposed to be signs of plague among marmots were actually physiological rather than pathological traits of the animal.

The enclosure of the shape-shifting character of *tarbagans* within the medical-materialist paradigm of plague-related knowledge found its epitome in the work of Smolev, a Kyakhta-based ethnologist who provided a rich record of Mongol and Buryat legends and myths. Acting in response to official interest in the alleged native knowledge of marmot-plague in the region, Smolev (1900) sent a short report to the Subsection of the Troitzossawsk-Kyakhta Section of the Amur Regions of the Imperial Russian Society of Geography, entitled 'Buryat Legends on Tarbagan'. There, he claimed that during his research he came across an 'already recorded legend', whose relation to the plague he wished to illuminate.

The myth Smolev recounted was a curious melange of the mythic variants on Erkhei Mergen recorded by Potanin in 1876; this incorporated the *chetkur* myth, which in Potanin's original account stood unconnected to the Erkhei Mergen myth. In this hybrid-variant, Erkhei Mergen bragged that he could shoot down the three suns ruling heaven with his bow and arrow; the boastful archer pledged that if he should not succeed he would cut his thumbs off and live underground, where for six months he would neither drink nor eat (Smolev 1900: 101–103). Finding himself thumbless and transformed into a marmot underground, the punished archer proclaimed: 'Now people will look for me as a treat, but I swear that should someone kill me with an arrow, then every time I shall go to the people and cause human disease, and death' (ibid.: 102). Smolev noted that this was clearly a prohibition against hunting marmots to avoid plague, an interpretation he supported by providing yet another, rather confused, variation of the same prohibition story. This recounted that Buryats were averse to hunting *tarbagan* with bow and arrow because once a man had hit a marmot with his arrow and whilst digging it out of its hole, to where it had managed to escape, he found a 'little man with bow and arrow' (ibid.: 102–103).

Smolev's motif of an arrow-armed marmot is strikingly similar to the story related two decades later by an international star of plague research in Manchuria, the Austrian doctor Heinrich von Jettmar. Before being posted to Manchuria, Jettmar was already an old hand in Transbaikalia, so the possibility of him actually having come across Smolev's report cannot be excluded. Whatever the case may be, Jettmar claimed that as the defeated mythic archer descended into his subterranean abode, in the shape of a marmot, he uttered the following threat: 'I will now retire for a long time under the earth, and there I shall not drink or eat. But I take with me my arrows. Woe to the wicked, who digs up my den and disrupts my sleep! My arrow will then meet the presumptuous disturbers of my rest!' (Kaminski 2010: 40).·

Grasping the chance for a bold medical interpretation, Jettmar did not shy away from the conclusion that 'these legends are probably the consequences of the observations on the epidemiology of plague in Mongolian natives: the *tarbagan* is the true carrier and keeper of plague, that is, of the "arrow" which meets all of those excavating the *tarbagans* or approach their *butans* or disturb the beast somehow' (ibid.: 41).

The medical-materialist exegesis of *tarbagan* mythology was endorsed by the highest authorities in plague epidemiology, like Petrie (1924: 400), who wrote: '[t]he inhabitants of the steppes – the Buriats [*sic*], Mongols, and Russian Cossacks – have long been acquainted with the danger of handling diseased *tarbagans*; and indeed their appreciation of the risk gives point in an interesting and unmistakable fashion to the *tarbagan* legends'.

This medical-materialist enclosure of marmot-related cosmology carefully ignored *tarbagan* myths that did not fit its reductionist scheme. It also avoided questioning why the work of other plague researchers in the area, whose ethnographic work spanned books and not mere pages (such as those by the French doctor and ethnographer Jean-Jacques Matignon (1895; 1899) and the Polish ethnologist Julian Talko-Hryncewicz (1899)), did not support the native knowledge hypothesis. It is through this selective engineering of evidence that the authoritative conclusion of William McNeill was reached. In his *Plagues and Peoples* McNeill (1976: 146) writes, in an Orientalist tone that his nineteenth-century sources would have endorsed: 'Nomad tribesmen of the steppe region, where these animals lived, had mythic explanations to justify the epidemiologically sound rules for dealing with the risk of bubonic infection from marmots'.

There is no doubt that these attempts at the medicalization of shape-shifting beliefs of native hunters were intended as gestures of donning what was seen as a primitive belief system with hygienic rationality. It is, however, precisely this ethnocentric and essentially colonial gesture that perpetuated the separation of indigenous Mongol and Buryat interactions with marmots from its epistemological autonomy. Projecting medical knowledge upon native mythological and demonological belief systems, this medical-materialist operation subsumed Mongol and Buryat modes of interacting with marmots within a pre-determined epistemological regime, which defined what is knowable, what cannot be ignored and what is simply imagined.

In order to press the point regarding the impairment of native epistemological autonomy, this chapter will now turn to an aspect of the native knowledge hypothesis not yet discussed here: the allegation that Mongols and Buryats knew not only how to protect themselves from plague-infested marmots, but also how to stop the spread of the disease among humans by means of draconian isolation measures.

This epidemiological fable originated in Beliavksy's 1895 article and has been a central narrative structure in medical and historical works on plague in Inner Asia to this day. During and after the First International Plague Conference held at Mukden in April 1911, Mongol and Buryat hunters were universally hailed as bastions of vigilance against plague contagion. Dr Martini, Germany's delegate to the Plague Conference, claimed that the alleged practice of sewing up the yurts with plague patients inside until no smoke rose from the top was 'excellent from the public health point of view'. For Martini, this 'tradition' was emblematic of a people able to manage public health as well as any modern nation: 'When that kind of procedure was operative, one did not require medical officers for health. It showed quite a virile public spirit' (Farrar 1912: 23). Similarly Roger Baron Budberg, a medical doctor and Manchurian old hand, wrote: 'Naturally one cannot speak of any immunity of the Mongols. The fact that the plague is not spread as an epidemic among them and that we do not hear of any sickness among them is surely because these nomads have known since ancient times about the infectious nature of the disease. If an incident appears, they certainly isolate the sick person immediately, as they do for cattle killed by an epidemic disease, and then move out of the infected area immediately' (Budberg 1923: 292–93).

All this may sound exhilarating yet it bears no relation to ethnographic reality. Or rather, it comprises a full reversal of that reality. For there is no doubt that Buryats and Mongols did, in fact, opt to keep individuals afflicted by various forms of evil alone in their family's yurt. Yet, paradoxical as it may sound to our contagion-habituated minds, this was not intended to protect non-inflicted persons from the sufferer in question. On the contrary, as historical-ethnographic evidence demonstrate, the isolation was meant to protect the suffering individual from the people around him or her (Ikeshiri 1943). Whereas, having a ritual source, the affliction could not spread from its victim to others, his or her non-afflicted social surrounding posed a great danger to the afflicted person, as it could further compromise his or her spiritual condition. Death of the afflicted individual was often believed to result from such unwarranted encounters. From an indigenous perspective, it was hence the healthy that endangered the ill, not the other way around. This is a subtle point that epidemiologists operating in Inner Asia at the turn of the century seemed unwilling to acknowledge, but which we cannot afford to ignore.

What is presented here, in an ethnographic nutshell, is a prime example of a medical-materialist impairment of the active aspect of native impotentiality: in order to account epidemiologically for Mongols' and Buryats' ability to live in a region where plague is endemic, 'ritual avoidance' had to be explained away as the 'avoidance of contagious disease' (Douglas 1993: 30).

In conclusion, rather than simply turning native reality on its head, the spectacle of autochthonous hygienism propagated by the native knowledge hypothesis was not simply based on the projection of mistaken science of plague onto native traditions, but actually defined life in Inner Asia as possible only to the extent that it spontaneously based itself on epidemiological principles of social organization. What Mary Douglas (1993: 30) described as the beneficial by-products of ritual action were not simply mistaken 'as a sufficient explanation' of native social life, but in fact rendered its biological precondition. What the native knowledge hypothesis really prescribed was that without adopting them as a total system of prevention, Mongols and Buryats would perish under the bane of plague, and Inner Asia would be but a windy, arid vastness void of human life.

Acknowledgements

Research leading to this chapter was conducted as part of my Andrew Mellon and Isaac Newton Research Fellowship at the Centre for Research in the Arts, Social Sciences and Humanities (CRASSH) of the University of Cambridge. I am grateful to the staff of the Russian State Library for their assistance with often non-catalogued material, and to Valentina Charitonova for hosting and supporting my research in Moscow. I would also like to thank Caroline Humphrey for many illuminating discussions on the subject, as well as Olga Bakich and Anastasia Piliavsky for their insights regarding were-marmots. I would finally like to thank the scholars who met at the University of Konstanz to give their comments on a draft of this chapter.

Notes

1. All translations from German are by Emily Stavridis, whom I would like to thank for her help and effort to retain the period nuance of these texts in English. All translations from Russian are mine. I would like to thank Nikolai Ssorin-Chaikov for his help in these; the romanization of Russian characters follows the British Standard system of transliteration. The transliteration of Chinese characters follows the Pinyin system.
2. V.A. Baruikin's 1905 identification of a plague bacillus in a marmot corpse was considered with suspicion, when not totally ignored, outside Russia (Baruikin 1909).
3. It is striking that the practice is conspicuously absent in Wu's ethnographic observations of marmot trapping from the summer expedition of 1911 (Wu 1911–1913).
4. Radde (1862) referred to Siberian marmots as '*bobacs*', not to be confused with today's *Marmota bobac*.

References

Agamben, G. 2011. *Nudities*. Stanford, CA: Stanford University Press.

Anonymous 1895. 'Special Correspondence: A New Disease'. *British Medical Journal* 2, 391.

Baruikin, V.A. 1909. 'Uzelkovaya forma chumui u tarabagana' [Nodular form of plague in tarbagan]. *Russkiĭ Vrach* 16, 538–40.

Beliavsky, M.E. 1895. 'O chum tarbaganov' [Regarding tarbagan plague]. *Vestnik Obshestvennoĭ Gigienui Sudebnoĭ i Praktichesnoĭ Meditsinui* 23, 1–6.

Benedict, C. 1996. *Bubonic Plague in Nineteenth-Century China*. Stanford, CA: Stanford University Press.

Budberg, R.B. 1923. *Lungenpest Epidemien in der Mandschurei 1910–11 und 1921*. Hamburg: Verlag Von Conrad Behre.

Cherkassov, A.A. 2012 [1867]. *Notes of an East Siberian Hunter*. Bloomington, In.: Author House.

Clemow, F.G. 1900. 'Plague in Siberia and Mongolia and the Tarbagan (Arctomys Bobac)'. *Journal of Tropical Medicine* 1900, 169–74.

Douglas, M. 1993. *Purity and Danger: An Analysis of the Concepts of Pollution and Taboo*. London: Routledge.

Dudchenko-Kolbasenko, I.S. 1909. 'Ob Izslêdovanïi chumnuikh zabolêvanïïv Zabaykaĭl'skoĭ oblasti v 1908 godu v svyazi s tarabagan'eĭ chumoĭ' [On the study of the plague disease in the Transbaikalia Oblast in the year

1908 in relation to tarbagan plague]. *Vestnik Obshestvennoĭ Gigienui Sudebnoĭ i Praktichesnoĭ Meditsinui* 45, 1045–89.

Echenberg, M.J. 2007. *Plague Ports: The Global Urban Impact of Bubonic Plague, 1894–1901*. New York: New York University Press.

Farrar, R. 1912. 'Plague in Manchuria'. *Proceedings of the Royal Society of Medicine* 5, 1–14.

Favre, A. 1899. 'Ueber ein Pestähnliche Krankheit'. *Zeitschrift für Hygiene und Infectinkrankheiten* 30, 359–63.

Gamsa, M. 2006. 'The Epidemic of Pneumonic Plague in Manchuria 1910–1911'. *Past & Present* 190, 147–84.

Gardner, C. 1895. 'Folk-Lore in Mongolia'. *The Folk-Lore Journal* 3, 312–28.

Golubev, G.N. 1962. *Zhitiye Danila Zabolotnogo* [The life of Danilo Zanolotny. Moscow: Molodaya Gvardiya.

Holy, L. and M. Stuchlik 1983. *Actions, Norms, and Representations: Foundations of Anthropological Inquiry*. Cambridge and New York: Cambridge University Press.

Ikeshiri, N. 1982 [1943]. *Da wo er zu (The Daur Nationality)*. Hohhot: Daur History, Language and Literature Society.

James, W. 2008. *The Varieties of Religious Experience: A Study in Human Nature*. Rockville, MD: Arc Manor.

Kaminski, G. 2010. *Pestarzt in China: Das Abenteuerliche Leben des Dr. Heinrich Jettmar*. Vienna: Löcker.

Lynteris, C. 2013. 'Skilled Natives, Inept Coolies: Marmot Hunting and the Great Manchurian Pneumonic Plague (1910–1911)'. *History & Anthropology* 24, 303–21.

Matignon, J.-J. 1895. 'La Médicine des Mongoles'. *Archives Cliniques de Bordeaux* 4, 515–23.

———. 1899. 'La Peste Bubonique en Mongolie'. *Archives de Médecine et de Pharmacie Militaires* 33, 463–86.

McNeill, W.H. 1976. *Plagues and Peoples*. Garden City, NY: Anchor Press.

Müller, H.F. 1900. *Die Pest*. Vienna: A. Hölder.

Nathan, C.F. 1967. *Plague Prevention and Politics in Manchuria, 1910–1931*. Cambridge, MA: Harvard University Press.

Petrie, G.F. 1924. 'A Commentary on Recent Plague Investigations in Transbaikalia and Southern Russia'. *Journal of Hygiene* 22, 397–401.

Pole, S.B. 2003. 'Marmot and Zoonotic Infections in CIS'. In *Adaptive Strategies and Diversity in Marmots*, ed. R. Ramousse, D. Allaine and M. Le Berre. Lyon: International Marmot Network, 13–18.

Potanin, G.N. 1881–1883. *Ocherki Severo-Zapadnoĭ Mongolii*. 4 vols. St Petersburg: V. Bezobrazov.

Radde, G. 1862. *Reisen im Süden von Ost-Sibirien in den Jahren 1855–1859*. St Petersburg: Buchdruckerei der Kaiserlichen Akademie der Wissenschaften.

Reshetnikov, A. 1895. 'O Chumê tarbaganov: perenesennoĭ na lyudeĭ' [Regarding tarbagan plague, tranferrable to humans]. *Vestnik Obshestvennoĭ Gigienui Sudebnoĭ i Praktichesnoĭ Meditsinui* 23, 6–9.

Skrzhivan, F. 1901. 'Nashi svêdênïya o tarabagan'eï chumê' [Our information on tarbagan plague]. *Russïi Arkhiv Patalogïi, Klinicheskoï Meditsinui i Baketeriologïi* 30 July 1901, 603–12.

Smolev, Y.S. 1900. 'Buryatkaya legenda o tarbagane' [Buryat tarbagan legend]. *Trudui Troichkosavsko-Kyakhtinskago Otdêleniya Priamurskago Otdêla Imperatorskago Russkago Geograficheskago Obshchestva* 3, 100–103.

Sticker, G. 1908. *Die Pest als Seuche und als Plage: Abhandlungen aus der Seuchengeschichte und Seuchenlehre.* Gießen: Töpelmann.

Strong, R.P. 1912. 'Report of the International Plague Conference'. In Mukden, April 1911. Manila: Bureau of Printing.

Summers, W.C. 2012. *The Great Manchurian Plague of 1910–1911: The Geopolitics of an Epidemic Disease.* New Haven, CT: Yale University Press.

Talko-Hryncewicz, J.D. 1899. 'O Chumnuikh zabolêvanïyakh v Mongolïi' [Regarding plague disease in Mongolia]. *Trudui Troichkosavsko-Kyakhtinskago Otdêleniya Priamurskago Otdêla Imperatorskago Russkago Geograficheskago Obshchestva* 1, 96–110.

Wu, L.-T. 1911–1913. 'Investigations into the Relationship of the Tarbagan (Mongolian Marmot) to Plague'. *North Manchurian Plague Prevention Service Report 1911–1913*, 9–62.

———. 1923. 'A Further Note on Natural and Experimental Plague in Tarbagans'. *Journal of Hygiene* 22, 329–34.

———. 1924. 'Plague in Wild Rodents Including Latest Investigations into the Role Played by the Tarabagan'. In *North Manchurian Plague Prevention Service Reports.* Tianjin: Tietsin Press Limited.

Christos Lynteris is a social anthropologist working on biopolitical and visual aspects of infectious disease epidemics. He is Senior Research Associate at CRASSH, University of Cambridge, and Principal Investigator of the ERC-funded research project Visual Representations of the Third Plague Pandemic. His recent publications include *The Spirit of Selflessness in Maoist China* (2013) and *Epidemic Events and Processes*, a special issue of *Cambridge Anthropology*.

Chapter 3

MANAGING PLEASURABLE PURSUITS

UTOPIC HORIZONS AND THE ARTS OF IGNORING AND 'NOT KNOWING' AMONG FINE WOODWORKERS

Trevor H.J. Marchand

Utopias offer a space for imagining alternatives to real times and places. The medieval *Land of Cockaigne*, the island utopias of Thomas More (1869 [1516]) and Aldous Huxley (1994 [1962]), Karl Marx and Friedrich Engels' *German Ideology* (1987 [1845]: 145) and William Morris' idyllic 'Nowhere' (Morris 1984 [1890]) are charters for good life and plenty, sagacious politics, social equality, a balanced education of mind and body, and pleasurable work. These tales of hope are devised in dialectical relation with select and polemical versions of the 'real' worlds in which their authors are immersed. The existing social, political and economic regimes are typically flattened to render a cardboard version of all that is wrong, thereby producing vulnerable caricatures that can be easily supplanted – on paper, at least – by new idyllic orders. In cultivating their knowledge of what exists *in potentia*, authors of utopias wilfully suspend for a temporary period their knowledge of the fuller spectrum of forces at play in daily life. Attaining a clear utopian vision involves the luxury of taking time out from the disorientating flux of quotidian demands and pressures. This means discovering a safe haven to ignore what is undesirable and to reflect, renew energies and redirect aspirations with, it is hoped, long-term, beneficial consequences.

In the way that utopia is narrated in relation to versions of 'reality', ignoring, too, can be understood as an enactment – a strategy – in relation to knowing. The acts of ignoring and of producing knowledge therefore exist not in oppositional relation, but rather in a mutually constitutive partnership (Hobart 1993; Dilley 2010: 176). Furthermore, both utopia and ignoring imply and produce kinds of absence, respectively manifested as non-place and the banishment or suspension of knowledge, whereas their counterparts – the real world and knowing – are conceived as presence, as being tangibly existent. Grounded in ethnography, this chapter will consider the relationship between all four terms and, more specifically, the variety of positions taken up by actors in the discursive spaces produced when the continuum between knowing and ignoring is intersected by that between world and utopia.

This research was carried out during fieldwork at the Building Crafts College (BCC) in East London, where, in addition to my role as anthropologist, I trained and qualified as a fine woodworker (2005– 2007). The two-year programme in fine woodwork supplied intensive skill training that progressed from basic hand tools to a more complex set that included power tools and milling machinery. For prospective trainees, discovering the existence of the BCC was an accomplishment in itself. Though it had been founded by the Carpenters' Livery Company in 1893[1] and was the oldest institution of its kind in the U.K., the College kept a low profile in contrast to England's better-known fine woodwork and furniture-making programmes, which included, for example, Bucks College, Rycotewood Centre and London Metropolitan University. The fine woodwork programme at the BCC was small by comparison and, at that time, the course information posted on its website was rudimentary. But those who found their way to its workshops – by serendipity, through word of mouth, or through deft investigation of the options – benefited from capable technical instruction and first-rate facilities. Perhaps the most appealing advantage of the BCC for those who trained there was the generous quantity of bench time in proportion to classroom teaching or textbook learning. Fine woodwork at this college was (and remains) first and foremost a hands-on education in independent creativity, problem-solving and making.

Term commenced in mid-September and ended in early July. The daily schedule imitated full-time work, starting at 8:45 A.M. Monday to Friday and finishing at 4:45 A.M., with a 45-minute lunch break and short tea breaks in the morning and afternoon. The curriculum aims were: acquiring good understanding and competent handling of tools; learning to conceptually plan the progressive stages of a wood-working project; and developing critical judgement of one's own work balanced by creative approaches to rectifying deficiencies. In combination, ample bench time, a well-stocked timber rack and normally patient instruction afforded trainees the chance to make mistakes and learn from them, and to repeat procedures until the logic was digested and the execution was incorporated in a more-or-less fluid assembly of stances, postures, gazes, grasps and movements. While still in the first year, a fellow trainee remarked that the college afforded 'the luxury of time to think about what we want to do. Rather than worrying about our futures, we have the good fortune to define what we want out of it'.

The concentration in the first year was on producing set pieces of architectural joinery using softwood, and the second year was dedicated entirely to the design and making of furniture in a variety of hardwood timbers. The emphasis on high-end, bespoke furniture was intensified from 2005 onward with the successive appointment of convenors with specializations in that branch of woodworking. By the end of the programme, the majority of the trainees aspired to become designer-makers of fine furniture, operating individual or communal workshops and, crucially, exercising control over the design, production and sale of their crafted wares. Notably, the college provided an incubation space for an assortment of personalized, but often compatible, utopian visions of work and life.

Of the twenty-four trainees I came to know across three annual cohorts, two-thirds were mature students and the remainder were school-leavers. All the mature trainees had completed secondary, and often post-secondary, education and came to carpentry from a variety of professional and employment backgrounds including business, real estate, consultancy, nursing, truck driving, media, fine arts and others. Only one had previous experience as a carpenter-joiner, while the remainder possessed little or no prior woodwork training. In an earlier publication, I coined the term 'vocational migrants' (Marchand 2007) to describe these mature men and women.[2] For all, the choice of woodworking was tightly woven into the pursuit of pleasurable work and a satisfying life.

One trainee, Richard, with postgraduate qualifications and nearly a decade's experience as a consultant in an environmental agency, told me 'I've never been happy with settling with what's there. I've always had an urge to be autonomous; a desire to live separately from those aspects of life that I don't like: crime, cars, traffic, noise and constant material consumption. As a craftsman, I hope to be able to work when I want and how I want'. He qualified his ambitions as entirely relevant to the contemporary world by insisting that 'my utopia is not rooted in the past'. Rather, through his activity, Richard hoped to provide an example to others of 'what might be' when the mindful energy of the body is mobilized, in place and in the present moment. 'Increased mechanization, increased mobility – both have been a turn for the worse', he continued. 'In some ways the world is devalued by being able to get to places more and more quickly. I don't ignore the technical benefits [of our age], but there are more of us wanting more and more. My instinct is to stop, find a better way to live, and hope some people take notice'.

This chapter focuses on four of my fellow trainees and their ambitions and utopian visions for work and life. Their issues and concerns as mature students and aspiring craftsmen, and the complexities and contradictions of their shifting positions and perspectives, are voiced in their dialogues with one another and in conversation with me. An exploration of the arts of not-knowing and ignoring is made through the ethnography of three core themes that profoundly marked our collective experiences at the college. These are presented in loose chronological sequence, beginning at the end point of our first year of training and finishing at graduation from the programme.

The first theme considers the ways that not-knowing was employed as a teaching and learning strategy in the college workshop. Next, the chapter explores the lack of business management tuition in the fine woodwork programme. It was intimated by the college that the course would prepare graduates to set out and set up as sole traders. Though a handful of lectures on the subject were offered, trainees generally felt let down by the absence of a dedicated module. In fact, however, their desire for that knowledge was contradicted by the effort they were willing to expend in attaining it. Trainees treasured their bench time above all else and, as one pointed out, there would have been reluctance to attend a classroom module. In effect, students passively colluded with instructors and administration in ignoring the critical importance of basic business and marketing skills to succeed, as well as the reality of the U.K.'s narrow and highly competitive marketplace for makers and sellers of bespoke furniture.

The final section offers an account of the trainees' participation and experience in the annual New Designers show in London. The stark contrast between the small, safe and intimate atmosphere of the college workshop and the bustling, competitive enormity of the outside world of design and making rattled utopian ideals of William Morris' 'pleasurable work' and Thoreau's 'Walden', or of becoming 'the village carpenter' (Rose 2001). Issues that had been put conceptually to one side while training at the college workbench now loomed large and could no longer be ignored. In that rapid realization (or admission), the short-lived workshop community fractured and utopias were tainted by real demands and obligations of making a living 'on the tools'.

Not-Knowing in Teaching

The final architectural joinery assignment in year one was a half-scale staircase in Scots pine (*Pinus sylvestris*), with a balustrade, bullnose treads and a starting step with a semi-circular end to support a newel post. When I finished my staircase in late May, Con, the first-year convenor, suggested I make a 'hanging sign' in American oak (*Quercus robur*). This had been a competition piece sometime in the early 1990s for joinery trainees around the country. The project included an elegantly curved bracket with chamfered edges and a horizontal arm from which the framed sign hung on brass eye hooks. As I proceeded, I discovered that the bracket was far more complicated than I had initially gathered from the official description, concealing a number of challenging geometries and joints, including a so-called 'mason's mitre' joint. In my workshop log, I recorded that 'this project is a little daunting, but there'll be much to learn from it'. Along the way I made an assortment of minor blunders that forced me to re-cut tenons and remake entire components; and this, of course, was all part of the learning process I had anticipated.

The part-time workshop instructor John W. was a retired civil engineer who had converted to fine woodworking at an advanced age. He brought to his craftwork and teaching the discipline, clarity, methodical precision and structural understanding of his former trade. When John W. was present, I actively sought his engineer's sagacity to resolve my latest troubles with the hanging sign. According to John, teaching something practical was a straightforward case of 'explanation, demonstration, watching and correcting'. Together, we explored a variety of options for making the tenons at either end of the curved bracket and, though he made his preference known, he encouraged me to get on with the solution I felt most comfortable with and confident about. 'I try to lead students through the process rather than just giving them the answer', he told me during our conversation on teaching and learning. 'I believe they will learn better ... if they can come up with their own solution rather than being told *the* solution. And they will remember that solution better as well'.

Con, the year-one convenor, likewise encouraged us to explore options and make informed choices, but his approach harboured a notable distinction. 'My teaching method hasn't really changed over the years', he told me in conversation. 'My mentors never gave me a straight answer. If you were interested in something, you'd find it'. In his instructor's role, Con regularly feigned 'not knowing' when we asked for advice on what tool to select for a task, about the physical properties of a timber species or how to resolve a technical problem. His contrived ignorance was an effective strategy to force us to think for ourselves. With a little effort and patience, the answers could be discovered by reading the photocopied handouts Con distributed and referring to the manuals in the college library; or by searching in the tool cabinet and experimenting with different methods. Con's not-knowing was sometimes construed by trainees as an exercise of power since, clearly, he was freely electing to withhold information and coercing us to labour for it. In turn, however, his persistent method was also productive of his trainees' cumulative knowledge and problem-solving capacity which, over time, built confidence and self-esteem. 'By doing this, I try to get across to the students that this is a *long* process', he explained. 'But I also try to put them at ease by reminding them that, while in college, they have the time; and I have the patience – if they have'.

With term drawing to a close, those who had finished making their architectural joinery projects were permitted to get a head start on the first of the year-two projects, namely a bedside cabinet of their own design. This was our first foray into furniture making and the first large-scale project in hardwood. The bedside cabinet project also liberated trainees to explore and foster their individual aesthetic preferences and, for many of us, it set in motion an evolution of our personal styles that would intensify and heighten the sense of competition during the second year. Everyone was keen to put their tool blades to hardwood and launch into furniture making.

Leading the pack, Toby and the young and talented Zahir were already well advanced with their bedside cabinets. I seized the opportunity to play 'apprentice' and harvest a few tips by assisting them in turn with the dry assembly of components they had prepared. Like Con, trainees too feigned 'not knowing' from time to time to gain fuller know-how in a faster, less costly way. But unlike for the instructor, not-knowing on the part of trainees was comprised, at least in part, of truly not knowing. Persuading another member of the cohort to explain, demonstrate or assist was calculated to be more efficient than consulting printed handouts for the details or assuming the risks of a go-it-alone, trial-and-error approach. 'Not knowing' where to find the information or 'not knowing' where to begin a task were the premise for asking others to show and lend a hand. Teenage Jack, for example, regularly took up a stool at Toby's bench, silently watching, assisting and learning (Marchand 2014). But when Jack's more direct requests for information or assistance were refused, Jack cunningly played to Toby's pride in his technical skill and humorously appealed to his seniority in age: 'I'm just a boy!', Jack would say with a devilish smirk. 'I haven't a clue how it's done!' This and similar tactics imputed hierarchy that exposed weakness or ignorance on the part of the less-experienced party, but if effectively deployed they opened up shortcuts to knowledge. Whereas Con's not-knowing was an (albeit productive) exercise of power, the students' often-exaggerated admissions of 'not knowing' were an exercise of dependency and subordination, but with a tactical eye on advancement in knowledge and position.

In my case, by exposing, and even embellishing, my lack of know-how and sharing my uncertainties about making my own bedside cabinet, I invoked a student–teacher hierarchy. In doing so, I hoped that Toby would impart some of the precious joinery expertise accumulated during his years as a door and window manufacturer. More significantly, I also hoped that his teaching would confirm the partial know-how I already possessed, thereby instilling a greater sense of self-confidence in my skill set. As David Pye asserted, craftwork constitutes a 'workmanship of risk' (1995). In working by hand with natural materials, 'the quality of the result is not predetermined, but depends on the judgement, dexterity and care which the maker exercises as he works' (ibid.: 20). Productive engagement with the constant risks inherent in fine woodwork demands, and in turn cultivates, a sense of 'confidence' – a state of being repeatedly invoked by woodworkers. Confidence evolves through regular, active practice in problem solving, autonomously discovering solutions and creatively repairing mistakes in the ways that both John W. and Con promoted through their teaching styles. Confidence as a woodworker therefore stems not from the narrow mastery of technical know-how alone (i.e., tool-wielding techniques), but from responsively orchestrating various kinds of knowledge and harnessing resources for moving a project forward. Such confidence enables woodworkers to take on ever more challenging commissions, expand their repertoire of production and, ultimately, to grow their business. Together, these activities breed in turn a greater sense of confidence.

During the short summer break, Richard accumulated on-site experience by assisting a handyman with a host of odd jobs; Anthony set up a back-garden workshop in his native Didcot; Toby reluctantly returned to manufacturing doors and windows; and other trainees, including Karl, grudgingly took on temporary contracts in their former places of work. In preparation for the next session's focus on furniture, David, the second-year convenor, assigned us a summer project to write a short, illustrated report on two established designer-makers of our choice. We were to individually investigate the makers' inspirations, how they built up a portfolio of work, where they sold their pieces and what timbers they favoured, and why. David's objective was to nurture a holistic view of the world of craftsmanship and design, including a better understanding of the business of bespoke furniture making. Most students, however, did not make the time or have the inclination to arrange a meeting with an established maker. At the time, this struck me as curious given that the exercise offered the opportunity to network within the professional community and to increase knowledge about marketing and financial survival strategies among self-employed artisans. This chapter turns next to issues of business and marketing, and the ways in which this field of learning was, for the most part, ignored or inadequately addressed by college staff and trainees alike.

Marketing Ignorance

My fine woodworking research included a long series of interviews with makers and other players involved with the craft. These included an informative meeting with Betty Norbury, who, at the time, was the undisputed doyenne of the U.K.'s handcrafted furniture market. I met with Betty over tea at the elegant Queen's Hotel in Cheltenham; she owned a shop in an upmarket quarter of the Regency spa town. Though not a maker herself, she exuded in equal measure a passion for fine timbers and skilled woodwork and an antipathy towards the general public who, she charged, were overwhelmingly ignorant of the craft. With steadfast ambition to promote the industry and give Britain's top furniture makers a venue for exhibiting and selling, Betty curated her first furniture show in 1981, and from 1994 onward she organized the annual *Celebration of Craftsmanship & Design*. In reference to her instructive, straight-talking book *Marketing and Promotion for Crafts* (1995), she told me: 'I make it very clear that I'm not telling you how to get rich. I'm telling you how to make a success of what you do so that you can live in a way that you want to live'. According to her, the key ingredient to success in the field is 'to hang in there' and build a reputation. The opening lines of her book spell it out bluntly: 'To succeed as a craftsman it is not enough to be good at your work... you have got to be a mixture of craftsman, salesman, public relations officer and packager' (Norbury 1995: 9). This includes cultivating the necessary social graces (i.e., personal presentation, social manners and the ability to convincingly communicate design ideas and craft expertise) in order to access the small, and often elite, target market and win their patronage.

However, in working closely with bespoke furniture makers, one of the major problems Betty identified was that many were incapable of marketing their own wares. 'They're obsessed...', she began. Then, amending her generalization, she went on, '*Some* are obsessed with the way it's made. There's no good them making something with the most wonderful dovetails in the world if somebody isn't going to cross the room to look at it', she said. 'You've got to capture their imagination with the piece'. She carried on while handing me a copy of her newest book, *Bespoke* (2007): 'When I put this together, you won't believe the number of photographs of dovetails I got sent... And a lot of the makers won't even invest in proper photographs!'

Indeed, my own conversations with numerous designer-makers confirmed that only a tiny minority of practitioners had any formal training in management, and many loathed the business of marketing and dismissed it as a distraction from their real work – making furniture. Betty's frank pronouncements on the industry's ignorance of marketing resonated with the college's continued neglect to incorporate elementary business training into the fine woodwork programme.

While excelling in technical tuition, BCC trainees complained that the programme sorely lacked an elementary module in marketing and business management: both key skills for the survival and success of a self-employed craftsperson. For the vast majority of trainees I worked alongside and interviewed, money was not the prime motivator in taking up the trade. Nevertheless, a basic understanding of business was deemed essential to pursuing autonomy as a craftsperson and fuller control over how and what one produced. Though the prospectus professed to equip students with such skills, the actual shortfall in this area of training was routinely pointed out to senior management by the elected student representatives – and with a greater sense of urgency as their respective cohorts progressed through the second and final year. Their pleas and constructive suggestions, however, had minimal impact on the curriculum. At the end of our first year, the director offered an hour-long talk on 'setting up a business'. All trainees conceded that it was informative and that the director covered impressive ground, but a single hour of general tuition was judged to be no more than a taster.

In the second year, David, the fine woodwork convenor, made earnest attempts to remedy the lack of connection with the business of furniture making. He scheduled two lectures by established U.K. designer-makers and one by a mature graduate of the college who had formerly worked in corporate marketing. Though these events put trainees in contact with current practitioners, many felt that the talks served a limited purpose. After the first lecture, Karl, a fellow trainee, remarked, 'The thing I'm *really* interested in is how people make that transition from training to actual furniture making for a living'. 'The guy didn't go into that at all', Karl continued with a note of frustration. 'He talked mainly about high-end furniture that gets shown in flash galleries. I felt completely detached from that'.

David also arranged a fieldtrip to the famous ERCOL factory in Princes Risborough for trainees to witness quality furniture making on an industrial scale. In combination, the talks by independent craftsmen and the factory visit gave trainees a somewhat clearer idea of the employment options that existed at either end of a spectrum, from cottage workshop to industrial manufacturing. The focus, however, was consistently on furniture rather than general carpentry and joinery which offer a greater range of employment opportunities. Despite the impressively sophisticated machinery at Ercol and the factory's congenial working atmosphere, the trainees, without exception, pined to emulate the 'independent craftsman' model. For the mature career-changers, assembly-line production (in all its forms), the lack of autonomy and the time clock were precisely the constraints they sought to escape. Anthony, a mature trainee with diverse work experience, voiced that position with a bite: 'Got to a point in life where I thought I had to do something for me. Got fed up of working for other people; being a small cog in a big machine; having no voice in how things work, and just being told what to do by people who were half my intelligence, if that!'

On a separate occasion, John W. delivered a pragmatic and well-informed talk on the practicalities and costs of setting up a workshop. Notably, John W. was the only college instructor at the time with an active furniture-making business. His lecture reviewed the essential tools and machines required for a workshop and then briefly elaborated upon other basic necessities for setting up a business. Especially salient items from the long list included securing adequate financing to cover start-up costs, finding affordable and appropriate workshop space, installing dust extractors and other equipment, buying a suitable vehicle for transporting raw materials and finished products, purchasing liability insurance, creating a website and devising a marketing strategy. To paraphrase John W.'s message on marketing, 'clients aren't likely to just turn up at your workshop and commission a bespoke chair or a table. They need to know you're out there and they need to be able to see the quality of your workmanship'.

The thoughts of trainees, however, became fixated on an earlier point in John's lecture, namely on his presentation of estimated start-up costs. For the basic tools and machinery alone, it was recommended that we budget at least £10,000. Monthly rents for workshop space would vary wildly depending on the square footage and on whether one had London in mind or a rural region; and, of course, proximity to potential markets had to be factored into that equation. Need for a vehicle and liability insurance further inflated the sum. The talk was geared to trigger productive planning for post–graduation, but the dispiriting reality of the high costs, the professional responsibilities and the vast skillset (beyond woodworking) required to survive as a sole trader flummoxed most thinking about the future. It was not that trainees had been clueless as to the financial implications, the determination and the effort needed to realize their dreams, but rather that most had deferred these unsavoury realities, choosing instead to channel their attention onto the tools and the workbench. It is this tactical deferment, or active ignoring, of the total picture and the risks of failure that is particularly relevant here.

John had done a commendable job of setting out the main issues, but again, students felt that one hour was far too little. There was no further formal tuition on managing and marketing a small business. The other workshop instructors were skilled in their craft, but they possessed minimal or outdated workplace experience and were therefore poorly equipped to mentor on those subjects. Trainees regularly produced cutting lists for their projects, but only occasionally were we required to cost materials, and never labour. Presumably, training in the past at the BCC was geared to skilling craftspeople for industry: upon entering employment, carpenters with the inclination to learn the business would do so during their on-site apprenticeship to a foreman, manager or senior colleagues. In recent decades, however, the fine woodwork programme at the BCC has attracted growing numbers of mature career-changers who seek a wider skill set that includes both carpentry technique and business acumen. This is a tall order to fill for most educational institutions – especially in a brief two-year programme.

Many trainees acknowledged this structural limitation, but the missing management module nevertheless remained a source of discontent. Halfway through the programme Richard confided that 'It's an area where I'm really lacking confidence in terms of knowing where to start', while Karl, by the end of the course, was wrestling with the sinking feeling that he still was not capable of accurately estimating the cost of materials for an item he might make. 'I've got a vague idea of what it should sell for', he said, 'but no idea what profit I'd be making'. Anthony, too, expressed disappointment: 'Like most educational institutions, the college didn't fill all the promises it makes in the prospectus. I had understood that we'd be able to come off the street with no carpentry and leave here with the ability to start our own business. That was my main agenda: to be my own boss!'

Offering a somewhat more nuanced perspective, Toby observed from experience that 'like other things they tried to offer us, we would have moaned about having to take a couple of days or a week to go and listen to someone talking [about] boring stuff. I'll bet you some us wouldn't have turned up. It's a bit of a catch-22 situation'. A couple of weeks after graduation Toby had to formulate a detailed business plan to secure a bank loan and he was forced to seek guidance and considerable assistance from friends and family with appropriate know-how. He complained at that point that this should have been part of the curriculum, 'but', he added quickly, 'I'm really not sure there was enough time'. The strength of the course, Toby believed, was its emphasis on the practical: 'I don't get on with theory, or the writing-up bit'. This sentiment was widely shared and bench time was universally cherished. I therefore concur with Toby that, despite the students' grievances, any bid by the college to substitute workshop time for more classroom instruction, including business training, would have met with staunch resistance.

Indeed, college administrators, workshop convenors and woodwork trainees innocently colluded in their various ways of selectively ignoring the realities of the U.K. marketplace for bespoke furniture and the limited opportunities for qualifiers to secure gainful employment in this specialized and arguably elitist vocation. The college continually deferred inclusion of a business management module and it kept no database on job placement or the career trajectories of its graduates. Understandably, resources for maintaining a database

would have been costly; but also, perhaps, it was simply too disheart-
ening or discouraging to know about the graduates' plight in a national job market where craftsmanship is undervalued and where, as
Betty Norbury observed, consumers remain fundamentally ignorant
of the excellence in U.K. design and making.

Instructors, for their part, had limited or outdated experience of the
day-to-day business of the trade. Their expertise was in teaching the
tools, not selling the wares. And by choosing to sideline tuition in conventional carpentry and architectural joinery for the art of furniture
making, programme convenors were actively ignoring the fierce competition in the trade over what amounts to a small handful of bespoke
commissions in proportion to the total volume of furniture bought and
sold each year in the U.K.[3] The knock-on effect was that students, too,
conveniently shelved critical thinking about the disjuncture between
the trade skills they were painstakingly acquiring and the reality of the
marketplace in which they would soon find themselves.

None of the trainees actively sought extracurricular instruction in
business management or marketing while on the course. In truth, the
intensity of the college schedule would have scarcely allowed for it,
and those truly dedicated to becoming successful entrepreneurs would
have had to enrol on an evening course. A few did take on odd carpentry jobs to earn money and gain practical experience, but only Richard
had set up a website to market his services before the end of the programme. This was somewhat ironic given his aversion to brash capitalism and placeless technologies, but he explained that even though he
was not interested in 'being "a designer" or a known craftsperson', he
needed 'to earn a living'. He wanted to sell his work but qualified this
by asserting that he would do so 'on [his] own terms'. Throughout the
two years, Richard and my fellow trainees held steadfast to utopian
ideas of autonomy, working creatively with their hands and producing
objects that clients would value and that would endure through time.

Of the two dozen fine woodwork trainees I met during my two years
at the BCC, only a tiny fraction went on to become sole traders making bespoke furniture for a living. All who succeeded in doing so had
benefited from the luxury of independent financial means to take the
plunge and weather the long and risky start-up period of establishing business networks and clientele. Of the remainder, the majority
have, to the best of my knowledge, persisted in the trade in one form
or another, either working for larger workshops specialized in batch
production, fitting kitchens or doing architectural joinery and site
carpentry – but sometimes landing a rare commission to make the
kind of furniture they learned to craft at the BCC.

New Designers: Utopia Capsized?

In November of year two, a brief meeting was organized between David, the instructor, and trainees Richard, Karl, Toby and me to discuss participation in the upcoming New Designers exhibition. This important annual event was held each July at the Business Design Centre in Islington, showcasing the talent of thousands of new design graduates from across the U.K. Anthony had opted out, claiming to be unconcerned with the 'designer-y' side of woodworking, and the three teenage members of our cohort were lacking in either confidence or initiative. Early in the New Year we received news that the BCC had been allotted a prime spot in the main exhibition space. Collectively, Richard, Karl, Toby and I decided that we would display our pieces against different wallpaper backdrops whose patterns and colours accentuated the individual styles we were developing over the course of year two. Alongside the strengthening alliances, a sense of excitement and anticipation grew over the following months. But so too did a sense of rupture, fragmentation and anxiety.

Richard authored the abstract for New Designers, entitling our submission *Modern Design with Medieval Roots*. He wrote: 'Our four graduating students exhibiting this year have all demonstrated exceptional talent in both designing and making. All four have exemplary craft skills. They can all make a beautifully dovetailed drawer, but that's just a starting point. Where they take their learning is up to them, and their outputs are as different as the people themselves – as you will see'. Indeed, as the second year progressed, individual design and stylistic preferences gelled and turned from random experimentation to deeply felt, personal expressions. I pursued a contemporary exploration of the British Arts and Crafts; Toby looked to bold landscapes and curvilinear forms in nature for his inspiration; Karl resurrected his Scandinavian heritage in the clean lines and elegant proportions of his furniture, and Richard brought his *bricoleur*'s eye to collecting and assembling his woodworking designs.

New Designers ran for four days in July 2007, attracting an estimated seventeen thousand visitors. We each displayed several pieces of furniture at the BCC stand, including our bedside cabinets, coffee tables and chairs. Initially uncertain about what we would gain from the experience, Karl concluded at the end that 'It was fantastic!' and Toby proclaimed that we had 'held our own' and we had attracted 'interest from the right people'. 'The biggest comment was how well it's made', Toby continued, 'and that all the design has come from us'. For Karl, the positive reception of his work gave him 'a huge boost of confidence'. 'And to be approached by potential employers saying that I should give them a call!', he beamed momentarily before adding '... but it would have been nice if I could've had some firm orders and money changing hands'.

While also relishing the attention, Richard was more acutely sceptical of flattery and fleeting promises: 'I'm here in the rarefied atmosphere of New Designers and I want it to be a success, but there's a whole lot more to making a success of it than just having a few positive comments at a design show'. Later in our conversation he reflected: 'There are people there who try to build you up – and I suppose by being there, you're asking to be built up'. Determined not to be swept away by the euphoria of the event, he asserted with vexation: 'I don't want to be pressured by some man who selfishly wants to commission me to make something, and then we start arguing whether I get 50 per cent or 60 per cent. I'd rather just hang a back door for someone – someone who I like – and be happy with it'.

This sentiment aptly captured the inner turmoil that beset each of us at New Designers, as well as our fellow trainees who visited the show and were simultaneously dazzled by the buzz of the crowds and the dynamism and accosted by the enormity of the world of design and making outside the college. It became quickly apparent to all that the event was the threshold between the security, camaraderie and indulgence in creativity we had enjoyed for two years at the BCC, and the brutal, brazen reality of the competitive marketplace into which we were being thrust. At the point when the business of marketing and selling and the demands for efficient and economic production can no longer be ignored, can dreams of self-autonomy and utopic ambitions for control over creativity and production be salvaged? Is pleasurable work a tenable pursuit?

Once uprooted from the college workshop, a tide of new beginnings engulfed each graduate with a matrix of responsibilities, hopes, burgeoning anxieties and uncertainties. Planning for the future became increasingly individual as camaraderie ruptured and the community dissipated. 'When I leave here', Anthony told me, 'I'm going to spend one, maybe two years being a 'wood butcher'. Just doing site furniture, kitchen fitting, to get a serious amount of cash behind me so that I can go on to do what I want to do: to build bespoke furniture for audiovisual systems. Produce big expensive stuff. All custom made – built in. There's a good market and people make a phenomenal amount of money. Lots of the people doing it can knock together a cabinet, but they're not real carpenters; whereas I can make stuff that will command premium dough'. Toby, too, had his eyes set on starting up his own business. 'I'm not afraid of getting up early and working weekends if I have to. But my biggest worry is getting a workshop and making the payments until I've got enough work'. Toby came to a space-sharing arrangement with his former employer in Potters Bar, hoping this would afford a measure of security against having to pay full overheads for an individual workshop. He counted on his first commissions coming through family, word of mouth and the networks he had already established in the trade. If need be, Toby was prepared to go back to manufacturing doors and windows in order to 'make ends meet and pay off the business loan' he was about to incur.

For Karl, our time at the BCC had been 'the most enjoyable two years' of his life. 'It's been a positive change', he continued. Reflecting back to a time before the course, he confessed, 'I couldn't have said what I would be doing in the next five years because I had been stuck in a rut for so long. But now I know that, in some shape or form, I'll be woodworking for the rest of my life'. Like others on the programme, Karl was deeply invested in 'being happy' with the things he made, and 'having an important role rather than a small part' in the process. Unlike Anthony and Toby, however, he had no immediate plans to 'go down the route of independent work just yet'. By his accounting, two years had not been enough time to get a full handle on the technical side of things: 'I can pick up tips on how to work faster and make better joints if I work with somebody'. He also was not prepared to dedicate the energy that one guest lecturer had forewarned was needed for marketing our work. 'For the time being, I want to keep away from doing all that marketing and self-promotion... I'm still building that confidence, I guess'.

'I'm constantly reminding myself', said Richard thoughtfully, 'that I'm not in this to be a fine furniture maker. I'm in this to have a good quality of life. So my ambitions in terms of status and financial position are minimal'. He admitted to being nervous about starting out on his own, mainly because 'I feel I know hardly anything. All I've learned is a bit of confidence to tackle things, and maybe get them wrong; and to think my way around problems, and learn the basics of how to join timber together. I'm fighting the scary knowledge that there's a huge amount that I don't know. I need to put that to the back of my mind and march forward regardless, because I don't think I could work for anyone again, and certainly not full time. I haven't got it in me any more'. Again, this spoke volumes to the act of ignoring as a strategy for managing knowledge, bringing a navigable formation to the kaleidoscopic flux of information and sensations that surround us, and getting on in a focused way with the task immediately to hand.

One thing about which Richard was fully confident was his newly acquired abilities to 'earn a living on the tools'. Impressively, he already had a busy rota of jobs scheduled on the heels of New Designers: 'I have to refurbish two brush-scrubbing tables and hang a new back door for someone. And I take up my workshop in Forest Hill on the 1st of August'. Reflecting on the two years past and pondering the future ahead, he told me: 'It's been the most remarkable and rapid two years of my life. It's been a process of learning I've enjoyed more than any other I've embarked upon – and I've done quite a few, though mainly academic. That said, I'm also ready to move on. My time is up. I'm ready to become the next thing that I am, being on my own'. He paused, and then he reinforced the line he was drawing between his future and the recent past: 'You realize that people go off their own way. And people you liked and worked well with, you may no longer work well with. It's just what happens. You develop new networks as you develop new skills'.

New Designers had proven to be a major catalyst in expanding individual networks and broadening the horizon of possibilities, as well as the realm of challenges and unknowns. It marked our 'banishment' from the college refuge where the real costs of setting up, the business of craft, changing technologies, the role of machinery and a scarcity of commissions for fine furniture could all be safely and tactically ignored. In the aftermath, actors were forced to gradually take up new positions in their relations with one another and in the world of work, and to recalibrate ambitions and expectations accordingly. For those who remained committed to the pursuit of pleasurable work and personal fulfilment, dreams and aspirations had to be dialectically engaged with changed circumstances and realities so that utopias could be reimagined, reinterpreted and narrated anew.

Conclusion

In contrast to my previous research focus on the ways that demonstrable skills are learned and mastered, writing this chapter incited more careful thought about what woodworkers selectively chose to 'not know' and to ignore while training. As I delved into the topic, it became apparent that, as an anthropologist, I too had been ignoring important dimensions of my field site: namely absences, active concealments or the marginalization of knowledge. Indeed, the act of relegating certain thoughts or activities outside thinking and doing, and denying specific skills a place in the repertoire, plays a fundamental role in constituting and shoring up ideals of craft, craftwork and what it is to be and become a craftsperson.

This exploration of the arts of ignoring and not-knowing began in year one of the course at the BCC, at the point when the emphasis of the fine woodwork programme shifted from architectural joinery to furniture. A few exemplary accounts of teaching and learning revealed how declarations of 'not knowing' were strategically employed by one workshop instructor to promote independent learning among his students; and how claims to not-knowing were tactically used by trainees, including me, to garner assistance, gain speedier access to know-how and get assurances from others for what they already knew how to do.

The next section of the chapter demonstrated that the need to market what one produces was actively ignored or neglected by many fine woodworkers – trainees and qualified practitioners alike. Not surprising, the art of making was heavily prioritized over the business of trade since handwork constitutes the core pleasure, and is imagined as the defining activity, of the craftsperson. The majority of mature career-changers on the programme had sought to escape, among other things, alienating capitalist relations and the brassy, boastful 'trumpet blowing' (in Karl's words) of the marketing world. At the same time, they admitted that business skills were necessary for realizing their ambitions to work autonomously and to maintain control over what they produced, from start to finish. While wishes for a dedicated business management module were unreciprocated by the college, closer consideration of the conflict revealed that trainees would have probably resisted this additional tuition because it would have infringed upon cherished time at the bench. The expectation of leaving the course with business know-how was therefore not matched by a dedication to acquiring it, and this observation was further substantiated by the fact that none of the trainees pursued extracurricular tuition in the subject.

While absorbed in producing flawless dovetail joints, steam-bending timber into exquisite forms and making cabriole legs, trainees and instructors ignored the potential impact an economic downturn would have on job prospects and potential earnings, as well as the growing competition from cheaper, and in some cases well-made, mass-produced imported furniture.[4] Equally unpopular to ponder was the real scarcity of clients willing to take the aesthetic risk of owning and displaying a unique piece of furniture, or with the pocket to pay and the patience to wait for it to be designed, made, polished and delivered. Access to that small and typically elite market requires not only technical woodworking competence, but, perhaps more crucially, social and cultural capital on the part of the maker. The salience of social class to success remained unspoken since, as opposed to commerce and trade, craftwork was idyllically conceived as a leveller – a vehicle for superseding 'useless toil' and economic disparity with fulfilment and universal happiness for those engaged in it.

In sum, not-knowing and ignoring were tactics for avoiding and managing what was either too much or unwelcome knowledge (Festinger 1957). By sidelining information, ring-fencing subjects of knowledge or evading certain activities, woodwork trainees were attempting to defer fears and anxieties about the world of work and disengage from unpalatable realities. Doing so allowed them to stay absorbed in learning hand skills and creative making; but notably it also gave freer rein to imagining alternative, idealized futures. The activities of not-knowing and ignoring therefore need to be recognized and studied as practised skills in their own right. They involve conceptual, embodied and emotional strategies for managing the world of stimuli, experience and knowledge. That managed realm of being, however, is vulnerable. When disagreeable realities obfuscate utopian visions, tensions are unleashed and rupture ensues.

Rupture was witnessed most dramatically during the New Designers show at the end of the course. That exposure to the frenetic marketing and business of design and production, and the sheer size of this commercial sector, inflicted lasting tensions and new competitions on the cohort of fine woodworkers, fragmenting social relations and fracturing utopian visions. In the aftermath, actors were forced to take up new positions, mobilize new social alliances, renegotiate their goals and aspirations, and reinterpret or reinvent the utopias they strived for. Encroachment of the world did not necessarily destroy idyllic aspirations; rather, it modified them. This recurring process is crucial for individual growth and development, and for crafting livelihoods that are both viable and pleasurable.

Acknowledgements

First, I thank my fellow trainees, instructors and college administrators at the Building Crafts College for sharing their ideas, experiences and passion for fine woodwork. Thanks to the ESRC (RES 000-27-0159) and SOAS for generously supporting my study of fine woodwork training in Britain, and to the British Academy Mid-Career Fellowship scheme for supporting my continuing research with carpenters.

Finally, many thanks to Roy Dilley and Thomas Kirsch for providing the opportunity to explore the arts of not-knowing and ignoring.

Notes

1. It was originally founded as the Trades Training School on Great Titchfield Street, West London. In 1948 it was renamed the Building Crafts Training School, and renamed again in 1993 as the Building Crafts College. In 2001 it moved to new and larger premises in Stratford, East London.
2. Of the twenty-four trainees in the three annual cohorts, just two were women. Both were mature trainees, one having left a job in the City and the other having left a senior management post with the NHS.
3. At the high end, bespoke furniture is detached from market logics and, like an artwork, the value is indexed to the author's name as they become established and cultivate a reputation among the small circle of general public 'in the know'. The pieces of some makers become collectibles, surpassing their functional use, consumed instead as aesthetic objects for contemplation and display.
4. Indeed, economic recession hit the U.K. in 2008, just one year after the trainees introduced in this chapter graduated from the fine woodwork programme.

References

Dilley, R. 2010. 'Reflections on Knowledge Practices and the Problem of Ignorance'. In *Making Knowledge*, ed. T. Marchand. Oxford: Blackwell Publishing, 176–92.

Festinger, L. 1957. *A Theory of Cognitive Dissonance*. Palo Alto, CA: Stanford University Press.

Hobart, M. 1993. 'Introduction: The Growth of Ignorance?' In *An Anthropological Critique of Development: The Growth of Ignorance*, ed. M. Hobart. London: Routledge, 1–30.

Huxley, A. 1994 [1962]. *Island*. London: Flamingo Press.

Marchand, T. 2007. 'Vocational Migrants and a Tradition of Longing'. *Traditional Dwellings and Settlements Review* 19, 23–40.

———. 2014. 'Skill and Ageing: Perspectives from Three Generations of English Woodworkers'. In *Making and Growing*, ed. E. Hallam and T. Ingold. London: Ashgate, 183–202.

Marx, K. and F. Engels 1987 [1845]. *The German Ideology: Introduction to a Critique of Political Philosophy*, ed. C.J. Arthur. London: Lawrence and Wishart.

More, T. 1869 [1516]. *Utopia*. London: A. Murray & Son.

Morris, W. 2004 [1890]. _News from Nowhere and Other Writings_. London: Penguin.

Norbury, B. 1995. _Marketing and Promotion for Crafts_. Ammanford: Stobart Davies.

———. 2007. _Bespoke: Source Book of Furniture Designer Makers_. Ammanford: Stobart Davies.

Pye, D. 1995 [1968]. _The Nature and Art of Workmanship_. London: The Herbert Press.

Rose, W. 2001 [1937]. _The Village Carpenter_. Hertford: Stobart Davies.

Trevor H.J. Marchand is Professor of Social Anthropology at SOAS and recipient of the RAI River's Medal (2014). He is trained in architecture (McGill University), anthropology (SOAS) and fine woodwork (Building Crafts College). Marchand conducted fieldwork with masons and craftspeople in Yemen, Mali and East London. He is the author of _Minaret Building and Apprenticeship in Yemen_ (2001), _The Masons of Djenné_ (2009) and _The Pursuit of Pleasurable Work_ (forthcoming); and editor of, among others, Making Knowledge (2010) and Craftwork as Problem Solving (forthcoming). He has produced and directed documentary films and curated exhibitions at the RIBA and the Smithsonian Institution.

Chapter 4

IGNORANT BODIES AND THE DANGERS OF KNOWLEDGE IN AMAZONIA

Casey High

In this chapter I consider how anthropology, a discipline that has increasingly adopted Foucauldian approaches to the question of knowledge and its production, might also account for ethnographic contexts in which ignorance takes centre stage. Based on fieldwork with Waorani communities in the Ecuadorian Amazon, I explore the mutual implication of knowledge and ignorance in Amazonian understandings of learning and being in the context of shamanism. Drawing on recent calls for ethnographically grounded studies of ignorance (Dilley 2010; High, Kelly and Mair 2012), I raise questions about the tendency to project our own anthropological preoccupations with knowledge onto ethnographic contexts in which the people we study insist on ignorance as a social value. I also examine how local concerns about ignorance, formal education and relations between older and younger generations require attention to the ways in which Waorani people understand knowledge to be inseparable from bodily experiences.

Conceiving an anthropology of ignorance requires not only a new approach to ethnography, but also some critical reflection on the history of how ignorance has been understood and debated by anthropologists. The interpretive practice of anthropology implies what Viveiros de Castro (2003: 3) describes as an 'epistemological advantage over the native' insofar as we claim to know about 'cultural' practices that

our informants assume to be 'natural'. In this process we attribute
meanings and functions to the illusions or 'beliefs' they hold about
themselves such that the very premise of anthropological knowledge
implies the delegitimation of the claims of 'natives' (Viveiros de Castro
2003: 4). At the same time, many anthropologists today embrace 'indigenous knowledge' as a valued object of ethnography. In describing
this 'traditional' knowledge in terms of cultural continuity and the
agency of informants, they attempt to remedy precisely the traditional
epistemological advantage alluded to by Viveiros de Castro. This state
of affairs reveals a certain tension between how anthropologists conceive of their own knowledge and how they relate to the knowledge
of others.

I compare this apparent tension in anthropology to anxieties about
the relationship between knowledge and ignorance in Amazonian
Ecuador, where my Waorani hosts make strategic claims of ignorance
about shamanism and lament the ignorance of young people. While
Waorani people are 'wilfully ignorant' of shamanism in part because
its practice is associated with assault sorcery (High 2012a), young
people are described as not having specific knowledge and abilities
as a result of lacking specific bodily experiences associated with previous generations. Drawing on Roy Dilley's (2010) notion of 'bodily
ignorance', I examine the transmission of knowledge in terms of a
Waorani ontological premise that refuses to separate knowing from
being. By exploring the kinds of knowledge and being that shamanism, school education, and the bodily capacities of elders entail, I describe how Waorani are less concerned with the loss of 'indigenous
knowledge' than they are with constituting the kinds of relations
with various 'others' they envision in a *comunidad* (community). Their
formulations of knowledge, its production and its absence challenge
the focus on cultural reproduction implicit in much writing on indigenous knowledge, memory and Amazonian ethnography.

Ignorance and Anthropology

While questions of ignorance have long been neglected in anthropology, it is important to recognize that this is at least partly the result of
its controversial presence in earlier anthropological debates. Perhaps
the most prominent anthropological discussion of ignorance was
sparked by Malinowski's claim in *The Sexual Life of Savages in North
Western Melanesia* (1929: 171) that 'physical fatherhood is unknown'
to his informants in the Trobriand Islands. Leach's equally famous

response to Malinowski in 'The Virgin Birth' (1966) provides a clue to why questions of ignorance have since fallen out of fashion in anthropology. For Leach, the Trobrianders' insistence that *baloma* spirits, rather than men, were responsible for pregnancy was akin to the Christian notion of the Virgin Birth, rather than actual ignorance of physical paternity. In warning against the tendency to take specific religious claims as the total knowledge (and thus ignorance) of a particular society, he noted that 'Western European scholars are strongly predisposed to believe that *other people* should believe in versions of the myth of the Virgin Birth. If *we* believe such things we are devout: if *others* do so they are idiots' (Leach 1966: 41).

Leach saw Malinowski's claim as an example of the resilience of nineteenth-century evolutionist assumptions about 'primitive societies' being ignorant of basic knowledge; the idea, for example, that the supposed promiscuity of primitive societies coincided with their ignorance of paternity. I mention this example here merely to illustrate how debates about ignorance in anthropology were, until relatively recently, centrally about the question of whether certain societies demonstrated or lacked certain forms of knowledge characteristic of Europeans. In this sense, anthropologists have since had good reason to eschew questions of ignorance in favour of a more relativistic approach to culture and, more recently, adopting 'knowledge' – rather than ignorance – as a primary ethnographic object. This is to say that non-knowledge ceased to be a viable category of ethnographic enquiry due to the moral and political connotations of ignorance in modern anthropology and Western thought more generally.

And yet, while anthropologists today are no longer interested in describing certain people as ignorant, there remains an implicit assumption that much of the whole enterprise of anthropology is about establishing what Viveiros de Castro (2003: 3) describes as an 'epistemological advantage' over the 'native'. Whether in describing social structures, interpreting culture or simply engaging in participant observation, the basic assumption is that anthropologists can and should come to understand things that their informants cannot. This, according to Viveiros de Castro, is in fact what distinguishes the 'native' from the anthropologist, as 'the latter may be wrong about the former, but the former must be deluded about himself' (ibid.: 4). What Viveiros de Castro is alluding to here is not simply an assumption of false consciousness on the part of 'natives' or their assumed failure to understand what anthropologists do, but a more general feature of how anthropologists tend to conceive of differences in terms of culture and representation. In positing culture as a plurality of perspectives on a single objective world, the 'multiculturalist relativism' of Western thinking 'supposes a diversity of subjective and partial representations, each striving to grasp an external and unified nature' (Viveiros de Castro 1998: 478). This multiculturalist understanding, and the epistemological advantage it implies on the part of anthropologists, has important consequences for how we think about anthropological knowledge and the knowledge of the people we study.[1] Despite the increasing focus on reflexivity in anthropology, this epistemological advantage that Viveiros de Castro describes continues to inform the project of interpreting culture and meaning:

> What makes the native a native is the presupposition, on the part of the anthropologist, that the former's relation to his culture is natural, that is, intrinsic and spontaneous, and, if possible, non-reflexive – or better still, unconscious. The native expresses his culture in his discourse; likewise the anthropologist, but if she intends to be something other than a native, she must express her culture culturally, that is, reflexively, conditionally and consciously. The anthropologist necessarily uses her culture; the native is sufficiently used by his[;] ... the anthropologist holds total sway over those reasons of which the native's reason knows nothing. She knows the exact doses of universality and particularity contained in the native, and the illusions which the latter entertains about himself – whether manifesting his native culture all the while believing he's manifesting human nature (the native ideologizes without knowing), or manifesting human nature all the while believing he's manifesting his native culture (he cognizes unawares). (2003: 3–4)

While this ignorance on the part of 'natives' remains an implicit assumption in certain conceptualizations of culture, the focus on 'indigenous knowledge' and 'agency' appears to indirectly address the epistemological imbalance described by Leach and Viveiros de Castro. Just as theorizations of agency in anthropology have challenged the notion that women, indigenous peoples and subaltern groups should be understood mainly in terms of marginality and subordination to structures of power, the central place of indigenous knowledge appears to be part of a similar political and ethical move within anthropology. Rather than debating whether or not certain 'natives' are truly ignorant of what the West upholds as 'truth' or 'rationality', today we describe other forms of knowledge, other ways of knowing that sometimes depart in significant ways from our own. My point is not to dismiss this movement towards knowledge as a key object of anthropological study or to call for a return to pejorative speculations about 'ignorant natives'. However, I suggest that, as ethnographers, we should also take seriously the claims our informants make about not knowing. While Malinowski and his predecessors appear to have spent considerable energy attempting to determine whether or not certain 'primitive societies' could truly be ignorant of Western standards of rationality, my interest in this chapter is to consider Waorani claims to non-knowledge on their own terms, to think about the ethnographic contexts in which ignorance is expressed, valued, contested and lamented by different people.

Approaching ignorance ethnographically in this way requires reconsidering how we tend to think about indigenous knowledge in places like Amazonia. One of the problems with placing indigenous knowledge at the forefront of anthropology is the tendency to associate 'knowledge' with an implicit notion of cultural continuity. This is particularly striking in studies of indigenous Amazonia, where ethnographic descriptions of indigenous knowledge and agency tend to focus on the resilience of Amerindian sociocosmological principles and the creative responses indigenous peoples bring to social transformation in the face of colonial history and powerful contemporary outsiders. This preoccupation with knowledge, whether in writings about shamanism, environmental knowledge or advocacy for the intellectual property rights of indigenous peoples, risks ignoring indigenous claims to non-knowledge.

In this context, any potential gap in knowledge is assumed to be a problem, a cultural deficiency or worse, an indication of the loss of 'traditional culture'. Like the exotic body imagery that has gained certain indigenous Amazonian peoples the status of 'authenticity' in the eyes of environmentalists and indigenous rights activists from around the world in recent decades (Conklin 1997), indigenous knowledge has an important political value that constitutes part of the changing 'middle ground' between Amazonian Indians and ecopolitics (Conklin and Graham 1995). As some groups are better able to seize on these expectations than others, and the governments of South American countries claim an interest in indigenous knowledge as part of a national heritage to be protected (Conklin 2002), alliances based on the cultivation and preservation of indigenous knowledge may prove just as fragile as those between indigenous people and environmentalists.

The central aim of this chapter, as outlined above, is to think about Waorani notions of knowledge and ignorance outside of conventional Western concerns about cultural continuity and acculturation. Rather than worrying about what I think Waorani people *should* know and piecing together their accounts as partial (or even deficient) knowledge, I examine the practical and conceptual implications of ignorance for Waorani people themselves. This perspective leads to a series of questions about the mutual implication of knowledge and

ignorance in a context where knowing and not knowing are inseparable from indigenous understandings of being and bodily experience.

Shamanic Knowledge and the
Dangers of Being a Shaman

In Amazonia, perhaps even more than in other parts of the world,
shamanism has come to be seen as a key site and source of indigenous
knowledge. Associated with specialized knowledge of plants, animals,
spirits and healing, shamans have featured prominently in studies of
indigenous cosmology (Harvey 2003; Thomas and Humphrey 1994;
Brightman, Grotti and Ulturgasheva 2012). For similar reasons they
are a focal point of ecotourism projects, ethnobotanical research and
heated debates about intellectual property rights. Shamans have come
to be defined, and in some contexts define themselves, as 'guardians'
of indigenous knowledge in ways that are redefining the relationship
between indigenous people and the state. In Brazil, for example, despite the ongoing conflicts between indigenous people and aggressive,
state-driven development policies, indigenous knowledge is now cast
as part of the country's national patrimony (Conklin 2002). Similar
concerns about indigenous knowledge can be seen in debates about
museum collections and the ownership of native 'culture' in North
America (Brown 1998, 2004). Whether in the context of national
debates about indigenous culture, global commercial interests or anthropological research, shamans have come to be seen as a key repos-
itory of knowledge.

   In Waorani villages shamanism is a manifestation of what we
would conventionally describe as 'indigenous knowledge'. But what
kind of knowledge does it consist of? Waorani shamans know a great
deal about plants and animals, and they know about them in ways
ordinary people generally do not. Like shamanic practices described
elsewhere, Waorani shamanism involves a form of communication between humans and animals. Shamans develop a special kin relationship with jaguars through dreams in which an 'adopted' jaguar-spirit
visits the shaman and speaks through the voice of its human 'father'
(Rival 2002; High 2012b). As it temporarily inhabits the shaman's
body, the jaguar-spirit tells its adopted father and his family where to
find game animals. Shamanic practices are associated with keeping
animals close to Waorani people, ensuring their abundant supply and
'*attracting* them back when they flee from people' (Rival 2002: 78). In
the Waorani language, shamans are called *meñi* (jaguar) or *meñera*

(jaguar father) or, in accusations of assault sorcery, *iroinga* (witch/sorcerer).[2]

In part as a result of the engagement with predatory jaguar-spirits that shamanism entails, and its association with sorcery, shamanic practices have become highly contentious in Waorani villages today. There are in fact very few Waorani who claim to be shamans, especially in the larger villages. While elders also describe sorcery as a cause of intergroup revenge-killings in past times, the establishment of permanent villages appears to have coincided with growing concerns about shamans carrying out sorcery against their neighbours. The proliferation of sorcery accusations in recent years should be understood in the context of a general transition from relatively autonomous Waorani households to the establishment of large villages since missionary settlement in the 1960s. These villages, the largest of which today incorporate up to two hundred people, bring together former 'enemy' families, people from other indigenous groups who intermarry with Waorani, and a range of non-indigenous Ecuadorians. This growth in the scale of Waorani villages and the intensification of intergroup relations they entail appears to have created fertile ground for sorcery accusations in a context where violence has a central place in social memory (High 2009).[3]

I initially came to understand Waorani fears and frustrations about sorcery and the apparent decline of shamanism as a result of missionary influences since the 1960s. The Waorani are best known for their relative isolation from other Ecuadorians until the late 1950s, when five North American missionaries were killed by Waorani while attempting to establish an evangelical mission along the Curaray River. With the help of a Waorani woman who had fled her people years before in the wake of intense violence between Waorani clans, the widow and sister of two of the deceased missionaries established a mission at Tiweno where, by the late 1960s, some five hundred or more Waorani had come to live for the first time among *kowori* (non-Waorani) people (Kimerling 1996: 181).

Although few Waorani today identify as Christian, most who lived at the mission settlement had converted to Christianity by the early 1980s (Yost 1981; Robarchek and Robarchek 1998), when the missionary organization was expelled from Ecuador.[4] The small number and marginal position of Waorani shamans today can be understood in part as a result of this process of missionization common to much of Amazonia (Vilaça and Wright 2009). However, rather than simply evidencing a loss of shamanic knowledge or indigenous 'culture' in the face of missionary teachings, the decline of Waorani shamanism

is also related to the seriousness with which Waorani people understand the consequences of shamanic practices. The problem for my
Waorani hosts is less one of losing shamanic knowledge than one of
preventing the kind of 'predatory' relations that shamanism involves.

As local concerns about shamans turning to sorcery appear to
have intensified in this context of social transformation, the status of
Waorani shamans was almost untenable in some villages at the time of
my fieldwork. My hosts often denounced shamanism on the grounds
that such practices constitute a threat to what they see as the ideal
conditions of village life. As one of my Waorani interlocutors suggested, 'Here we live well; we have no shamans'. His comment voiced
a common concern about assault sorcery, which is often lamented as
the cause of sickness and death. Although Waorani generally attribute these misfortunes to sorcery, few claim to know a great deal about
how shamans carry out their attacks. What is clear to them, however,
is that shamanism involves a highly dangerous two-way relationship
between the shaman and his 'adopted' animal spirit in which human
and nonhuman perspectives can be exchanged, confused or in dispute (Fausto 2004, 2007, 2012). Whereas Waorani people ordinarily
identify themselves as victims of predatory human and nonhuman
forces (Rival 2002), many fear shamans may invert this relationship
by adopting the predatory perspective of a jaguar-spirit. The result of
this reversal of perspectives, according to my hosts, is sorcery, a process that involves a shaman domesticating his spirit animal 'like a pet',
sending it to harm people (High 2012b).

Shamans become potential killers when, through their anger or
jealousy, they adopt the predatory perspective of jaguars or other animals. Since to see the world from the jaguar's point of view is to be
a killer, Waorani people who become jaguar-shamans are seen as a
source of danger, even when they are respected elders with famous
biographies in local lore. This dual perspective has made the social position of shamans increasingly untenable in contemporary Waorani
communities where, after decades of revenge-killings between rival
families, shamanism is seen as an obstacle to the local ideal of peace-
ful sociality. As a result, few self-proclaimed shamans remain in the
villages in the western part of the Waorani reserve where I work. Fear,
suspicion and outright hostility towards shamans appear to be widespread across many of the more than thirty present Waorani communities, where people who are socially distant or perceived to be selfish
and untrustworthy are rumoured to practise assault sorcery.

With the rampant speculation that circulates about who is responsible for sorcery attacks, it is no surprise that few Waorani claim much

knowledge about them. On a recent visit to a Waorani community, two brothers complained to me that their mother was ill as a result of the sorcery of a shaman living nearby. When I asked them why their neighbour would want to harm other people in the village, they explained that the man was sad and 'angry' (*pii*) that his own son had recently died, and as a result performed sorcery against their mother out of jealousy. The same man, who was rumoured to have become a shaman only recently, while living in a distant *kowori* community, was also blamed for the death of a child in the village. People commented that seeing other families prosper with many children made the man feel a kind of jealous envy that eventually led him to attack his neighbours.

Although the kin of these victims, and the surviving victims themselves, identify specific shamans who they say are responsible for assault sorcery, they rarely have much to say about how the attacks are carried out. My questions in this direction were usually met simply with claims to ignorance, such as *aramai* ('I don't see') or *iñinamai* ('I don't hear'), followed by moral evaluations of the act itself, such as *wiwa keranipa* ('they do badly') or *ononki wentapa* ('he/she killed without reason'). This is because to claim knowledge about the actual techniques of shamanism would be, I suggest, tantamount to claiming one's own ability as a shaman, thus opening oneself up to potential sorcery accusations. In this context, not knowing can be seen as a strategic defence against unwanted, negative attention: a way of denying relations that are considered to be inappropriate (Chua 2009).

While the emphasis on not knowing about shamanism may in part be a strategic denial in the context of sorcery accusations, I suggest that this form of ignorance also has an ontological dimension. Contrary to the assumption that shamanism is centrally premised on a specialized body of accumulated knowledge, Waorani people envision shamanism more as a particular state of being that implies relations with nonhuman entities. Beyond strategically denying inappropriate relations, these claims to ignorance are expressed with the awareness that 'knowing' about shamanism is not altogether distinct from 'being' a shaman. In a context where 'knowledge' and 'experience' are not theorized as separate, knowledge about the practice of sorcery would necessarily imply a predatory perspective. As Viveiros de Castro (2004) observes in Amerindian shamanism more generally, 'Shamanism is a form of acting that presupposes a mode of knowing, a particular ideal of knowledge'. In contrast to 'the objectivist folk epistemology of our tradition', in Amazonian shamanism '[t]o know is to personify, to take on the point of view of that which must be known' (Viveiros de Castro 2004: 468).

Waorani explain that people often become shamans not as a conscious choice, but as a consequence of events outside their own control. One risks becoming a shaman as a result of a life-threatening accident or illness, such as suffering a severe malarial fever, becoming a victim of sorcery or surviving a plane crash. As can be seen in the above example, the man accused of sorcery is described as having become a shaman after experiencing tremendous emotional pain. Such experiences, whether an accident or other personal trauma, may lead people to see the world from the perspective of a predatory jaguar. In Carla Stang's (2009) description of the Mehinaku in the Brazilian Amazon, changes in emotional consciousness, marked by excessive fear or desire, have the potential to collapse ontological boundaries and cause people to enter into different worlds. In Mehinaku understanding, people risk coming to see the world from the perspective of spirits or animals, rather than that of living humans.[5] In a similar way, Waorani do more than simply acquire a kind of knowledge about the world when they become shamans: they become a different kind of being in the world. They carry out assault sorcery because, like jaguars, they see people as animal prey.

For Waorani people this shamanic perspective is not as much a form of knowledge as it is an ontological state that allows people to engage in different kinds of relations. In contrast to positivistic scientific traditions that seek to fill in knowledge gaps by accumulating facts with the aim of moving ever closer to a universal truth, Waorani shamanism is part of a cosmology that assumes the ways in which people experience the world to be inherently transformative. Although some shamans are known to be particularly powerful and experienced, Waorani anxieties about them focus less on the level or degree of their ability than on the question of whether one is or is not a shaman. Put another way, it not a question of whether a person is 'more' or 'less' shamanic or knowledgeable, but what perspective they bring to relations with other people.

Waorani seldom question whether one's point of view is 'real' or 'true', but are concerned instead with the moral implications and effects of the perspective taken in a given relation. That killers and, at times, shamans experience the world from the jaguar's point of view is not a point of debate or speculation, even for Waorani who have converted to evangelical Christianity. It is simply a manifestation of the dangers inherent in a transformative world in which various kinds of agency are not restricted to human beings. Some Waorani explain that they converted to Christianity in the 1960s precisely because they hoped it would protect them from the sorcery of shamans. This ontological premise sheds some light on current efforts to quell shamanism in Waorani villages. Not knowing about shamanism is not only a strategic claim, but also a desired state of being that confers a person's moral position within a wider set of relations. Like positioning oneself as a victim, in this context being ignorant is part of embracing a fully human perspective.

Bodily Ignorance and Waorani Ways of Knowing

Waorani understandings of shamanism and assault sorcery illustrate how ignorance, seen in the context of actual social relations and cosmology, cannot simply be reduced to the loss of indigenous knowledge, much less a pejorative sense of moral or intellectual deficiency. Not knowing about shamanism is in many ways a strategic claim that confers a commitment to what most Waorani people consider to be a desirable form of sociality. It is an important part of living in what my hosts describe as a *comunidad* that brings together several Waorani groups who were engaged in intense mutual hostilities a few decades ago.[6] Of course, it would be misleading to construe the cultural value placed on not knowing about shamanism as the only, or even the primary place of ignorance in Waorani communities. Just as any ethnography of knowledge should account for multiple and in many cases contrasting forms of knowledge in a given social context, there are multiple meanings and values attributed to ignorance.

This section considers how, in contrast to the ignorance people claim about shamanism, Waorani elders in some contexts lament the absence of knowledge among young people. At the same time that Waorani efforts to stem the threat of shamanism embrace ignorance as an indigenous expression of discontinuity with past violence, recent social transformations have also led to certain anxieties about the kinds of knowledge and skill that Waorani fear may be lost from one generation to the next. While their concerns about the failure of certain forms of cultural transmission reveal a clear contrast to the strategic ignorance of shamanism described in the previous section, indigenous understandings of learning and bodily experience also point to the same ontological premise that emerges in shamanism. Both of these contexts reveal how, in Waorani understanding, questions of knowledge and being are mutually constituted.

It is difficult to ignore the ways in which the social and political lives of Waorani people have transformed radically in the past few decades. Elders often recount stories from the period that preceded the arrival of missionaries, a time they associate with the relative autonomy of individual households, the hardships of intense interclan revenge-killings and the invasions of *kowori* outsiders. The causes of this violence and the relative isolation that some Waorani still struggle to maintain have sparked considerable interest and debate among missionaries, anthropologists and other outsiders. Various scholars have pointed to colonial history (Cipolletti 2002), sociobiology (Beckerman and Yost 2007) and ethnopsychology (Robarchek and Robarchek 1998) in attempting to explain the remarkable degree of 'pre-contact' violence between Waorani people. However, they generally agree that, in the years prior to missionary settlement, the frequency of intergroup spear-killings accounted for a remarkably high proportion of deaths among the Waorani, whose population was only around five hundred in the 1950s (Yost 1981).[7] Today elders remember not only how they lost many kin to revenge-killings, but also how they feared the intrusion of *kowori* – whom they assumed to be semi-human cannibals.

Today, some fifty years after U.S. missionaries established the evangelical mission, most Waorani live in multi-family villages with airstrips and state-supported schools. While the bulk of missionary activity ended in the early 1980s, today young people learn Spanish at school and make regular visits to Ecuadorian cities, and most men at some point work on temporary contracts for oil companies operating on Waorani lands. The oil industry, which has intensified and expanded its activities on Waorani lands considerably since the 1960s (Stoll 1982), has had a major social and ecological impact that is felt in even the most remote Waorani villages. While changes like these are not unique to the Waorani or to Amazonia more generally, the prominent place of violence and group autonomy in Waorani social memory gives particular salience to the contrasting generational experiences of elders and young people (High 2015).

Elders embrace many of the changes they have seen since missionization, a period they describe in Spanish as *civilización* (civilization). For them, *civilización* refers not only to a time when many Waorani converted to Christianity, but also to the relative peace, the intensification of relations with *kowori* people and the rapid expansion of the Waorani population. Above all, discourses of *civilización* draw a contrast between this sense of expanding social relations and the violence and isolation they ascribe to previous times. However, elders and many young people do not simply remember the past as a time of hardship and suffering. Deceased kin and the elders (*pikenani*) who survived the period of raiding prior to the mission are also associated with a sense of freedom and independence by which even young Waorani people today distinguish themselves from other indigenous groups and *mestizo* (non-indigenous) Ecuadorians. Ancestors are associated with the skill and strength that my hosts say allowed them to maintain their autonomy in the past and provide abundant food to their kin. Elders today, both men and women, are celebrated in a similar way, as are the few 'uncontacted' groups who live in voluntary isolation within the Waorani ethnic reserve (High 2013).[8] Elders and uncontacted groups are emblematic of the value Waorani people generally place on the idea of being *durani bai* ('like the ancient ones').

But how do Waorani reconcile the notion of being 'like the ancient ones' with an equally important notion of being 'civilized' and living in close contact with *kowori* people? This is a context where generational changes come to the fore: where young people who attend Ecuadorian schools become knowledgeable and skilled in things that their parents and grandparents are not. In many cases elders acknowledge young people's abilities to interact with *kowori* people and technologies in more productive ways than they can. This recognition is one of the key reasons that urban Waorani political leaders are almost invariably young men who speak reasonably good Spanish and have completed at least a basic school education. However, it is increasingly apparent to elders that young people also lack certain abilities associated with being 'like the ancestors'. This is a concern that elders expressed repeatedly during my fieldwork, despite their statements in support of *civilización* and formal education. They sometimes lament young people not having the strength or skills expected of young adults, who in the past were expected to carry out nearly all subsistence tasks and other household responsibilities from an early age (Rival 1996; High 2006).[9]

Rather than referring to a sense of ignorance or knowledge in the abstract, in alluding to the perceived deficiencies of young people, elders say that they 'don't see' (*aramai*) or that they 'don't hear' (*iñinamai*). In this context and in others, they refer to non-knowledge as a consequence of the absence of specific bodily experiences. At one level, for example, young people know less about the forest because, as students who spend most of their time in school or in the village, they lack the same sensory experience of 'seeing' and 'hearing' in the forest and gardens that older adults demonstrate. It is perhaps not surprising that, in a society that traditionally depends on hunting, gathering and small-scale gardening, there is an emphasis on the body as a source of knowledge. What became particularly noticeable during my fieldwork, however, is that parents and elders do not see school education as directly responsible for what they see as the deficiencies of young people. In contrast to Western ideas about the effects of school education, they do not envision direct competition between these two kinds of knowledge, with one potentially replacing the other. Nor do they say that young people fail to listen to the detailed stories that elders tell about their ancestors while sitting around the cooking hearth in the evenings.

Instead, on several occasions during fieldwork I heard parents complain that young people today 'don't know' certain things because their bodies are deficient. They explained that the current generation of boys and girls is weaker than previous ones, who were stronger and better able to withstand hard work in the gardens and long treks in the forest. In their view, young people are weak in part because, unlike elders, they were never whipped with a jungle vine after male elders returned from peccary hunts. Men and women often recall how, in their childhood, they suffered these painful lashes from their father or grandfather. Elders explain that this practice made children strong enough to hunt peccaries and carry out tedious gardening work themselves one day. Being subjected to whippings is understood as a way of transmitting knowledge or ability from one person to another through specific bodily practices, whereby children acquire the capacities of adults.[10] Rather than being a form of punishment to correct mistakes, the whipping of children reveals a particular understanding that bodily experiences constitute the acquisition of specific kinds of knowledge and agency (High 2010).[11]

Some elders say that they stopped whipping children during the missionary period – the time of *civilización*. The resulting lack of embodied knowledge appears to have had a particular impact on young men, who are said to be unable to hunt peccaries with spears and to be ignorant of many aspects of life in the forest. So why, given this understanding of knowledge as constituted through (painful) bodily experience, do few parents today whip their children? In response to this question, one father told me that he does not whip his children because their arms and legs are too weak and would break from the impact of the lashes.[12] He explained that young people cannot withstand the whippings because today they eat too much 'foreign food' (*kowori kengi*), referring to the rice, noodles, oatmeal and other *kowori* foods they eat in school lunches and during trips to frontier cities. In this sense, their bodies are seen as deficient in terms of both knowledge (lacking specific bodily experiences) and their very constitution. This is particularly significant in a society where consanguinity is understood to be made within household groups through the shared consumption of food and drink in everyday life (Rival 1998; Overing and Passes 2000).

The idea that young people are becoming physically and culturally deficient as a result of recent changes resonates with studies elsewhere in Amazonia, where older generations of men are understood locally to have grown larger, stronger and more capable than men today, who have never experienced specific rituals after warfare (Conklin 2001). What is clear in these cases is that men are seen as unable to 'actualize their masculine potential' (Conklin 2001: 155) as a result of not experiencing specific bodily transformations. The problem is not just that young men and women today are failing to fulfil their expected gendered roles, but also that they lack specific embodied capacities attributed to previous generations – capacities that are in fact central to indigenous ideas of what it means to be a proper Waorani person. Whereas young Waorani are seen as being less 'hard' or 'strong' (*teemo*) than elders, the few remaining uncontacted groups are said to have remarkable physical abilities and knowledge due to their strict diet of 'Waorani' foods and because, in contrast to 'civilized' Waorani who live in villages, they continue to whip their children.

In discussing this state of affairs, Waorani elders appear to be voicing concerns about young people's lack of bodily knowledge, or their 'bodily ignorance' (Dilley 2010: 184). Roy Dilley develops the concept of bodily ignorance in attempting to redirect discussions of ignorance from conventional questions of epistemology to those of ontology:

> My point is that in the absence of culturally specific bodily techniques and mastery of bodily forms, this ignorance or not-knowing, if we can call it such, is construed in ways that indicate fundamental moral problems of definition about what it is to be human. An absence of 'bodily knowledge', as we coin it, is not simply a form of ignorance; it is often related to questions of being. (Dilley 2010: 184–85)

In the hierarchical context of Senegalese craftworkers that Dilley describes, knowing or not knowing specific forms of knowledge is a social function of the division of labour, whereby learning is transmitted within bounded social groups and ignorance is part of what maintains the gulf between different social statuses. As specific skills and knowledge 'are conceived as being linked to particular lines of descent traced back to the mythological originators of a trade' (Dilley 2010: 184), people who do not master their natal craft are seen as 'lesser exemplars of craft being' and their ignorance 'relates to the whole being of the person, not just to an inquiring mind or an ability to see the world' (ibid.).

In the relatively egalitarian context of the Waorani, the bodily ignorance of young people is conceived as a failure with respect to indigenous understandings of personhood. While young people, no matter
how weak or ignorant they appear to elders, are still considered to
be Waorani, their perceived deficiencies are often compared to those
of *kowori* people – an explicit measure of moral failure. The strong
moral connotation of the word *kowori* can be seen in its reference not
only to non-Waorani 'enemy/others', but also cannibals who prey on
Waorani, the true measure of proper people. In the worst of cases, a
young person risks being called *kowori bai* ('like a *kowori*') when he or
she transgresses specific expectations of Waorani sociality. So whereas
in Dilley's discussion of specialized craftsmen, 'the weaver who cannot weave is a lesser kind of weaver-person than one who can' (2010:
184), for Waorani people bodily ignorance implies a kind of deficiency
at a more generalized level of what it means to be a person. In both
of these cases, however, ignorance has important ontological dimensions that extend beyond questions of knowledge.

Learning and Being in School

Although Waorani once associated *kowori* people relatively unam-
biguously with predatory violence and generally avoided them, today
they tend to praise their medicines, manufactured goods and skills,
such as the ability to fly aeroplanes and drive cars. For Waorani people
these skills and knowledge are in no way exclusive to *kowori* people, at
least not in principle. During fieldwork my hosts repeatedly expressed
their curiosity about objects and abilities they wanted to know more
about, whether this was the process of manufacturing an aluminium
pot, piloting the small aeroplanes that often arrive in their villages, or
space travel. Increasingly confident that some *kowori* can be trusted
in certain things, they see this new knowledge as attainable through
their interaction with Ecuadorians and other outsiders. Their desire to
attain new technologies and new knowledge may have contributed,
among other things, to the increasing Waorani preference for interethnic marriages with indigenous groups who have more extensive
contact with the national society.

While the younger generations are seen as lacking in certain forms
of knowledge as a result of not having been whipped by elders and
eating too much *kowori* food, they also are expected to learn new and
important knowledge in school. But what is it, according to parents,
that children 'see' and 'hear' in the context of formal education? In

school, Waorani students are understood to inhabit a *kowori* world – this is in fact the whole point of formal education for Waorani people: to learn Spanish and to become familiarized with skills and knowledge that are relatively unknown to older people. More specifically, they are expected to hear and see things in the presence of *kowori* teachers, who are predominantly *mestizos* or indigenous people from other parts of Ecuador. Parents hope that this education will allow students to en-gage *kowori* people more productively in the future and lift Waorani people out of their relatively marginal social position in Ecuador.

At the time of my primary fieldwork (2002–2004), teachers spent a considerable amount of time reprimanding students for their poor study skills and admonishing parents for doing little to encourage their children to study at home. In some ways the teachers were right in their assessment of the situation. Many Waorani parents, despite the strong support they voice for schools and the sacrifices they make to keep their children in them, do not pressure young people to do their homework or to improve their performance at school. While part of this may be the result of the generational transformations described above, whereby elders have relatively little knowledge of the content of formal education, it also reflects a strong emphasis on personal autonomy in a cultural context in which parents rarely make specific demands on young people. They do, however, place considerable em-phasis on their children's school attendance. For these parents, the kind of learning that occurs in school is primarily the consequence of a physical presence in the school and among *kowori* teachers. The assumption is that if young people attend the classes they will some-how automatically learn the *kowori* skills and knowledge that elders see themselves as lacking.[13]

It emerged in my discussions with parents that, in their view, if children attend classes and fail to learn, it is clearly because the teach-ers are in some way failing to demonstrate the abilities and knowledge expected of them. This is because, for them, learning is less about co-ercive discipline or an abstract process of acquiring knowledge than it is about learning from the presence of people who demonstrate their knowledge by carrying out specific practices (Bloch 1991). This is much the same way I came to understand Waorani approaches to teaching and learning in the home and in the forest: adults generally teach by example, by demonstrating certain skills and knowledge, whether this is the ability to weave a makeshift basket in which to carry fish home or identifying bird calls or the traces of animals on hunting trips. The assumption is that people, young and old, will learn by being in the presence of others who demonstrate these abilities, rather than being repeatedly instructed and corrected. In this way, processes of learning and cultural transmission should be understood in the context of specific forms of sociality that are not always appreciated or recognized in formal school education.

The conflicts that emerged between Waorani parents and *kowori* teachers at the time of my fieldwork reveal some of the tensions between formal schooling and the mutual implication of knowledge and being in Waorani understandings of learning. One of the major complaints from parents was that teachers in the village were drinking too much, to the extent that some either missed their lessons or appeared drunk in the presence of students. At one point teachers were also hosting late-night parties in which teenage students joined them in drinking *tiname* (cane liquor). The central concern for parents was not just that the teachers' behaviour would prevent their children learning in school, but that they were learning one of the *kowori* practices that is most despised by elders. While Waorani people value many of the technologies, objects and practices they associate with *kowori*, the consumption of alcohol is one of the key practices by which elders distinguish Waorani from non-Waorani people. As a particularly *kowori* state of being, drunkenness is described in stark contrast to the distinguishing characteristics of the *pikenani*, whose revered knowledge and skill are seen as antithetical to being drunk or 'crazy' (*dowenta bai*). The Waorani were until recently almost unique among indigenous peoples in Ecuador for their lack of alcohol, preferring to drink even their manioc beer (*tepe*) almost entirely unfermented.

It is in this context that Waorani parents and elders raised serious concerns about teachers drinking. They worried that students, rather than learning to read, write and engage in other valued *kowori* ways of knowing by their presence at school, were becoming *kowori bai* (like *kowori* people) as a result of the presence of drunk teachers. Despite their usual deference to the authority of teachers in village affairs, several parents denounced the teachers at a village-wide meeting and successfully petitioned the educational authorities in the regional capital to have one of the teachers dismissed from the school. Waorani understandings of school education, and learning more generally, again illustrate the ways in which knowing and being are mutually implicated. In a context where highly valued new knowledge is sought precisely from people whose moral standing as *kowori* 'others' is constantly in question, it is perhaps no surprise that formal education raises certain problems in Waorani villages. The central question, for my Waorani hosts, appears to be how to become skilled in reading, writing and other abilities without becoming 'like *kowori*'.

Conclusions

Anthropological approaches to ignorance demand much more than the age-old questions about what is known and what is not in a given society. In the context described here, such an approach requires attention to Waorani understandings of learning, the body, and the moral implications of knowledge and being in a changing world. Seen as a form of 'indigenous knowledge' or 'traditional culture', shamanism is often valued as an important expression of cultural continuity in places like Amazonia. For many Waorani, however, shamans are contentious and dangerous figures who have the potential to carry out assault sorcery by engaging the point of view of predatory jaguar-spirits. In this context, where knowing about shamanism is not entirely separable from being a shaman, ignorance of such practices confers a certain commitment to a fully human perspective on social relations. The idea that rejecting or denying certain forms of knowledge can constitute 'strategic ignorance' should be familiar in many if not most of the ethnographic contexts described by anthropologists. The knowledge economies of the modern world, in fact, which are increasingly focused on the creation of strategic gaps in knowledge, could equally be described as 'ignorance economies' (Roberts and Armitage 2008). However, an anthropology of ignorance should recognize that ignorance is not just strategic; nor does it necessarily mark a state of social or intellectual deficiency. It is also produced and conceived and acquires meanings in ways that depart significantly from economies of knowledge familiar to the West.

The point is not simply to recognize that different societies have different 'ignorance economies', but also to consider how the different kinds of not-knowing found in a given ethnographic context, strategic or otherwise, relate to ontological questions about what a person is. Like the multiple forms of knowledge alluded to by Leach and many scholars since, the different values of ignorance may appear contradictory. In the brief examples presented here, Waorani claims to ignorance about shamanism confer one's place within indigenous understandings of personhood, while at the same time and in the same place indigenous concerns about bodily ignorance raise the spectre that certain young people may be becoming deficient, to the extent that they are sometimes compared to *kowori*. Even in situations where people lament the absence of knowledge, questions of 'knowing' and 'being' prove inseparable and are closely linked to bodily experience. By locating ignorance at the interface of indigenous understandings of knowledge and being, it has been the aim of this chapter to illustrate how we might come to understand the ways in which not-knowing is valued, lamented and contested in social life. At the very least, ethnographies of ignorance should make us ask what 'indigenous knowledge' means to so-called 'natives' and what its absence implies for their own ways of being.

Notes

1. Viveiros de Castro describes how this 'multiculturalist' cosmology is but one way of thinking about difference. His formulation of Amerindian perspectivism, for example, describes a 'multinaturalist' cosmology that, in contrast to Western cosmology, supposes 'a spiritual unity and a corporeal diversity' where 'culture or the subject would be the form of the universal, whilst nature or the object would be the form of the particular' (1998: 470).

2. These attacks, referred to in this chapter as 'sorcery' or 'witchcraft', are sometimes described by Waorani using the Spanish word *brujería*, meaning 'witchcraft'.

3. It is also worth noting that, since the 1970s, many Waorani have intermarried with Quichua-speaking indigenous people, who are known for their powerful shamans in Amazonian Ecuador and elsewhere in the Upper Amazon (Reeve and High 2012). In most cases these Quichua spouses move to a Waorani village after marriage.

4. While the missionaries were affiliated with the Summer Institute of Linguistics (SIL), one the women who established the Tiweno mission remained among the Waorani until her death in 1994.

5. See Londoño Sulkin (2005) for another Amazonian example of how immoral behaviour is attributed to nonhuman perspectives.

6. Waorani use the Spanish word *comunidad* to describe their villages and to convey a sense of mutual participation in periodic collective activities, many of which are closely related to a local school. In contrast to the sense of collective unity by which many outsiders imagine 'indigenous communities', there remains a high degree of autonomy among households and clusters of closely related households in large Waorani villages.

7. In part as a result of the decrease in revenge-killings and the growth of large families in villages since mission settlement, the current Waorani population is estimated to be around 2,500.

8. These 'uncontacted' groups are the subject of considerable interest and debate among the Waorani and in Ecuador more generally. Waorani people until recently described all people living in voluntary isolation in their territory as Tagaeri, in reference to the man Tagae who fled deep into the forest with his followers after refusing mission settlement. Today these groups are more often described as Taromenani, a group of mysterious

origins who apparently decimated and possibly incorporated the remaining Tagaeri in recent years. Some Waorani have been involved in ongoing violent conflicts with these 'uncontacted' people since the 1980s, culminating in large-scale attacks on isolated longhouses in 2003 and 2013 (Cabodevilla 2004; Cabodevilla and Berraonda 2005; High 2015).

9. This is part of a wider Waorani emphasis on individual autonomy evident in many aspects of social and political life (High 2007).

10. This notion of bodily knowledge appears to have at least some historical depth among the Waorani and elsewhere in Amazonia. For example, according to the account of an early evangelical missionary who met Waorani people in the 1950s, one of the first Waorani men he brought to a large Ecuadorian town asked to be beaten by a tractor driver so that he would acquire the ability to use the machinery in his home village (Wallis 1960: 256).

11. Fisher (2001: 122) describes another Amazonian example of how, in indigenous understanding, social qualities are created through 'bodily states'.

12. Rival (2002: 162) makes a similar observation regarding Waorani views on dietary changes leading to 'soft' bodies.

13. In recent years a number of Waorani women and men have become teachers in their own communities. It remains to be seen how this will affect Waorani understandings of the role of schools in their villages.

References

Beckerman, S. and J. Yost. 2007. 'Upper Amazonian Warfare'. In *Latin American Indigenous Warfare and Ritual Violence*, ed. R.J. Chacon and R.G. Mendoza. Tucson: University of Arizona Press, 142–79.

Bloch, M. 1991. 'Language, Anthropology and Cognitive Science'. *Man* 26, 183–98.

Brightman, M., V.E. Grotti and O. Ulturgasheva 2012. *Animism in Rainforest and Tundra: Personhood, Animals, Plants and Things in Contemporary Amazonia and Siberia*. Oxford and New York: Berghahn.

Brown, M.F. 1998. 'Can Culture Be Copyrighted?' *Current Anthropology* 39, 193–222.

———. 2004. *Who Owns Native Culture?* Cambridge, MA: Harvard University Press.

Cabodevilla, M.Á. 2004. *El Exterminio de los Pueblos Ocultos*. Quito: Cicame.

Cabodevilla, M.Á. and M. Berraondo (eds) 2005. *Pueblos no Contactados ante el Reto de los Derechos Humanos: Un Camino de esperanza para los Tagaeri y Taromenani*. Quito: Cdes and Cicame.

Chua, L. 2009. 'To Know or not to Know? Practices of Knowledge and Ignorance among Bidayuhs in an "Impurely" Christian World'. *Journal of the Royal Anthropological Institute* 15, 332–48.

Cipolletti, M.S. 2002. 'El Testimonio de Joaquina Grefa, una Cautiva Quichua entre los Huaorani (Ecuador, 1945)'. *Journal de la Société des Américanistes* 88, 111–35.

Conklin, B.A. 1997. 'Body Paint, Feathers, and VCRs: Aesthetics and Authenticity in Amazonian Activism'. *American Ethnologist* 24, 711–37.

———. 2001. 'Women's Blood, Warrior's Blood, and the Conquest of Vitality in Amazonia'. In *Gender in Amazonia and Melanesia: An Exploration of the Comparative Method*, ed. T. Gregor and D.F. Tuzin. Berkeley: University of California Press, 141–74.

———. 2002. 'Shamans versus Pirates in the Amazonian Treasure Chest'. *American Anthropologist* 104, 1050–61.

Conklin, B.A. and L. Graham 1995. 'The Shifting Middle Ground: Amazonian Indians and Eco-Politics'. *American Anthropologist* 97, 695–710.

Dilley, R.M. 2010. 'Reflections on Knowledge Practices and the Problem of Ignorance'. *Journal of the Royal Anthropological Institute* 16, 176–92.

Fausto, C. 2004. 'A Blend of Blood and Tobacco: Shamans and Jaguars among the Parakanã of Eastern Amazonia'. In *In Darkness and Secrecy: The Anthropology of Assault Sorcery and Witchcraft in Amazonia*, ed. N.L. Whitehead and R. Wright. Durham, NC: Duke University Press, 157–78.

———. 2007. 'Feasting on People: Eating Animals and Humans in Amazonia'. *Current Anthropology* 48, 497–530.

———. 2012. *Warfare and Shamanism in Amazonia*. Cambridge and New York: Cambridge University Press.

Fisher, W.H. 2001. 'Age-Based Genders among the Kayapo'. In *Gender in Amazonia and Melanesia: An Exploration of the Comparative Method*, ed. T. Gregor and D.F. Tuzin. Berkeley: University of California Press, 115-40.

Harvey, G. 2003. *Shamanism: A Reader*. London and New York: Routledge.

High, C. 2006. 'From Enemies to Affines: Conflict and Community among the Huaorani of Amazonian Ecuador', PhD Dissertation, London School of Economics.

———. 2007. 'Indigenous Organisations, Oil Development, and the Politics of Egalitarianism'. *Cambridge Anthropology* 26, 34–46.

———. 2009. 'Remembering the Auca: Violence and Generational Memory in Amazonian Ecuador'. *Journal of the Royal Anthropological Institute* 15, 719–36.

———. 2010. 'Warriors, Hunters, and Bruce Lee: Gendered Agency and the Transformation of Amazonian Masculinity'. *American Ethnologist* 37, 753–70.

———. 2012a. 'Between Knowing and Being: Ignorance in Anthropology and Amazonian Shamanism'. In *The Anthropology of Ignorance: An Ethnographic Approach*, ed. C. High, A. Kelly and J. Mair. New York: Palgrave Macmillan, 119–35.

———. 2012b. 'Shamans, Animals, and Enemies: Locating the Human and Non-Human in an Amazonian Cosmos of Alterity'. In *Animism in Rainforest and Tundra: Personhood, Animals, Plants and Things in*

Contemporary Amazonia and Siberia, ed. M. Brightman, V.E. Grotti and O. Ulturgasheva. Oxford and New York: Berghahn, 130–45.

———. 2013. 'Lost and Found: Contesting Isolation and Cultivating Contact in Amazonian Ecuador'. *Hau: Journal of Ethnographic Theory* 3(3), 195–221.

———. 2015. *Victims and Warriors: Violence, History and Memory in Amazonia.* Urbana: University of Illinois Press.

High, C., A. Kelly and J. Mair (eds) 2012. *The Anthropology of Ignorance: An Ethnographic Approach.* New York: Palgrave Macmillan.

Kimerling, J.A. 1996. *El Derecho del Tambor: Derechos humanos y ambientales en los campos petroleros de la Amazonia Ecuatoriana.* Quito: Abya-Yala.

Leach, E. 1966. 'Virgin Birth'. *Proceedings of the Royal Anthropological Institute of Great Britain and Ireland* 1966, 39–49.

Londoño Sulkin, C. 2005. 'Inhuman Beings: Morality and Perspectivism among Muinane People (Colombian Amazonia)'. *Ethnos* 70, 7–30.

Malinowski, B. 1929. *The Sexual Life of Savages in North-western Melanesia.* London: Routledge.

Overing, J. and A. Passes 2000. *The Anthropology of Love and Anger: The Aesthetics of Conviviality in Native Amazonia.* London and New York: Routledge.

Reeve, M.-E. and C. High 2012. 'Between Friends and Enemies: The Dynamics of Interethnic Relations in Amazonian Ecuador'. *Ethnohistory* 59, 141–62.

Rival, L. 1996. *Hijos del sol, padres del jaguar: Los Huaorani de ayer y hoy.* Quito: Colleción Biblioteca Abya-Yala.

———. 1998. 'Androgynous Parents and Guest Children: The Huaorani Couvade'. *Journal of the Royal Anthropological Institute* 4, 619–42.

———. 2002. *Trekking through History: The Huaorani of Amazonian Ecuador.* New York: Columbia University Press.

Robarchek, C.A. and C.J. Robarchek 1998. *Waorani: The Contexts of Violence and War.* Fort Worth: Harcourt Brace College Publishers.

Roberts, J. and J. Armitage 2008. 'The Ignorance Economy'. *Prometheus* 26, 335–54.

Stang, C. 2009. *A Walk to the River in Amazonia: Ordinary Reality for the Mehinaku Indians.* New York: Berghahn.

Stoll, D. 1982. *Fishers of Men or Founders of Empire? The Wycliffe Bible Translators in Latin America.* London: Zed Press.

Thomas, N. and C. Humphrey (eds) 1994. *Shamanism, History, and the State.* Ann Arbor: University of Michigan Press.

Vilaça, A. and R.M. Wright (eds) 2009. *Native Christians: Modes and Effects of Christianity among Indigenous Peoples of the Americas.* Surrey: Ashgate.

Viveiros de Castro, E. 1998. 'Cosmological Deixis and Amerindian Perspectivism'. *Journal of the Royal Anthropological Institute* 4, 469–88.

———. 2003. '(Anthropology) and (Science)'. *Manchester Papers in Social Anthropology* 7.

———. 2004. 'Exchanging Perspectives: The Transformation of Objects into Subjects in Amerindian Ontologies'. *Common Knowledge* 10, 463–84.

Wallis, E.E. 1960. *The Dayuma Story: Life under Auca Spears*. New York: Harper and Brothers.

Yost, J.A. 1981. 'Twenty Years of Contact: The Mechanisms of Change in Wao (Auca) Culture'. In *Cultural Transformations and Ethnicity in Modern Ecuador*, ed. N.E. Whitten. Urbana: University of Illinois Press, 677–704.

Casey High is a senior lecturer in social anthropology at the University of Edinburgh. His fieldwork with Waorani communities in Amazonian Ecuador has focused on violence, memory and indigenous politics. His research interests also include linguistic anthropology and the interface between Amazonian cosmology and development. He is the author of *Victims and Warriors: Violence, History, and Memory in Amazonia* (2015) and has co-edited *The Anthropology of Ignorance: Ethnographic Perspectives* (2012) and *How Do We Know? Evidence, Ethnography, and the Making of Anthropological Knowledge* (2008).

Chapter 5

WHAT DO CHILD SEX OFFENDERS NOT KNOW?

John Borneman

Ignorance, Information and Knowledgeability

The issue of what child sex offenders know and of what they are ignorant was central to research I began in 2008 on the legal and therapeutic treatment of child sex offenders in Berlin, Germany.[1] Over the course of a year, I sat in on four therapy groups at KiZ (*Kind im Zentrum*, Child in the Centre), Berlin's largest centre for therapy for offenders and abused children. I followed the offenders, males between the ages of thirteen and seventy-two, in those groups as they were asked, under the threat of legal prosecution or, for those who had already served their time, the threat of *Sicherungsverwahrung* (preventative detention for reasons of security) or *Führungsaufsicht* (supervised release) to talk about themselves and what they did, in front of each other and two therapists, a man and a woman.[2]

Child molesters present acute challenges to knowledgeability, a term I will develop in the context of this chapter. In therapy they are asked to come to know themselves through introspection and empathic understanding in a process that is never fully complete. Yet if the therapists are competent and the treatment is at all successful in working through the offenders' defences, they come to know themselves differently and better than they had before. To use this knowledge not merely to control impulses and alter behaviour, or to change one's relation to children, but also to transform the self, is a demand of a much higher order, and one the criminal justice system seems to increasingly make before allowing the offenders to freely enter social life.

That transformation is in fact the official goal of the German penal system. As stated in the Criminal Legal Code, amended on 16 March 1976, rehabilitation aims 'to enable prisoners to live in the future a life of social responsibility without illegalities; it should also serve to protect the general public from further criminal acts'. The alternative to this transformation is to act on habit or its avoidance alone and risk mindless repetition of scenarios based on past experience. Hence offenders are subject to strong incentives to change, but, given the public scepticism about this possibility of change, they are subject to equally strong incentives to deny the accusations and avoid the full weight of the social stigma attached to molestation. Without some degree of transformation, and the ability to show signs of rehabilitation, however, reintegration into the social will usually be made impossible.

To know exactly what happened in sex abuse is elusive, in part because it is based on memories of an act. One must reconstruct the act and experience of abuse after, often long after, something happened. This retroactive reconstruction through memory work would seem to give force to the argument that most sex abuse lacks a materiality independent of the diffusion of meanings and discourses drawn from and promulgated by the various actors involved. From this perspective, the act materializes only in its subsequent performance in which speech is central. Yet, as I hope to demonstrate in what follows, the actual act of abuse, aspects of which usually remain opaque, can serve as a material referent for the memory work entailed in understanding the crime of abuse.

Following arrest for child sex abuse, few men ever admit fully to the accusations at this early stage of the ritual process. When child sex offenders in Germany enter therapy, which most of them do – as a legal right, a duty and a condition of sentencing – they usually have several individual sessions before joining a group. Therapists insist that they admit to their offence before entering the group; that is, that they admit to knowing something. All offenders withhold some things, however, both as a strategy to protect themselves from the accusation, a motivated ignorance of the facts, so to speak, and because to assimilate their experience into the crime of sex abuse is a self-incriminating process.

When I write of ignorance, I am referring only to not-knowing that is motivated – that is, to 'motivated ignorance'. To leave the state of ignorance is to become informed, but information alone will not suffice to make one knowledgeable. Therapy is supposed to enable the accused to recover both what he does not know and what he does know but is withholding. In both cases, to become knowledgeable is never merely a matter of elaborating that about which he is ignorant; nor is it a matter of making explicit what is implicit. To become knowledgeable is also a process of recovering bits of information – images, sensations, feelings, thoughts, speech – that have been made unavailable to memory or repressed. And after the suspect recovers these disconnected experiential bits, they must be combined into interconnected wholes, what Wilfried Bion (1984: 7) called transforming 'beta elements' into 'alpha elements'. That is, the accused must recover information that he has made difficult to retrieve, certain memories that he has made unavailable to himself, and think through the connections between these different bits of information. For the man accused of child molestation the process of discovery and recombination requires both introspection and establishing a relation of empathic understanding in his thoughts with the child he has molested.

To summarize: confronted with an accusation of sex abuse, suspected child molesters are asked first to recall and then to organize the details of an experience or experiences in a way that responds to the accusation. But that accusation is of 'sex abuse' – an alpha element, an already coherent, organizing concept. If the accusation is true, the suspect knows he will be placed in the category of the modern untouchable, outside the moral bounds of the human. Hence the first reaction to be expected, when accused of child molestation, is to protect oneself from this charge: to deny it. And that is what men accused of child molestation tend to do. In any institutional setting in German society, however, whether the home, the school or the workplace, such denial is rarely accepted. The accusation alone is grounds for an inquiry. Indeed, it often mandates an investigation, usually by some agent of the state, someone acting for or authorized by the law. Such an investigation, even before it has reached the criminal justice system, is the beginning of a ritual process in which the suspect repeatedly answers questions that entertain the possibility, or more likely presume, that he is hiding something. They do not presume, however, that he is ignorant, but only that he is motivated to ignorance.

Accusations are based on the experience of a child or youth. Nowadays, children are given the benefit of the doubt as to the veracity, or at least partial veracity, of their accusations. In northern Europe, at least, the long history of dismissing children's complaints as fantasies of adult abuse is over. Today even those cases of children's complaints based largely on fantasy are usually assumed to warrant an investigation to determine their truth. And following some very public scandals in German schools and churches in 2010, educators have become increasingly active in encouraging children to come forth immediately when they suspect adult misbehaviour, in a policy publicized as 'zero tolerance'. Hence it is no longer always the case that most statements of abused children are gathered long, even years, after the transgressive act. In the period of the research discussed here, however, most accusations were still made years after the violations, in which case they are not statements of children but statements of youths or even adults who claim to remember what happened.

In any event, it would be highly unusual for that happening to have been immediately experienced as abuse, although it may have been experienced as transgressive, harmful or injurious. To classify the act as abuse the child must do precisely what Bion (1967: 110) describes as thinking under the pressure of thought: transforming beta elements into alpha elements. This transformation takes time, both because language itself tends to be inadequate to contain the experience of abuse as a child and because children's testimony of sex abuse, being central to the recovery of the event, is usually based on an experience of ambivalence. The experience is, first of all, confusing, often with an adult with whom they identify, and then also painful, perhaps even simultaneously pleasurable. Only in retrospect and with some external assistance, after children or inexperienced youths attain a certain maturity, do they have the linguistic categories, the emotional capacity and the confidence in their own integrity to turn what happened into an experience that makes sense as criminal abuse.

If the victims are still children when the accusations are transformed into testimony for the court, an adult – e.g., a mother, school counsellor, psychologist or therapist – usually becomes the primary interlocutor in reconstructing the memory of a transgressive experience into one of sex abuse, and in producing evidence for the court. Fathers or close father-substitutes are the most frequent child molesters. In those cases, if the abuse is revealed during the child's latency stage, it is the mother who frequently serves as adult interlocutor. Once puberty is reached, however, mothers usually become complicitous in the abuse. In those cases, third parties outside the family instead intervene to help the youths or adults form a coherent picture of what went on.

This process of recovery of memory means that the suspected child molester must respond to an accusation about a violent transgression that he is charged with initiating, based either on the accusation of someone who is not capable of making the charge without the mediation and support of other adults, or on the accusation of someone who has reached a maturity that enables her or him to remember and now construe the experience as a connected whole. It is important to emphasize the temporal and adult mediation of the experience of abuse because adults today are highly motivated to protect children from an unmediated experience of sex in the first place. Moreover, this motivation to mediate the child's experience is one that many adults will insist they are ignorant of.

These conditions of recovery might create the impression that a true representation of the experience of abuse, in word and image, is impossibly elusive. Elusive, yes; impossible, no. However difficult it is to create a true representation, this seemingly elusive experience contains within it a truth that is capable of being grasped. That truth is necessary for the victim, in particular, because without knowing what experience exactly is behind the symptoms of sex abuse, one cannot address the consequences and effects of abuse. By the time that experience enters the ritual process of rehabilitation of the offender, it invariably includes the social mediation of what happened.

This is all to say that the experience of the transgression, for the abused child and the offender, is fully intersubjective, redefined through relations and interactions with various adults subsequent to the initial act. Children are ambivalent about this mediation, for it in many ways takes away an initial experience by fixing its referents in adult terms. By seeking to make this experience fully discursive in adult language, it robs the child's unconscious. But to rob the child's unconscious is part of the process necessary to achieve the coherence of the category of 'abuse' on which the court relies. The focus of this chapter will be more narrow: not on what the victims of sex abuse experience or know but on how the offenders come to know, and what they then in fact do know, in light of what we know about the intersubjective experience of the child. Consider this problematic through Uwe's attempt to arrive at knowledgeability of his act of incest.[3]

The Case of Uwe

The case of Uwe, a 37-year-old man accused of incest, is in many ways atypical of German sex offenders in therapy. He never disputed the descriptions of his daughter or ex-wife, and he was not arrested but only threatened with legal proceedings. What he shares with other men in therapy is the struggle with coming to know what went on, and it is this aspect of his case, the relation of knowing to the materiality of the act of abuse, that will be the focus in what follows.

Many of the men in group therapy do not talk much; some do not seem to even like to talk.[4] Uwe was most extreme in both respects. Although he was always alert and appeared to listen well, he went through entire two-hour sessions saying things like, '*Nichts neues*' (Nothing new), or '*Ich weiss nicht, was ich erzählen soll*' (I don't know what I should tell). In response to a therapist's question, 'Anything new?', he says '*Eigentlich nicht*' (Actually not) or '*Bei mir gibt's nichts*' (Nothing much happening with me). 'And at work?' asks the therapist. '*Eigentlich auch nicht viel, nichts passiert*' (Actually, also not much, nothing happened). When therapist #1 asks, 'Have you seen your children this last week?' Uwe replies, '*Gar nicht*' (Not at all).

This consistent recourse to the negative may seem like the result of defences against self-revelation such as repression or denial. Repression would mean he is making his experience unavailable to conscious thought; denial would mean a refusal to admit what occurred. But, after a year of observing Uwe, I concluded that he was neither repressing his experience nor in denial of the events. What he did, as he arrived at an understanding, alarmed him like a natural disaster would. He understood that he had committed an act considered so heinous that even murderers are treated with more sympathy. He truly wanted to know what he had done and how he had come to do something considered so despicable: something that, if he had committed the abuse he was accused of, was absolutely repulsive.

Uwe usually came to therapy directly from work – odd jobs repairing or building things. Despite his reticence to say anything, he brought a tense, anxious presence to the group simply by how he looked: typically, tattered jeans with holes at the knees, a hooded zip-up sweatshirt and fashionable, frameless glasses sitting above an unkempt, straggly beard. All of this adorned a thin, reedy body with a long, elegant neck, dimples, a wan, pleading smile directed at whomever addressed him, and quirky hair, which stood straight up, defying gravity, as if it were electrified.

I often strained to understand the speech in these groups. Many of the men mumbled or swallowed their words, talking in fragments comprehensible only within the larger contexts of their lives about which nobody listening knew. Uwe muttered softly, often mouthing words that did not come out in distinctive sounds. The other men repeatedly asked, 'What?' And they admonished him to speak up. Therapist #2 suggested that Uwe practise talking loudly to himself in front of a mirror. At his workplace, fellow workers had nicknamed him '*Der Stumme*' (the Mute One). 'Here we have to speak', said therapist #1. 'Can we do something to help you?'

Uwe shook his head to say no and raised his eyebrows helplessly.

After about four weeks in therapy, Uwe had still not spoken about what he had done. The other men in the group were curious, but also a bit angry at his reticence, and they began to needle him. Uwe reluctantly explained: 'My daughter, who was 4½, discovered that she could gratify herself [*Selbstbefriedigung*]. I helped her, *muschispielen* [play with the pussy]'. His ex-wife noticed that their daughter had discovered this. He talked to her about it, and she said, 'We all do that. But let's see if she does it at school also. You should have forbidden this'. The daughter apparently then played with herself at school also. '*Muschispielen* was not my intention', said Uwe. 'I wanted to distract her [*ablenken*], to play with her to divert her attention. It didn't work out. Then, I thought, stroke her behind, her legs, her feet, to take her mind off the vagina. This concept "*muschispielen*" was hers, she discovered the formulation herself. Shortly before Christmas, my ex-wife said our daughter could stay overnight, but I wasn't there. Then it came out. She turned to the juvenile authorities for advice, and she and I agreed I would come here to KiZ'.

The initial goal of therapy is to bring into words the deed, thereby externalizing it as an object about which the offenders then can think critically and create the possibility for changing their relation to that deed. Over time the therapists tried several approaches with Uwe.

In a series of sessions, they reconstructed Uwe's biography, and looked for some event in his life that might have prefigured the abuse. They asked about his relations with his parents, his early sexual experience, his time in school, vocational training and work history. His parents divorced when he was six, and he was raised subsequently by his father, now deceased, whom he regarded as 'somehow a friend'. His childhood was unremarkable, he said, but he did not want to speak much about that period. He instead skipped over it to talk about his military service. He served as an orderly with the Red Cross in preparation for catastrophes, but he had done this kind of work before. It was nothing exceptional for him, he said. He felt prepared for the experience; it did not shock him.

When asked about his sexuality, he becomes visibly uncomfortable: he leans forward, then back, rubs his hair, looks up, exhales. He describes playing doctor as an eight-year-old with his stepsister, who is three years older, as 'nothing bad'. Sex was spoken about at home, he says: nothing unusual there, either.

Therapist #2 asks who was more active in playing doctor, his step-sister or himself, and he does not seem to understand the question, before finally conceding, 'As far as I remember, she was more active. She examined me'. Therapist #2 asks if his sister already had breasts and pubic hair. 'Yes', he says. One usually plays doctor much younger than that, explains therapist #2, twelve is particularly old for such a game. 'We didn't know each other before that', Uwe says, as if they would have played doctor earlier, had they met.

'Were you discovered?' asks therapist #1. 'Yes, I think so'.

'What was the reaction?' 'More amused than anything'.

'Did they forbid it?' 'We didn't do it often', he says, and explains that he had an interest in sex, but it was not exciting for him. For his sister, however, he grants that the play was about sex. Yet the family, he says, talked and even joked about this later, always with amusement.

Searching for other sexual experiences, he describes discovering a few years after this doctor-play that he could masturbate. He says he discussed it with his father, with whom he lived at the time, even though his mother remained closer as a confidante. After completing the sixth grade of elementary school he spent more time alone and no longer sought out close friends. He had no childhood crushes, he says, because he did not seek out a girl.

How did he experience his first love? asks therapist #1. Uwe explains that in his early twenties he was asked by a woman who worked in the government office in charge of driving licences whether he had a girlfriend. When he said no, she advised him to search for one, and offered to help him write a personal advertisement for the newspaper. The woman who responded became his wife. They were engaged three months before marrying, and remained together for another three years. Asked to describe his ex-wife, he says she is open, sociable and approaches people easily.

Asked to describe what he put in the advertisement, he says, 'Loyal, somewhat odd, shy, in treatment'. He laughs. The woman, his future wife, was a nurse, and she said she was seduced by his description of being 'in treatment'. 'When I met her', he says, 'I could talk a lot, not like now'. They soon had a daughter, and then a son.

But his wife was always dissatisfied, he says. She insisted on moving frequently, to different parts of Germany. They first moved to Kassel, where they could buy a house cheaply. He moved there first and prepared the house. Within weeks after his wife arrived, she wanted to move again. At that time, pregnant with a second child, she revealed to Uwe that she was attracted to women. They moved back to Berlin and found a house there, which he painted and renovated. Then came the divorce, he says, and she insisted that he leave the house. She wanted, says Uwe, their son for herself.

When asked to account for his own transgression, Uwe explains, 'It was because I was fixated on my daughter, without establishing that I was her father'. He distinguishes between his initial feelings for her, how they developed and how he sees them now. After the separation from his wife, he enjoyed joint custody, but the children largely lived with their mother. When he arrived to pick them up, his daughter initially avoided him, hiding and not wanting to go with him. He realized he had to do something to change this, he explains, and offered his ex-wife to take care of the children more often. That proved convenient for her, as she had begun to go to evening classes. Over time the daughter then developed a deep intimacy with him, and started in fact to resist returning home to her mother. She began to say things like, 'I want to remain with you forever'. On reflection, he notes that back then he had devoted all his time to taking care of the children, and to creating closeness with his daughter, instead of taking care of himself. He also ignored his friends.

'And your son?' asks therapist #2. 'Our relationship has been more constant', he explains. 'It was different. He knew that I was his father. And there was a time when he was with me more than with his mother'. Shortly after the birth of the second child Uwe's ex-wife sought a new relationship, and found a female partner. When asked by another man in the group if it bothered Uwe that his wife 'turned lesbian', he says, 'Yes', adding, 'At some point she would have noticed that she wasn't interested in men'.

In a session that followed the attempt to create a biographical sketch, the therapists concentrated on some details of Uwe's sexual experience. An entire session was devoted to his relations with his sister. Therapist #1 asked what the age difference meant, that the sister was twelve and he nine. 'This is hard for me,' Uwe prefaced his remarks, 'generally hard [to talk about my experience with my sister]. I never had problems with her. We understood each other before we had sex play and after it also. She left then, started her own family'.

Therapist #2 interjected, 'It's not about a problem. You were the little brother. What was your feeling for her, and what did you feel in this close sexual contact with your sister? Children experience this in different ways. A nine-year-old boy is still a young child; a twelve-year-old girl can already be quite grown-up. Uwe replies, 'We slept together in the same bed, and I never noticed her physical proximity. It was a game for me'.

The therapists sense that he is being evasive, and therefore are suspicious of his insistence that his experience with his sister was neither
sexual nor ultimately traumatic. 'Not a sexual game?' Asks therapist
#2. Uwe answers, 'There was no sexual sensibility back then'. 'And for
your sister?' Uwe concludes, 'The sexual experience was very pleasant
for her, for me it was a game. She was my stepsister, we were not related. And we didn't grow up together. She lived with us in our family
for only three years'. 'Did you not feel exploited?' asks therapist #2. He
shakes his head to say no.

In another session, the therapists ask the men to fill in a question-
naire. One question reads: 'Your sexuality, it did not play any role, but
instead...'

Uwe first says, 'I have no idea. I wanted to distract her [Uwe's
daughter]'.

'From what?' asks therapist #1.

'From masturbating', says Uwe. He adds, 'I'm guilty in that I continued to stroke her while she masturbated. I thought it was something private, but she was with me. She wanted attention'.

'You encouraged her in this', says therapist #2. 'Would she have
masturbated if your ex-wife were there?'

Tears begin to roll down Uwe's cheeks, and he wipes them away. 'I
stroked her because I thought it would get her thinking about something nice [*etwas Nettes*], something else, and then she would stop'.

'But stroking her did not set any boundaries', says therapist #2.

'That's my problem', says Uwe. 'I have to learn how to have authority. Or I have to pay attention to what I am feeling also'.

'You sound helpless', say therapist #1. 'You have to learn to say no.
And what about your son, do you discipline him?'

'No, I also don't set boundaries with him', says Uwe, and he begins
to cry again.

'Do you make any decisions?' asks therapist #1, visibly frustrated.
He reminds Uwe of an event he has mentioned in another session,
about how Uwe responded to a physical assault by a co-worker by
smiling at him. 'You never resist', he tells him.

'Yes I do', Uwe defends himself.

'When?' 'I moved house a number of times'.

Therapist #1 returns to probing Uwe's sexual fantasies: 'What do
you think about when you have sexual feelings?'

'I do it alone'.

'What do you think about?' the therapist repeats.

'A woman'.

In perhaps a third of the sessions, the therapists keep returning to the question of why Uwe encouraged his daughter to fondle herself. Most of the time, he gives the same answer: 'I wanted to distract her'.

Once therapist #2 asks, 'Did her wish shock you?'

'Yes,' he says, 'looking at it that way. In that moment, when it happened, [however,] my expectation was that it was something nice. It was like play'.

Another time, the therapists distinguish between setting boundaries and distracting, and ask, 'If the goal was to stop your daughter from pulling down her pants and playing between her legs, then why would *stroking her* help achieve this?' Uwe is silent.

Therapist #1 says, 'For six months your attempt to distract didn't work. Did you try something else?'

'I wanted her closeness', replies Uwe.

'Why didn't you share this problem with your wife?'

Uwe remains silent.

Increasingly Uwe's ex-wife refused to talk with him and prevented him from having any contact with the children: no letters, and she refused to answer his telephone calls. For a while, she let him see his son but not his daughter. The social worker who is to mediate his relationship with his family informs him that his daughter does not want to see him any more. But then he learns from his son that his daughter has begun complaining: if her brother can visit him so should she be able to. The therapists counsel patience.

After I had finished my year of observation of the group, Uwe continued therapy with other incest abusers for another year. His ex-wife, the therapists told me, was happy in her new relationship. They described the daughter, whom they had observed in a separate therapy session, as a lively, delightful child, not affected as far as they could tell by the early history of masturbation in front of her father. The children now have two mothers, and they have cut off all Uwe's contact with his daughter. He seldom sees his son any more either. Near the end of therapy, he reported that his ex-wife had informed him that she planned to leave Berlin with her new partner and the children.

I asked the therapists to give me a final sketch of Uwe's development. They were ambivalent in their final diagnosis. On the one hand, they agreed that Uwe had a minimal sexuality, if any, and that his drives appeared consistently weak. On the other hand, one therapist suspected he might have an orientation towards children, in which case he should have been treated in a group with men who had abused unrelated children or young people rather than in a group of men who had committed incest. Following a new trend in German psychology to classify paedophiles as a third sexual orientation along-side hetero- and homosexuals, one therapist considered that he might be a *'Pädosexueller'* (the third sexual preference), but she had no fur-ther evidence for this ascription. The other therapist was more scepti-cal of this claim.

The Limits of Empathy

Uwe never did go on trial. But if he had, and if a judge had arrived at a verdict, she would have had to first engage in the process of assessing the truth of various utterances, a process of making objective and explicit the various motives and perspectives of the experiences of the child and the adult. Such a legal process of producing and evaluating evidence is similar to that of the humanist or social scientist engaged in reaching an understanding of the truth, except that the human sciences have few if any absolute restrictions on the kinds of evidence to consider, while the court makes all sorts of restrictions on the ad-missibility of evidence.

Whatever conclusions are arrived at in understanding the case of Uwe and his daughter, they will not be the result of the uncovering of the 'truth of sex' in the sense of Michel Foucault (1978: 7), which he hyperbolically describes as the 'existence of a discourse in which sex, the revelation of truth, the overturning of global laws, the proclama-tions of a new day to come, and the promise of a new felicity are linked together'. The 'truth of sex' about which Foucault writes was, argua-bly, the dominant ordering discourse in certain institutional settings from the late-nineteenth to the mid-twentieth centuries. It still exists, and speculation about Uwe as *'Pädosexueller'* – an ontological cate-gory; an attempt, in Foucauldian language, at 'subjectivation' – is part of this discourse. Indeed, on the surface, Uwe's experience interpreted through this discourse, and through the entire ritual rehab process, seems to have been oriented to producing a certain kind of sexual sub-ject. Yet the therapists who treated Uwe struggled with experiences of his that could not be subsumed within the discourse on sex and ulti-mately were inconclusive about how to define him as a sexual subject.

There are also obvious similarities in Uwe's case with the processes that Foucault perspicaciously wrote about, such as the 'pedagogiza-tion of children's behavior' and the attempt to produce a sexuality in Uwe through what appears to be a confessional setting (Foucault 1978: 103–10). But the formal similarities between confessional and therapeutic settings are not borne out in Uwe's experience. The therapists are most intent on finding out what actually happened and what Uwe's motives were in his relations with his daughter that might have led him to encourage her to masturbate. They go through a lengthy set of questions that might lead Uwe to define himself as a sexual subject, but they do not end there. Their intent is ultimately to elicit from him an explanation in his own words rather than a particular 'confession'. To follow Foucault's analytic lead here, as does Judith Butler in her influential book *Bodies that Matter*, would lead one to a question about how 'regulatory power produces the subjects it controls' (Butler 1993: 23) or to understand 'the matter of bodies as the effect of a dynamic of power, such that the matter of bodies will be indissociable from the regulatory norms that govern their materialization and the signification of those material effects' (Butler 1993: 2). In other words, bodies are 'indissociable' from regulatory norms, based on knowledge that is an effect of power.

Yet 'the process of materialization' (Butler 1993: 9) of Uwe's body and that of his daughter cannot be followed by reading the effects of regulatory norms in discourse. Even after their bodies are marked by the act of transgression, noticed in the school and talked about with Uwe's wife and later by Uwe himself in therapy, the materiality of the interaction between Uwe and his daughter is separable from the regulatory norms expressed in language. Indeed, the therapists must keep the deed separable from the language they use and from social norms or they are not doing their job, which is one not of labelling or interpellating but of open discovery. The norms, which certainly exist, are not cited like law, as Butler defines the performative workings of regulatory power, but are merely one interpretive reference in everybody's attempt to interpret the meaning of the exchange between Uwe and his daughter.[5]

The word *muschispielen*, for example, which comes to be used by the girl (as Uwe relates) to describe a form of precocious sensual play, is the effect of a dynamic of power only if one reduces all of the young girl's interactions with adults to dynamics of power. The word does not appear to be the reiteration of anything for the girl, but instead nominates a novel act that confounds its participants despite their knowledge of the word. Uwe's encouragement of this play, and later, his difficulty of bringing the deed into speech, is due precisely in part to the absence or ambiguity of regulatory norms, and to the difficulty of interpreting them. Likewise, the process of uncovering what happened is not brought under a single rule or under language as such. The attempts of therapists in this case to understand Uwe's deed as an expression of sexuality ultimately went nowhere.

That is because the therapists held onto a conception of the event's materiality – that something did happen even though it may be difficult to get at – as that which Uwe must reference and work through. By asking questions only of the discourse of sex and its production through a matrix of knowledge/power, Foucault's analytical focus elides the materiality of the intersubjective. There is a truth in Uwe's case, but it is not an effect of the discourse. The truth has an integrity, not as an *effect* of the efforts of Uwe and the therapists to bring the act into speech, but one that can be approached *through* these efforts. If the theoretical goal of the therapists is to bring Uwe closer to the truth of his experience, Uwe's goal is ultimately knowledgeability: to understand his act through introspection and empathic understanding. If that is our goal as readers, we would be wise to replicate Uwe's efforts.

What did go on for those six months in Uwe's relations with his daughter? What is the truth in the materiality of the events? Uwe's explanation is consistent for what he agrees, in retrospect, is a transgression: that he wanted to distract his daughter from what she called '*muschispielen*'. Why, then, as the therapists repeatedly ask, did he stroke her other body parts when she engaged in this sex play? It remains a mystery where she learned the word '*muschispielen*', though it is highly improbable that she learned it from her father or her three-year-old brother, the only males she had contact with. It is likely that she heard it in interactions with girls or women, including her mother, or she put the two words '*Muschi*' and '*spielen*' together into a compound noun, as is allowed in German syntax. At any rate, *muschispielen* is merely a label for an activity, a symbol for the child's attempt to please herself, initially only in her father's presence.

Uwe has no answer for why his daughter discovered this behaviour in interaction with him, or why he seemed to encourage what most adults today would call masturbation. When asked, he repeats his initial motive: he stroked her in order to distract her ('*um abzulenken*'). That motive is indeed plausible, but it seems too transparent and partial an explanation. It seems too transparent because Uwe's motives in other domains remain generally hidden to himself, and though he may not have a large ego, he nonetheless has feelings and interests that are not merely reactive to those of others.

It would also be a mistake to assume that Uwe is pursuing certain interests because of a rational calculation, or carrying out a desire based on either a rational understanding of his passions or an innate drive that he cannot properly control. As has been discussed, Uwe has no particular passions and little 'inner passion', and he seems hardly a 'rational choice' type. Throughout therapy it proved difficult for him to retrieve a sense of his own self-interest. He makes few decisions but mostly follows the initiatives of others. When therapist #2 challenged Uwe about not making decisions and failing to defend himself, Uwe became agitated and insisted, 'Yes I do'. 'When?' asked the therapist. 'I moved house a number of times', replied Uwe. Yet earlier Uwe had complained about his wife's wish to constantly move house, suggesting that even this decision was not based on his initiative or interest, though, when cornered by the therapist to defend himself, he recalled it as such.

It might be asked here, following D.W. Winnicott (1965), if Uwe is showing in therapy a false self protecting something from disclosure: that something could in fact be an interest in sex with children. But there is evidence of only one such example in his life, that of his relations with his daughter, and one experience is hardly enough evidence to infer a primary interest in children or a sexuality based on such interest. The therapists' discussion of whether he had a '*pädo-sexuelle*' orientation was ultimately inconclusive, as there was insufficient evidence to infer a particular sexuality of any kind.

A more promising approach might be to ask not about his formation as a sexual subject but about how his experience is relational and leads to a strongly intersubjective sense of self. In therapy, Uwe is always smiling at the other men in the group, even when they are saying things critical of him. He smiled the same way, apparently, at work when a co-worker struck him. This smile might be a way of protecting himself from disapproval by others, but it is also a sign of empathy. Rather than assert his own interests and indulge in his own feelings, he consistently tries to intuit and share the feelings of the other. His authentic self seems all too eager to feel the other's interests or perspective rather than his own. Even when another man asks him whether he is disappointed or angry that his wife has left him for a woman, to 'become lesbian', as he puts it, Uwe does not react angrily. He merely admits his disappointment – in a single word, '*Ja*'. And then he goes on to account for his ex-wife's motives: eventually she would have discovered her sexual interest in women anyway. In other words, rather than dwelling on his own disappointment or accusing his ex-wife of trying to punish him, he offers the other members of the group a statement of empathy for her reason for leaving him.

Could it be that Uwe was reacting to his 4½-year-old daughter out of the same sense of relation: both protecting himself from disapproval and being empathic? That is, as his daughter begins playing with herself, Uwe enters a dilemma, knowing that society would think this is wrong, therefore trying to distract her, but also not risking her disapproval by affirming her interests in her own body by stroking her bottom, arms and legs. He admits to his pleasure in this tactility, but that does not imply he was motivated by self-interest or passion. That pleasure, so he reasoned, was limited and solely a result of his daughter's initiative.

His explanation – intending to distract her from something done on her initiative – was of course self-serving, assuming that his child had a will clearly demarcated from his own. In turn, however, was the daughter not taking her cues from her father, and performing for him? And to what extent is the *muschispielen* an attempt by the daughter to relate to her father in the absence of her mother? The most likely explanation is that Uwe in his sorrow and abandonment elicited an emotional reaction in his daughter, and that she therefore was reacting to his suffering.

The daughter's full motives are more difficult to interpret without a record of what she thought or felt, of how she was experiencing Uwe's co-participation, or, in his words, his 'attempt to distract' her sex play. To be sure, the daughter may indeed have discovered masturbation on her own; it may be a product of her own fantasy and discovery of her own body. The fact is, however, she made this discovery initially only in front of her father. His presence appears crucial and causative of her behaviour. Uwe's wife had left him; he was lonely, quiet, needy, but unwilling or incapable of expressing himself in words. His only joy seemed to be the visit of his children. He suspended all other activities and friendships. Therefore it is most plausible to assume that Uwe did in fact elicit his daughter's reaction, but that both his message and his daughter's reaction were unconscious.

In sum, to become knowledgeable in a way that approaches the truth of what really happened, to know the materiality behind the story, we must foreground what is communicated unconsciously, taking into account that which could not become material information for a court of law. This is true especially in cases of the sex abuse of children. Such diverse psychoanalytic approaches as those of Melanie Klein and Jacques Lacan have maintained that most adult communication with children is unconscious, even more so when the children are very young. This is because a great deal is learnt before children acquire language, and in that early phase of life, children initially take over from adults their unconscious. Jean Laplanche (1989) develops this line of thought most fully, arguing that the adult's excitation is subject to 'intromission' or 'implantation' by the child, resulting in a 'message' that in translation creates the child's unconscious – communication that is not dependent on words.

Uwe claims that he became more nonverbal after his divorce. It follows that after his separation from his wife, his communication with his daughter and son also had come to be primarily nonverbal, meaning that he communicated largely by mood and look – his wan smile, his searching, pleading eyebrows. Lacking speech, he probably thought that his smile and his eyes were telling his daughter little about his inner state, which in any event was not transparent to him either. But rather than project onto Uwe her own feelings, which, as a child, were highly susceptible to adult influence, she was more likely to be engaged in interpreting and translating his messages, however subdued and subtle in expression. She, the prescient child, in other words, understood his desire better than he himself did. She inferred from his nonverbal communication that the message was a desire for what he described to the therapists later as 'something nice' (*etwas Nettes*). In short, neither Uwe nor his daughter were acting out of any conscious self-interest or stable drive or desire; nor were they, in those six months of transgression, the subjects of any authoritative discourse. They were acting out understandings reached through an intersubjective process of largely unconscious communication.

What makes Uwe's case so unusual is that his offence seems to be due in part to an excess of empathy. Since the 1980s, most programmes of treatment for sex offenders have included a component on empathy, based on the assumption that sex offenders lack empathic skills. They lack the capacity to know emotionally what the child is experiencing within the child's frame of reference. Therefore they are not easily convinced of having harmed a child when told that they use children for their own sexual pleasure, imposing on them an adult sexuality for which children are by nature unprepared. More recently, scholars have amended this assumption, arguing that sex offenders are not marked by the lack of empathy generally but by the lack of empathy for their particular victim only (Brown, Harkins and Beech 2011: 15). Uwe's relations with his daughter do not appear to fit this model, yet because he seemed to encourage his daughter's sex play, his transgression was considered abuse.

From the daughter's point of view, was it the 'sex' that was damaging, or the social elaboration and interpretation of this sex as abuse? Uwe has in fact not engaged in abuse, which would have overwhelmed the senses of his daughter. Nor did he engage in deprivation or neglect, which would have starved those senses. There is no evidence that the daughter found her sex play troubling, at least according to the therapists who treated her (as discussed above), even after the scandal around the accusation of her father's abuse. Why the sex abuse did not result in symptoms may be in part a result of her father's empathy, which in turn led him to not overreact to her precocious sexuality. The same might be said for the early intervention in the child's behaviour by the mother, the kindergarten teachers and the therapists, whose empathic responses to what happened foreclosed the possibility that play might become abuse in her memory.

Nonetheless, the expert professionals – child psychologists, therapists and judge – all agreed that Uwe was motivated to ignore the potential harm he was inflicting on his daughter. Almost from the start of therapy, Uwe concurred about the question of harm, though he persisted in doubting that his motivations were sexual. The unknowability of whether Uwe was actually harming his daughter while he himself was sure of his nonsexual motives is probably what, I suspect, often drove Uwe to tears. Acting out of what he thought was empathy, he could not bear the thought that he had harmed his daughter. Even after therapy, he was left with a fundamental uncertainty about the consequences for his daughter of the sex play during her childhood. An explanation incorporating his unconscious motivations, as is attempted here, might have provided him with a perspective from which to understand better his motive of distraction. But the therapists did not probe his action as part of an unconscious exchange with his daughter. Rather, they insisted that his explanation of 'distraction' was merely a rationalization of a sexual motive that they are ultimately never able to clearly define.

Yet we should not lose sight of the goal in Uwe's therapy: to overcome his resistances and arrive at a transparency of self that would not tolerate his silences or possible self-deceptions. Therapy and the law approach Uwe's ignorance through a critical discourse of the self that is not merely confessional, not satisfied with a particular historical 'truth of sex', but intent on finding out 'what really happened'. This critical discourse is also not primarily oriented to classification of sexual types but instead calls for Uwe to engage in a relentless revelation of what is most authentic in himself through an examination of his history and actions in their finest details.

As has been described above, empathy with his child is necessary for Uwe to arrive at an understanding of the meaning of his interactions with her. But empathic understanding finds its limits when he is asked to say no, to authorize an action that entails not a mimetic relation to the other but a negative judgement. Initially his inability to be sufficiently introspective, to more fully understand his function as parent, limited his ability to go beyond his self-understanding as a supportive, empathic, facilitating person. He should have broken with

his own self-understanding of what being supportive and facilitating means. To become informed and knowledgeable of this requires
of him a reflexive interpretation that works through his own unconscious transference with his daughter. In this process he would have,
to paraphrase his own words, become a father who says no, both to
himself and to his daughter.

Given the outcome of events, it is obviously too late for him to rec-
tify his inaction now. Most important, however, is that from today's
vantage point, what happened appears to have caused his daughter
no harm. Yet the fact that his ex-wife moved to another city, and, with
the support of the social worker in charge of his case, removed his
daughter and son totally from his care, introduces another context
into his daughter's memory of what happened. That removal may in
fact lead the daughter to assume she is the cause of the separation
and thus guilty of betraying her father. In that case, the materiality of
what happened will be transformed through memory into a different
kind of abuse.

Final Reflections

In conclusion, what can be learnt from this case study and this particular framing of ignorance? There remain three major questions:
What is the relation of the materiality of the abuse to knowing? After
this analysis, do we readers leave the state of ignorance? And what do
we now know; are we now knowledgeable about incest and child sex
abuse?

Information itself cannot overcome the motivated ignorance surrounding child sex abuse. To the extent child sex, child sex abuse and
incest are taboos, they are structured in part by silences that one
might characterize as integral to a regime of ignorance. There is indeed a systematicity to the knowledge and ignorance surrounding
any taboo, an uneven distribution of knowledge and differential relations of intimacy and distance to the tabooed object. More important
for understanding abuse than this regime, however, is access to resistances to knowing and understanding how they are strengthened or
overcome. Those resistances elide the materiality of what happened.
Therapy relies on this materiality to come closer to the event. Uwe's
case sheds some light on this process.

To become knowledgeable in such issues, we, the readers, looking
in from the outside, must reckon with three minimally triadic relations, each of which mediates specific tensions about which we might

be motivated to remain in ignorance. That is, we must overcome certain personal investments and resistances that lead us to prematurely foreclose understanding of how these tensions work. There is the Oedipal dynamic of mother, father, daughter; the treatment dynamic of client, therapist, law; and the phantasmatic dynamic of media, sex offender, reader.

For contemporary critics of the family, especially many feminists, the Oedipal dynamic assumes the father's guilt, making it difficult to understand the frequently compromised position of the mother and the agency of the child (cf. Bell 1993). For contemporary critics of the state and law, this example can serve as an important reminder that the threat of imprisonment through law does in fact shadow the treatment, but the state in Uwe's case neither overreacts nor is entirely absent. Rather, the state seems to allow various social actors and institutions to work their way towards an understanding and to reckon with the transgression without making the deed into an illegality. This enables the mother, the father and the daughter to resist identification with a single event that might create the trauma they seek to contain.

Finally, there is the triad that constitutes the relation of publicity – that is, the issue of how such events enter the public sphere. This triad is more important for our resistances to knowing than is the regime of ignorance. We are very well informed, but we are not knowledgeable in part because the contemporary tabloid culture plays with and on the taboos surrounding incest and sex abuse, substituting a tabloid description of surface reality that creates a phantasma, inclusive of distorted images (silhouettes, angry faces, frames of faces partially anonymized), for the chaotic set of actual interpersonal relations which place the transgressive act in a processual context. Tabloid descriptions rely on key affective terms, modes of depiction and illustration, which are decontextualized from any understanding of the human relationships that motivate them.

Kinderschänder, Pädophiler, Inzesttäter (child molester, paedophile, *incest abuser*) – the figures of male sexuality that in Germany currently receive the most attention and provoke the most horror – require no interpretation. An empathic identification with the child victim is called forth to accompany the repulsion and reticence to empathize with the offender. To be sure, both empathy and repulsion have their place: both are attempts to contain the emotional transference that is entailed in establishing a relationship to the act of incest between parent and child. Yet the process of containment remains an unstable one: the goal is not to fix the male figures either as good and worthy of empathy or evil, but to be able to oscillate between the two reactions of empathy and repulsion.

Incest, as many have argued, is an aporia at the heart of the human condition (Borneman 2012; Godelier 2004; Laplanche 2009). The child needs protection from the very people who are responsible for its care, but this protection is always endangered by intromission of the desires of the parents. Adult abandonment of the child results in an inability to form attachments; if the adult gets too close the child is overwhelmed by this intimacy, and therefore unable to form new attachments. The incest taboo, then, regulates this paradox with parricide: to avoid this aggression against the child, parents are asked to prepare their own child to murder them in order for the child to become its own parent in the future. The horror of this dynamic is, as far as we know, specific to the human species. That we cannot overcome or supersede this dynamic is one of the reasons we are motivated to be ignorant about it, and resist knowledgeability.

Acknowledgements

Parts of this research were delivered as a keynote address at the University of California, Berkeley, in May 2012, and then discussed at the University of Konstanz, Germany, in August 2012. I want to thank the organizers and participants of both events.

Notes

1. This chapter is a shortened and reoriented version of a longer work on the rehabilitation of child sex offenders (Borneman 2015: 142–59).
2. I also worked in a minimum-security prison one day a week, where some of the men were or had served time, and there I had access to the archives of the Ministry of Justice, of all convicted sex offenders in Berlin from the years 2001 to 2008.
3. The case of Uwe is one of the thirty-five cases of offenders whose therapy sessions I attended. It is not representative but chosen for how it exemplifies certain problems about which the public are well informed but resist becoming knowledgeable.
4. To retain the real-time sense of the sessions, they are described here in the ethnographic present.
5. Butler's basic argument that the body does not preexist ideation is well taken, but the use of norm in determining 'cultural intelligibility' cannot be equated with the 'citation of law'. Likewise, regulatory norms are

merely one element and not determinative of the process of *'assujetisse-ment'* (subjectivation) (Butler 1993: 15). Butler writes, 'The force and necessity of these norms ... is thus functionally dependent on the approx-imation and citation of the law' (Butler 1993: 14). While the logic be-tween law and norm may be formally analogous, the specific modes and contexts of citation, approximation or assumption have such radically different functions in different cultures and in different cultural occa-sions as to obviate the utility of the analogy. Certainly KiZ therapists are aware of all sorts of regulatory norms, but the variety of deeds that are subsumed into the category of sex abuse – e.g., rape, kissing, fondling, viewing internet pornography – constantly challenge the applicability of these norms. Moreover, the therapists do not have the enforcement authority that such Foucauldian theory would attribute to them. As they treat Uwe, they are also trying, in all good faith, above all, to come up with a narrative that can help him account for his actions.

References

Bell, V. 1993. *Interrogating Incest: Feminism, Foucault, and the Law*. New York: Routledge.

Bion, W. 1967. *A Theory of Thinking: In Second Thoughts*. New York: Aronson.

———. 1984. *Learning from Experience*. London: Karnac Books.

Borneman, J. 2012. 'Incest, the Child, and the Despotic Father'. *Current Anthropology* 53, 181–203.

———. 2015. *Cruel Attachments: The Ritual Rehab of Child Molesters in Germany*. Chicago: University of Chicago Press.

Brown, S., L. Harkins and A.R. Beech 2011. 'General and Victim-Specific Empathy: Associations with Actuarial Risk, Treatment Outcome, and Sexual Recidivism'. *Sexual Abuse: A Journal of Research and Treatment* 20, 1–20.

Butler, J. 1993. *Bodies that Matter: On the Discursive Limits of 'Sex'*. New York: Routledge.

Foucault, M. 1978 [1976]. *The History of Sexuality: An Introduction*. New York: Pantheon.

Godelier, M. 2004. *Métamorphoses de la parenté*. Paris: Fayard.

Laplanche, J. 1989. *New Foundations for Psychoanalysis*. Oxford: Basil Blackwell.

———. 2009. 'Inzest und Infantile Sexualität'. *Psyche* 6, 525–39.

Winnicott, D.W. 1965 [1960]. 'Ego Distortion in Terms of True and False Self'. In *The Maturational Processes and the Facilitating Environment: Studies in the Theory of Emotional Development*. Madison, CT: International Universities Press, 140–52.

John Borneman is Professor of Anthropology at Princeton University. He has taught at Cornell University (1991–2001) and has been a guest professor in Sweden, Norway, France, Germany, England and Syria. His most recent publications include *Syrian Episodes: Sons, Fathers, and an Anthropologist in Aleppo* (2007), (as co-editor) *Being There: The Fieldwork Encounter and the Making of Truth* (2009), *Political Crime and the Memory of Loss* (2011) and *Cruel Attachments: The Ritual Rehab of Child Molesters in Germany* (2015).

Chapter 6

PROBLEMATIC REPRODUCTIONS

CHILDREN, SLAVERY AND NOT-KNOWING IN COLONIAL FRENCH WEST AFRICA

Roy Dilley

This chapter examines the production and reproduction of ignorance within parts of the French colonial apparatus and within networks of social relations among colonial officers in West Africa. I have pointed out in publications elsewhere how the early forays of the French military into West Africa during the period of colonial conquest (up until the end of the last decade of the nineteenth century) were sustained in large measure by not knowing in detail about the enemy (Dilley 2007, 2010). Various forms of knowledge were nonetheless important, such as the enemy's military capability, their tactics and modes of operation, their lines of communication and supply routes, the geography of the terrain, and so on. These were basic facts whose importance was instilled in officers through military training, and they were essential for successful military engagement. Beyond these aspects of knowledge, however, the early colonial regime was more based on ignorance and the power that this affords. It was only during the later stages of annexation and the establishment of a colonial administration that a need for detailed knowledge of the colonized peoples, their languages and cultures, their modes of livelihood and so forth was thought to be necessary. I have sketched out in earlier publications the ways in which the colonial regime and its officers attempted to fill those gaps in their knowledge about other places and other peoples; these publications also examine the ways in which ignorance and not-knowing are not extinguished by the forward march of knowledge; rather, they show how knowledge and ignorance as a mutually constituted pair of concepts are produced and reproduced over time with regard to specific colonial objectives and colonial knowledge practices, and to the particular interests of social actors.

I intend in this present chapter to push my analysis of aspects of the French colonial regime in a slightly different direction. I am concerned here not only with sets of relationships between knowledge and ignorance, but also with how non-knowledge is created through various sorts of social process: through contradictory pressures operating within a colonial regime, and through the activities of individual officers, who might be driven as much by desire and passion to conceal and dissimulate as by intellectual bafflement or opacity. I seek to investigate the production and reproduction of non-knowledge not merely as a consequence of the pursuit of knowledge, but moreover as an artefact of colonial relations, of a regime of governmentality. As Foucault argues (2007: 273–77), the state (here the colonial state) is a form of practice, a way of governing, a way of doing things, a way of knowing and indeed not-knowing things. The significant practices of colonialism here include the mechanisms of government and everyday social relations among officers; and this analysis of them considers the effort that is expended in creating holes, positive absences or zones of non-knowledge. The role of desire, passion and affect in the constitution of zones of ignorance has to be highlighted. Desire here relates to those areas that cannot be known because, for instance, it would be too painful to do so, or it would be more convenient or politically expedient to ignore them, or they escape someone's grasp because of a lack of motivation to apprehend them. Alternatively a person might simply revel in their state of not-knowing by turning their head away from something, or by pretending not to know.

In this chapter two problematic areas for the French colonial regime in West Africa will be considered. The first topic is the offspring of colonial officers and indigenous women, who are sometimes referred to as 'concubines' and known locally as *moussos*; that is, women taken as officers' wives in accordance with local customary practice – *mariage à la mode de pays*, as it was known. Whether these children of empire were recognized or not by their fathers was one concern; what to do with these children was an additional headache for the administration. Knowledge of them was as problematic as ignoring them.

The second area examined in this chapter is slavery within West Africa, especially how the colonial regime regarded such a practice and how individual officers reacted towards the existence of 'captives' in specific contexts. The Third Republic's ideals of *liberté, egalité et fraternité* informed the central planks of the 'civilizing mission' of French colonialism, and slavery was one of the main targets to be eliminated (see Conklin 1997). Yet, the practical realities of life in the African bush made these ideals sometimes difficult to live up to and problematic to impose on local populations; and furthermore the peccadilloes of individual officers sometimes worked against the moral high ground staked out by governments and political leaders in the metropolitan centre. This chapter attempts to analyse, therefore, the way in which aspects of French colonialism, as a system of relations, sustained and reproduced not-knowing. It also attempts to examine how individual officers, caught within the contradictory currents of colonialism, indulged themselves not only by entertaining 'concubines' but also by retaining domestic 'captives', keeping Paris and their families back in France in the dark about practical, local arrangements at French posts, thus obscuring from official scrutiny the dependency of local administrations on slavery. The desire for secrecy around the issue of slavery resulted in metropolitan France not knowing of these aspects of empire; the passion engendered by officers' relationships with local women set up a tension between knowledge generated (including 'knowledge' in a Biblical sense) in the isolated social networks within the confines of a colonial outpost, on the one hand, and not-knowing in the wider social and cultural world that found these facts unacceptable and unpalatable, on the other. The contradictory processes of knowing and concealment, of withholding social facts and dissimulation in the face of an officially proclaimed pursuit of knowledge, run through the system of relations of colonial life.

Crewe and Barot – What to Do with a *Mousso*

This chapter will turn shortly to the issue of children of empire, but first I would like to consider a logically prior stage in this process: namely, the relations and temporary unions between European men and indigenous women. When viewed comparatively, this example reveals different fault lines in the construction of ignorance in the colonial systems of Britain and France. At the beginning of the twentieth century, the upper echelons of the British Empire were apparently plagued by the problem of ignorance with regard to sexual liaisons between colonial officers and local women in the colonies. The famous Crewe Circulars of 1909, issued by the then British Secretary of State for the Colonies, Lord Crewe, illustrate the gap between not-knowing at the centre of colonial power and the concealed knowledge of those on the peripheries of empire (see Hyam 1986a, 1986b, 1990). Lord Crewe's first memorandum of 1909 condemned the practice of taking local women as 'concubines' by officers stationed in the colonies and sought to prevent these unwholesome unions, often referred to as 'country marriages'. The dim view of concubinage taken by the Minister was soon modified once he had heard the reaction from the colonies: officers were outraged and declared they would simply not be able to perform their functions properly over long tours of duty without the relief and support that 'country marriage' provided them. It was part of standard practice in the colonies that men should take native women in this way. Lord Crewe's second circular, dispatched soon after the first had had its initial impact, explained that while the practice of concubinage was not to be encouraged, London would try to turn a blind eye as much as possible to what was happening on the ground.

In France, by contrast, the subject of liaisons with native women was not something to be hidden from view in quite the same prurient way as in Britain. Indeed, a semi-official guide published in 1902 by Dr Louis Barot from Bordeaux – a medic in the colonial army – entitled *Guide pratique de l'européen dans l'Afrique occidentale* offered colonial officers, administrators, traders, colonialists and travellers to West Africa practical tips on living and working in the region.[1] One section of the *Guide* was dedicated to the issue of native women, and it gave advice on contracting temporary unions or *mariages à la mode de pays* by listing the ethnic categories of the region's peoples with accompanying notes on the suitability of their womenfolk as native brides. The book described their physical features, their stereotypical temperaments and cultural dispositions, and their supposed capacities as potential spouses. Rather than ignoring the issue or pretending that it did not exist, the *Guide* was forthright in recommending country marriage for the progress of French colonialism. 'The whole problem', it stated, 'of adapting our races to these climates lies there; it is by creating mulatto races that we most easily Gallicize West Africa'.[2] The emerging 'intermediate race' would act in the space between the colonizer and colonized: it could understand, it was argued, European civilization but yet would remain close to and in contact with local populations. The policy would produce, therefore, a kind of class of petty bourgeoisie that was conceived in racial terms: a population with the intelligence of the European and the physical strength of the African. Another acknowledged benefit of country marriages was that they would provide a more hygienic form of relationship between men and women, since serving officers would not need to rely on prostitution for sexual relief. An additional benefit of country marriages remarked on by British officers on the ground was encapsulated in their use of the term 'sleeping dictionaries' to describe native wives,[3] referring to the way in which a European's knowledge of a vernacular tongue could be improved through the expertise offered by indigenous women. This practical advantage deriving from relations with local women was acknowledged by French officers too.

The British and the French structures of colonialism differed markedly therefore, particularly with respect to their systems of knowledge and their regimes of ignorance regarding relations between local women and male colonialists. The prurient sensibilities of the British that led to a desire not to know the sordid details of everyday life at colonial outposts contrast starkly with the recognition of sexual passion felt by men left to fend for themselves in up-country stations in French territories. Local knowledge generated by colonialists through their interactions with populations on the ground was handled differently in official circles in the capital cities of each of the colonial regimes. Desire drove ignorance in two opposite directions.

Children of Empire

The French colonial authorities were well aware of the phenomenon of mixed-race children, the product of colonial officers and local women in Africa. As the moral atmosphere of the early colonies changed over the course of the nineteenth century, the idea took hold that European and Africa populations should be segregated. Racial mixing increasingly came to be seen as social and political problem, and the fear of the discontent of the new category of *métis* children was a potential threat. Saada points out: 'By blurring this crucial dividing line [between European and Africa], the existence of the *métis* posed a problem of classification and threatened the stability of the most basic categories of the colonial social order' (2012: 19). From the 1890s onwards, social activists began to describe the problems confronting mixed-race children, especially the fact that many European fathers abandoned their offspring after their tours of duty in Africa. The emerging '*métis* question' came to refer to children born outside marriage whose fathers failed to recognize them as their own and abandoned them.[4] A debate then followed as to what the legal status of these children would be. Under French law, legitimate children inherited their father's status, but this was not the case for illegitimate ones. In the colonies, illegitimate and unrecognized *métis* acquired the native status of their mother; they were not therefore, in contrast to legitimate and recognized children, French citizens but native subjects.

The children's legal status as 'native subjects' was regarded as problematic to colonial philanthropists, who pointed out that their 'real identity' was rooted in their physical appearance, their 'French blood' and their early French upbringing (see Saada 2012). To address this problem, mixed-race children were often removed at an early age from what was perceived to be unwholesome native households and were placed in special schools where they were brought up speaking French and learning French culture and manners. These educational institutions were referred to by colonial administrators as *Ecoles des otages* in West Africa or more generally as orphanages (*orphelinats*), even though the children were rather confusingly neither hostages nor orphans. Children educated in this way would provide, so it was thought, future generations of local clerks and administrators, teachers and other functionaries, who would maintain the colonies in good working order. This strategy was the materialization of Dr Barot's ideas about an intermediate mulatto race (see White 1999).

New decrees were issued by the French government to deal with the question of citizenship, such as the one produced in 1912 that offered French citizenship to native-born French West African subjects 'who approach us in education, adopt our civilization and our customs, or distinguish themselves by their service' (White 1999: 127). As White goes on to point out, over the following ten years only ninety-four French subjects were granted citizenship in this way. On 8 November 1928, another decree was passed in France that granted French citizenship to a specific category of *métis* children born in the French colonies. Citizenship was now to be granted to those children who had one parent (virtually always the father) that could, in the absence of firm knowledge, be presumed to be of 'French race'. This law was drawn up to deal with the growing problem, specifically in Indochina, of *métis non reconnu*; that is, children born out of wedlock and not recognized by their European fathers, who had subsequently abandoned them.[5] The new decree was an attempt by the colonial system to deal with an acute concern over the relations of reproduction it had itself created. Although the fathers were *de jure* 'unknown', as Saada observes, their identities were in fact often known. This is clear, she points out, from many long lists of names of *métis* drawn up by philanthropists or government officials (Saada 2012: 44). Institutional ignorance served a useful purpose in protecting the identities of officers.

That this decree gave a new legal status to the unrecognized offspring of colonial officers is just one aspect of not-knowing, ignoring
and unknowing in the highly charged colonial domain that included
sexual relations with native women and the children of empire who
resulted from these unions. The decree did nothing to help abandoned
children fill in the gaps in their knowledge about who their fathers
might have been; and in many cases too, the children would have been
estranged from their mothers since they no longer lived with them but
were housed in 'orphanages'. There were only a few genealogical facts
entered in the colonial records and registers, and indeed the regime
did not seem concern itself with such knowledge. However, this area
of not-knowing had a particular significance for the children of empire. It not only fed into the way a child constructed his or her own
identity, but led to significant political implications for the individual:
namely, whether the person was considered to be a native subject or
a French citizen. A child's degree of racial admixture, an estimation
of the proportion of French blood in their veins, could be judged, the
authorities presumed, by the colour of their skin; but this was only
one factor to be assessed. The decree addressed the problem of the lack
of specific genealogical knowledge by placing a burden of proof on the
individual to show that he or she had been placed in a special colonial
school, had undergone a French education and had been moulded by
contact with French civilization. To meet these requirements was sufficient for the individual to qualify for citizenship and all the benefits
that such a status would bring. One dubious benefit that accrued some
years later was that during the Second World War, large numbers of
French citizens were repatriated for their own safety from Indochina
to France, and this number included those children of empire granted
citizenship under the 1928 decree. However, they had no first-hand
knowledge of the mother country, and many of them had to be for-
cibly moved to Europe, despite their having no acquaintance with
its lifestyle (see Saada 2012; Badji 2011). These children, pawns in
a game of colonial ignorance, had their own sense of not-knowing
increased by enforced migration.

This example illustrates the process by which regimes of ignorance within colonialism were sustained and indeed developed over
the course of time by, in this case, liberal-minded philanthropists and
well-meaning activists who sought to improve the condition of those
they considered most disadvantaged by the colonial system of 'marriage' and parenting relations. These measures were introduced to
help alleviate the systemic problem of children of empire who were
ignorant of their own family backgrounds, and whose existence was

only begrudgingly acknowledged by the administration. Yet, in the wake of these measures, other areas of not-knowing were produced, and the burden of proof of citizenship was shifted onto the unrecognized *métis* children themselves.

The situation of children of empire in West Africa was much the same as in Indochina. By 1916, it is estimated that nine out of ten French men in the region had abandoned their mixed-race progeny, usually when they were still very young. However, not all fathers abandoned them, and those who recognized their offspring often faced dilemmas in providing for them. The case of a French warrant officer in 1918 illustrates the level of anxiety felt by one individual over the fate of his children. The example also shows how such cases were dealt with by the colonial authorities, and how the system of categorization in use by administrators to 'know' and to order the populations they administered led to uncertainties for all parties (see White 1999: 38 et passim; and Document 9 G35 in Archives Nationales de la République du Sénégal).

Due to return to France at the end of his tour of duty, the warrant officer in question attempted to make provision for his two *métis* children, whom he had left at their mother's house in the town of Kaédi in Mauritania. Before his departure from West Africa in 1918, he wrote to Henri Gaden, then newly appointed as the Commissaire de la Mauritanie, asking permission to have his children accepted at the orphanage in Kayes, the military headquarters of French Sudan (Mali), a different administrative region of West Africa from Mauritania. The officer pointed out that his salary was insufficient to support his children at the school and requested that an allocation be granted to him from the budget of the Mauritanian government. This problem then became the subject of official correspondence between Saint-Louis (in Mauritania) and the Governor General's office in Senegal, and the case revolved around the colonial issue of 'race': the 'race' of the mother, and the colour of the mixed-race child. The surprised reaction to this case of both Henri Gaden, the head of the territory of Mauritania, and Gabriel Angoulvant, the Governor General of Senegal, suggests that there were no clear procedures or precedents to follow.

In response to the warrant officer, Gaden pointed out that his office in Mauritania was willing to grant to these two children an allocation equivalent to that normally awarded to '*métis de la race maure*'. The children in this case had a European father and a 'black' mother – i.e., she was not a '*maure*' ('Moor'). Gaden added that 'an abandoned child born to a European and a female Moor can live normally in the maternal home without their colour being an issue'; but this was not the case, in his view, regarding a '*race noire*' family, who tended to discriminate against *métis* children because of their colour, and they were made to feel inferior. For this reason, Gaden went on, it was not necessary to have special schools among the Moors, who looked after their *métis* children in the maternal homestead; but they were necessary in the Soudan (French Sudan) among 'black' populations. The warrant officer's two children were eventually placed not at the school in Kayes, the father's preferred option, but in the hands of a village chief, who acted as their tutor. The chief received thirty francs per month from the budget of Mauritania for their upkeep (see Document 9 G35 in Archives Nationales de la République du Sénégal).

Faced with a problem for which there were no obvious guidelines, Gaden allowed his views on this case to be informed directly by social and political policies aimed at treating the different populations or 'racial groups' in the region under different dispensations. The '*politique des races*' had first been defined under the governorship of William Ponty and, according to this policy, populations from the Soudan were black, and less developed in their social and cultural institutions and in their forms of religion than the Moors from the desert margins (see Cohen 1971 and Gann and Duignan 1978). This latter population was 'white' and more advanced and practised not the '*Islam noir*' of the Soudanese but a supposedly more refined version of the religion. Each 'race' was subject, too, to different tax regimes. This *politique* also extended to how children of mixed race (either European-Moor or European-black) were treated, how they were brought up and how they were educated. Gaden reproduced the prejudices of colonial racial stereotyping in handling this case, and he applied policies relevant to each specific racial group in accordance with Ponty's original ideas. Without doubt, Gaden's compromise satisfied neither the father nor the mother, and there is no record of whether it suited the two children involved.

Hiding the Known and Pursuing the Unknown

Individual colonial officers faced a range of dilemmas as regards their own children born of indigenous women. Most commonly the fathers were concerned to control the spread of knowledge about their offspring within their own networks of family and friends, in order to protect their relatives and themselves from the prejudice and moralizing of the metropolitan bourgeoisie. In his letters to his father, Henri Gaden never discussed any detail concerning his domestic arrangements involving local women, and certainly not the possible existence of *métis* children. It would appear that the eventual revelation of some of these facts to his father by one of Henri's fellow officers during a visit to the family home in Bordeaux in 1907 put an end to the correspondence between father and son, and it appears to have severely undermined their relationship.[6]

In French academic circles there is a well-known case of a colonial officer turned ethnologist who was caught in a circle of deceit and secrecy about two children he had had with a Baoulé woman from Ivory Coast.[7] In 1899, Maurice Delafosse, then a colonial officer, noticed a girl in the court of his friend, the chief of Abli in Baoulé country. Named Amoïn Kré, the girl was the chief's niece. She became Delafosse's *mousso* or wife by a country marriage and the relationship lasted for five years. They produced two sons, Henri in 1903 and Jean in 1906. Delafosse did not at that time recognize these two boys and, on his transfer from Ivory Coast to the colony of Upper Senegal and Niger, wanted them handed over to the church mission in Dabou. Amoïn was extremely unhappy about Delafosse's transfer and more specifically about his wish to have both boys brought up by missionaries. Despite complaints about her treatment to the Governor, she eventually gave up resisting and the children were sent to the mission. Delafosse sent her money for their upkeep. Amoïn went on to enter two further *mariages à la mode de pays* after her relationship with Delafosse ended.

In the meantime, Maurice Delafosse had been courting a French woman, Alice Houdas, the daughter of Octave Houdas, the Professor of Oriental Languages in Paris, and on the eve of his marriage in 1907 the suitor found himself in a dilemma. Having withheld all knowledge of his two illegitimate and unrecognized sons in West Africa, Delafosse had a pang of conscience days before the marriage ceremony. Admitting to a chequered past to his future wife, Delafosse had his children hastily recognized through the appropriate civil process. The two *métis* sons, Jean and Henri Delafosse, later became important political and administrative figures in the Ivory Coast after its independence.

The curtain of ignorance that officers tried to draw around the existence of their *métis* children in West Africa no doubt fooled other members of their families back in France; but they also fooled themselves. Henri Gaden, who had at least two children over the course of his numerous tours of duty in the region, could hardly discuss the matter in letters to his close friend and confidant, Henri Gouraud. Never too coy to discuss their sexual conquests of women with each other, these two men found it difficult to admit that spreading their wild oats across the continent had had repercussions. They refer only tangentially to the existence of their children just after they are born, and discuss very briefly arrangements for leaving some of them with the White Fathers at the mission station in Kissidougou (in Guinea); but over the period of forty-five years of correspondence between the two friends, they are never mentioned again.

The story of one of Gouraud's sons in West Africa is poignant. Moreover, it illustrates the gulf of knowledge that existed between the child's understanding of his own position in the world and the recognition of that position by the colonial administration. A clue to what happened to one of Gouraud's children appears in Owen White's book *Children of the French Empire* where the case of a boy at the orphanage in Segu (Ségou, Mali) is reported. The boy insisted on signing off his letters to his 'second mother', Madame Pion-Roux, as 'Paul Gouraud', 'using the surname of his father, a captain in the colonial infantry. Since his father had not recognized him, however, Madame Pion-Roux referred to him as Paul Koulibaly – the surname of his true mother, who had abandoned him'.[8] The details of this child were also reported in the anthropological survey of 1910, which was published in 1912 under the title 'Enquête sur les croisements ethniques' in *Revue Anthropologique* and was based on details submitted by the doctor at the medical post at Segu. The child's family background is noted: Paul G ..., of mixed race of the first degree, the product of a union between Saran Koulibaly, black, and M. G...., white, that conformed to local customs; Saran Koulibaly, born in Kita, was of Bambara extraction; M. G... was a captain of the colonial infantry. Neither party had been 'married' prior to this union, which had produced three children, the oldest a boy (Paul) and two younger sisters, now dead. Paul's age was estimated as twelve years, which would date his birth to around 1898, prior to Gaden's reference to him in his letter of 10 December 1898 to Gouraud (see Anonymous 1912: 392).[9] It would appear that only three of Gouraud's children survived to be recorded in the records of the orphanage (see Dilley 2014: 139); perhaps the fourth one that Gaden referred to in his letter to Gouraud had died while in the care of the White Fathers at Kissidougou before reaching Segu.

This case highlights the asymmetries of knowledge, power and ignorance between the different parties involved. The son, Paul, knew somehow or other that his father was Henri Gouraud, a fact shared with the colonial authorities even though the father had not recognized him. The authorities at the *Ecole des otages* knew that the son knew, but insisted that he should appear not to know, and certainly insisted that this fact would have no bearing on his official status in the colony. He was *métis* and a native subject (this case was prior to the decree of 1928). The ignorance of the colonial regime and the power it wielded had trumped the knowledge held locally by the school, his teachers and the boy himself. In fact, it had the power to cast doubt over the veracity of boy's story and his claim to be something other than what he appeared to be.

It is not known what eventually happened to Gouraud's unrecognized child, but Gaden's children do reappear in official documentation at the end of his life: in his last will and testament, Gaden left part of his house in Saint-Louis to his two '*enfants naturels*', Henri and Amélie. He had by this time recognized them both as his offspring, who were married and living in France in 1940; his son bears the Gaden family name and his daughter the surname, Espagne, of her husband. It appears that Gaden set up an elaborate web of relations between West Africa and France through which the lives of his children in Europe were supported and financed. Known only to select members of Gaden's extended family, the existence of his children was a closely guarded secret, and today his surviving co-lateral relatives have only the dimmest knowledge of them, or at least they possess a knowledge dimmed by the passage of years and a hesitancy no doubt to recognize and accept the results of Gaden's 'African adventures'.[10]

Reproduction of Slavery

The second topic of this chapter is the problematic set of relations that surround slavery, and especially the production and reproduction of slaves in areas governed by the French. Part of the ideological justification of European colonial intervention in West Africa and elsewhere in the nineteenth century was to suppress the trade in slaves. This referred not just to the commerce across the Atlantic Ocean to the Americas, but also to the internal trade between different peoples and polities of West Africa and the Sahara. For many a decade in the nineteenth century it had been a difficult task to implement on African soil laws forged in Paris. Although the transatlantic movement of slaves tailed off quickly after the abolition of slavery in the mid 1800s, by the 1900s colonial officers still had to face the realities of servility and bondage in the territories they administered. Again, the creation of ignorance about the practices of slavery in Africa and the control of the flow of knowledge within the colonies and between a colony and the metropolitan centre were crucially important at two levels. At one level, the system of colonial relations that stretched across two continents and the fog of communication between the centre and military outposts in the late nineteenth and early twentieth centuries meant that ignorance found many suitable niches in which to thrive. Indeed, ignorance operated within the colonial regime to help sustain it as an institutional set-up and in the reproduction of its social relations. At the second level, slavery was not just a practice to which officers turned a blind eye, but one they actively engaged in by reconstructing the conditions of servitude within the confines of the distant bush outposts. These were facts which they kept hidden from their superiors in Paris.

The reproduction of servile relations was particularly prominent in the way in which native women were procured by and for officers and ordinary soldiers. One way was through *mariage à la mode de pays*, whereby an officer would make the customary prestations to the bride's family prior to marriage. However, the dividing line between bridewealth payments and the exchange of commodities to acquire slaves was not always clear to all serving military personnel. In the minds of some officers this practice was akin to purchasing the woman as one would a slave, and there were cases brought to court in which men later tried to sell their *moussos* on to another man, as though they were trade slaves.[11]

Another mode of reproduction of slavery came in the form of acquiring booty after battle. To the victors went the spoils of war, and these included the women of the defeated troops who were often taken as captives by the French and their locally recruited auxiliaries. This practice caused much anguish in Paris and was even the subject of an administrative report in 1894, which did, however, little to suppress the activity. The report threw its hands in the air over the question: 'what reward can we give [to African soldiers and auxiliaries] in exchange for services rendered ... if not booty, that is to say, slaves[?]' (Klein 1998: 108). Gaden reported something similar in a letter to his father on 25 December 1897, stating that the main reason why Malinke men volunteered for French military service was not the salary – for they did not receive one – but the chance of sharing in the division of war booty. In a single military campaign, a Malinke man could gain in war booty a profit equal to that produced by a year's labour in local agriculture or commerce. But the distribution of captives as war booty was not confined to the locally recruited auxiliaries; in fact, the officers often got the first choice of slave women after battle. Indeed, Gaden himself benefited from this perk when he managed to take one of the daughters of Samory Toure, the last major Muslim resistance leader in the Soudan who was captured by him in 1899.[12]

Gaden reflected on the role of slavery in his letter of 25 December 1897 to his father back in Bordeaux:

> And you find [French] soldiers here exploiting this sentiment [encouraging recruitment of local men to gain war booty]. It is rather surprising to see Frenchmen of the 19th century, who cry one to the other that we have come here above all to bring about the triumph of the cause of civilization, of progress, etc... You see here the beautiful tirade, in Jacobin style – [yet] we support ourselves by captivity in order to advance and maintain our position here. The end justifies the means, they say, but one has to confess that we are not content within ourselves about this. As regards my position, I left with much pleasure all my preconceptions at St Louis, [and] I find that we are perfectly right to proceed in this way. (Henri Gaden to his father, 25 December 1897, Centre d'archives outre-mer, Aix-en-Provence [henceforth CAOM]; all translations are mine)

The irony that the civilizing mission of French colonialism was founded in part on the uncivilized practice of slavery was apparent to Gaden; but more than this, he was proud to flaunt his newfound principles of relativism and challenge his parents' bourgeois preconceptions. Gaden's descriptions of the state of the slave trade were aimed at what he considered to be the ignorance of the metropolitan French, who congratulated themselves on having triumphed against slavery in the cause of civilization.

'Illusions!' cried Gaden. '[T]he bourgeoisie, who know absolutely nothing about this, and who, when captives are discussed, dream of chains, of ropes around their necks, of slave-drivers who, whip in hand, make them work, have been taken in by a collection of emotive words. This is simply grotesque' (letter to his father, 20 June 1895, CAOM).

Gaden's glee in being able to '*épater la bourgeoisie*', and particularly his parents, is obvious. The challenge he throws down to them revolves around issues of knowledge and ignorance. Gaden's insights into how the system of recruitment of African auxiliaries worked were deployed for his own political purposes; but the colonial administration would not have wanted to see information about the slaving practices of colonialists being circulated in France. Moreover, dissemination of knowledge about colonial slavery would have made the colonial administration look ignorant about practices in West Africa for which they were responsible; but to admit to knowing about slavery and doing little to suppress the practice would have undermined the foundations of its civilizing mission. This was a dilemma for the

colonial regime. Gaden's purposes were different: to expose the ignorance of his parents and others about what he considered the true
state of slavery in Africa: it existed but was not as harsh, in his view,
as the Paris press and humanitarian activists made out.

While colonialists reproduced forms of servility from which they
themselves benefited, they also had to confront the realities of enslavement of one local group by another, and the onward sale of slaves
within the region or across the Sahara. Questions were raised not
only about the morality of these practices but also about the part they
played within local political economies. These latter concerns underscored the difficulties associated with abolishing local slave trading,
which was a viable and in some ways valuable element in an economic
system. Henri Gouraud, as the commander of French colonial troops
in Niger, announced in May 1901: 'slaves should be confiscated,
turned over to French authorities and returned to their villages. All
the same, we can close our eyes if Bayero or Aouta [two neighbouring
areas] keep some slaves for themselves because it is necessary to give
them an interest in restraining the movement' (quoted in Klein 1998:
140). A clandestine slave trade continued in the region until 1905.

Ignoring the uncomfortable truths of slaving was the pragmatic response of most colonial officers. In 1895, Gaden justified to his father
this practice of strategic ignorance: 'One thing to respect absolutely in
all of this country is slavery .... It is much more gentle than one might
generally believe it to be . ... [T]he best way to repress it is to pacify
the country' (Henri Gaden to his father, 21 May 1895, CAOM). Gaden
elaborated on the subject of tolerating trade in slaves:

> In banning the sale of trade captives in our markets, the caravans sim-
> ply go elsewhere .... The result of these repressive measures will be to di-
> minish our commerce and push the chiefs such as Samory ... to an even
> greater devastation [of the local populations]. Our colony, pacified, will
> never be a centre for the production of captives. In tolerating the trade,
> we tolerate simply therefore the purchases by our blacks who contrib-
> ute to the populating of our colony. To defend the trade is to indulge in
> hollow words *without obtaining any practical result* .... Send us therefore
> people who [will] command the country for the good of the country
> and not for [the good of] the schemers who only seek the applause of
> the ignorant crowd that is France. (Henri Gaden to his father, 7 June
> 1895, CAOM, original emphasis)

For example, while no doubt being ignorant of the fact, France had indeed helped populate an area on the Niger with resettled slaves under
the rule of a Soudanese ex-postal and telegraph worker in the colonial
service. The ruler, Mademba Sy, appointed by the colonial administration, was given slaves by Colonel Archinard to populate his newly

established mini-state. They were to work for the ruler for three days of the week, after which they laboured for their own profit.[13]

On their fourth posting to West Africa, Gouraud and Gaden faced other thorny problems over servitude, but this time in Chad. The Sultan of a territory south of Lake Chad had signed a treaty with the French some years earlier that allowed him to continue to take slaves from certain neighbouring areas, and this trade formed an essential part of the revenues for his kingdom. One stumbling block in the Sultan's relations with the colonialists, however, was his desire to use revenues obtained through the sale of slaves for the payment of co-lonial taxes. Gaden, the officer responsible for the Sultanate, baulked at this suggestion, as he did at the idea that he might accompany the Sultan on his tax-raising tour of the territory.

But there was another problem. The Sultan had been wily in ne-gotiating the treaty with the French, for the document did not men-tion 'workers of two sexes', a 'beautiful euphemism' Gaden thought to refer to eunuchs. And the Sultan went on to exploit this omission. Eunuchs came from the ranks of captives, although freemen might volunteer for the status and undergo the operation at the hands of the local blacksmith. The Sultan had a large retinue of eunuchs, many of whom occupied important offices of state and carried prestigious titles. A contentious issue with the Sultan arose because eunuchs were an important human commodity sold and transported across the Sahara to Mecca and Constantinople, where they could also enjoy a privileged status in foreign service. This trans-Saharan trade came under increasing scrutiny in the early 1900s, and Gaden wrote a quasi-anthropological account of the production, function and distri-bution of eunuchs within the regional economy. Colonial officials in Dakar and Paris had become, however, very concerned that the immi-nent publication of Gaden's article would highlight a morally dubious institution and point to shortcomings in their administration of the region. Gaden sent Gouraud a draft of the article, and his friend re-plied with the question: 'if yes or no, as to whether eunuchs are still produced in Baghirmi?' The report gave the sense that the Sultanate *had been* a great supplier of eunuchs, but Gouraud wanted Gaden to insist 'on the impossibility that the production of eunuchs continues'. Gouraud also removed a passage where Gaden praised the beauty of the women and the number and quality of the eunuchs in the king-dom. 'It is quite useful in your thesis', Gouraud lectured Gaden, 'to recall ... the details of all the Baghirmi atrocities and that one of the sultans had 1000 eunuchs' (letter from Gouraud to Gaden, 20 June 1906, CAOM). This would surely make a better impression on those

readers in France who would be keen to see evidence of the civilizing mission of French colonialism and the suppression of the barbaric
practice of producing eunuchs. Despite the fact that the Sultan was
very keen to push ahead with the production of more eunuchs after
the harvest of 1904, Gaden bowed to pressure and included a note
in the published version of the text to the effect that no further eunuchs were produced from the time of the French occupation; but he
retained the passage about the beauty of local women and the quality
of the eunuchs in Baghirmi.[14]

In these cases of slavery, the politics of secrecy are compounded
by the need to maintain a viable, and ideologically tenable, colonial
policy in the eyes of the population in France. Colonial officers in
bush postings manipulated the flows of information in order to secure the benefits of practices that were wholly antithetical to the ideals of the colonial project in which they were engaged. The colonial
system, moreover, could not admit to itself that it relied upon the
enforced servitude of others in order to achieve its goals. Military
success was predicated upon the enslavement of those on the losing
side of a campaign, and ignorance or contrived ignorance of this
predicament was the easiest way to deal with it. Furthermore, turning a blind eye to the practices of local rulers and their patterns of
trade was easier than replacing a whole economic system with one
that did not rely on slavery.

Concluding Remarks

It has been argued in this chapter that colonialism should be seen as a
regime of power and knowledge. There is nothing new in that. There
has also been an attempt here to analyse it as a regime of ignorance
or non-knowledge, and the effects brought about by this regime are
as significant as those that result from the operations of knowledge.
The march of ignorance accompanies the progress of knowledge; ignorance does not flee in the face of an all-conquering knowledge, but
they are fellow travellers that journey in tandem. Moreover, it has
been argued here not only that knowledge and ignorance are mutually constitutive, but that colonialism as the practice of governmentality invokes its own structures of non-knowledge through a complex
interplay of social and political relations. Furthermore, passion and
desire are equally productive of ignorance; an appetite for not-knowing can be as seductive as a thirst for knowledge. Men driven by desires produce relations of knowing and not-knowing, of openness

and secrecy, about local women, about domestic captives and so forth. Passions provoked dilemmas for the colonial regime and individual colonialists about what should and should not be known, and indeed what should or should not be made known to others.

For example, the enlightened and humanitarian policy in 1928, provoked by the passionate concerns of social activists, to extend French citizenship to *métis* children of empire not-recognized by their fathers produced in its turn further consequences for all parties involved. Ignorant of who their fathers might have been, such children had to provide information on their schooling, their upbringing and their linguistic abilities in order to claim citizenship rights. The children now had to address these areas of their lives from a new perspective. The children themselves were also constituted as new areas of uncertainty and new objects of knowledge. Up to this point, the children's existence had focused on their immediate lived experiences, but now their lives became new objects of scrutiny: that is, lives that now had to be retrospectively registered and documented for legal purposes. Their lives as lived thus became lives to be documented. They came to be known through the fragments of what had been revealed earlier about them.

A similar process of documenting the lives of children of empire prior to the 1928 decree produced effects as much by means of what was *not* recorded in colonial registers and files as what was recorded in them. Children had to pretend officially to be ignorant of the identity of their fathers, and could not use their fathers' surnames. Paternity and other genealogical information were registered in one set of records – those of the orphanages – but this knowledge could not be extended into areas of life that were significant for the child; that is, with respect to his or her social identity and political status. They were not for instance registered as social 'facts' within the 'civil state'. These details were not admissible as facts; they were not recognized as items of legitimate knowledge in their own right.

Turning to the second issue examined in this chapter, it is apparent that slavery produced its own dynamic in the production of ignorance. Slavery was recognized as something that should be known and reported to the colonial administration. However, it was also something from which colonial officers could derive benefits while withholding knowledge of its existence from the authorities. In addition, it was perhaps better politically for the colonial administration to admit a lack of knowledge of the details of the practice of slavery in specific locations than to claim knowledge about it but do nothing to change the situation. In this way, the regime in its ignorance could maintain a moral high ground and sustain its posture over the ideals of colonial intervention and civilization.

Individuals and institutions attempted in many ways to divert the flows of knowledge for their own political purposes. Much labour went into the creation of zones of ignorance, into the production and reproduction of absences, and much work had to be done to insulate one zone and political purpose from another. So, for example, Henri Gaden's attempts to '*épater la bourgeoisie*' with stories of slave trading in West Africa were at once gestures to show his distance from and contempt for petty moralizing of the metropolitan chattering classes, and attempts to inform his parents that slavery was not what it seemed from the perspective of France. This relationship between ignorance and knowledge had to be managed with respect to the specific targets of knowing and not-knowing: the colonial administration would not have wanted to learn of Gaden's posturing with his newfound knowledge; nor would Gaden have wanted the administration to learn of the purposes to which he put that knowledge. While one might agree with Agamben (2011) that it is not always possible (or even necessary) to describe the contents of a zone of ignorance, what one can do is point to the effort that both institutions and individuals go to in producing and reproducing these zones and their absences. Knowledge and ignorance are not only the result of abstract epistemological relations; they are set within a politics of systems of colonial control and within the domain of human emotions and desires – to hide, to conceal and to not-know.

Notes

1. The Preface was written by Louis-Gustave Binger, the one-time explorer of Africa and then colonial administrator at the Ministry of Colonies in Paris.
2. Quoted in White (1999: 51).
3. Tony Kirk-Greene, personal communication, Oxford 2004. For further discussion of this and related points see Weatherston (1997).
4. See Saada (2007) and Badji (2011) for further details.
5. See Saada (2012) and Badji (2011) for further details.
6. For further details on Gaden's letters to his father see Dilley (2014: 5 et passim).
7. See Louise Delafosse's biography of her father, *Maurice Delafosse: le Berrichon conquis par l'Afrique* (1976) and Dilley (2014: 139) for more on this story.

8. My thanks to Owen White for pointing out this reference to me, and for a good deal of other invaluable help in trying to trace Gaden's and Gouraud's offspring; see White (1999: 83).
9. Gaden's letters (including one of 8 January 1899 in which the children are also mentioned) can be found in the Fonds Gouraud, Ministère des affaires étrangères et européennes, Centre des archives diplomatiques, Paris.
10. For further details of the points discussed here, see Dilley (2014: 417–19).
11. See, for a broad discussion of this and other issues, Klein (1998).
12. For further details see Dilley (2014: 100 et passim).
13. For further details see Dilley (2014: 45–46).
14. The offending part for Gouraud, that remained in the published version, was: '*Renommé pour la beauté de ses femmes, le Baguirmi le fut aussi pour le nombre et les qualités de ses eunuques*'. See Gaden (1907: 441).

References

Agamben, G. 2011. *Nudities*. Stanford, CA: Stanford University Press.

Anonymous. 1912. 'Enquête sur les croisements ethniques'. *Revue Anthropologique* 22, 337–406.

Archives Nationales de la République du Sénégal (Building administratif, Dakar, Sénégal).

Badji, M. 2011. 'Le statut juridique des enfants métis nés en Afrique Occidentale Française de parents inconnus: Entre idéalisme républicain et turpitudes coloniales'. *Technologies, Droit et Justice* 61, 257–83.

Barot, L. 1902. *Guide pratique de l'européen dans l'Afrique occidentale à usages des Militaires, Fonctionnaires, Commerçants, Colons et Touristes*. Paris: E. Flammarion.

Cohen, W.B. 1971. *Rulers of Empire: The French Colonial Service in Africa*. California: Hoover Institution Press, Stanford University.

Conklin, A.L. 1997. *A Mission to Civilise: The Republican Idea of Empire in France and West Africa, 1895–1930*. Stanford, CA: Stanford University Press.

Delafosse, L. 1976. *Maurice Delafosse: Le Berrichon conquis par l'Afrique*. Paris: Société française d'histoire d'outre-mer.

Dilley, R.M. 2007. 'The Construction of Colonial Knowledge Practices: The Case of Henri Gaden'. In *Ways of Knowing: New Approaches in the Anthropology of Knowledge and Learning*, ed. M. Harris. Oxford: Berghahn, 139–57.

———. 2010. 'Reflections on Knowledge Practices and the Problem of Ignorance'. *Journal of the Royal Anthropological Institute* 16, 176–92.

———. 2014. *Nearly Native, Barely Civilized: Henri Gaden's Journey across Colonial French West Africa (1894–1939)*. Leiden and Boston, MA: Brill.

Foucault, M. 2007 [1978]. *Security, Territory, Population: Lectures at the Collège de France, 1977–1978*. Basingstoke: Palgrave Macmillan.

Gaden, H. 1907. 'Les États musulmans de l'Afrique Centrale et leurs rapports avec la Mecque et Constantinople'. *Revue des Questions Diplomatiques et Coloniales* 24, 436–47.

Gaden's letters to Gouraud (1898–1939), in the Fonds Gouraud, Ministère des affaires étrangères et européennes, Centre des archives diplomatiques, Paris (MAEE).

Gann, L.H. and P. Duignan (eds) 1978. *African Proconsuls: European Governors in Africa*. New York and London: Collier Macmillan.

Gouraud's letters to Gaden (1901–1939), in the Fonds Gaden, Centre d'archives outre-mer, Aix-en-Provence (CAOM).

Hyam, R. 1986a. 'Empire and Sexual Opportunity'. *The Journal of Imperial and Commonwealth History* 14, 34–89.

———. 1986b. 'Concubinage and the Colonial Service: The Crewe Circular (1909)'. *The Journal of Imperial and Commonwealth History* 14, 170–86.

———. 1990. *Empire and Sexuality: The British Experience*. Manchester: Manchester University Press.

Klein, M.A. 1998. *Slavery and Colonial Rule in French West Africa*. Cambridge: Cambridge University Press.

Saada, E. 2007. *Les Enfants de la colonie: Les métis de l'Empire français entre sujétion et citoyenneté*. Paris: Editions de la Découverte.

———. 2012. *Empire's Children: Race, Filiation, and Citizenship in the French Colonies*. London: University of Chicago Press.

Weatherston, R. 1997. 'When Sleeping Dictionaries Awaken: The Re/turn of the Native Woman Informant'. *Post Identity*, 1. http://hdl.handle.net/2027/spo.pid9999.0001.106. Accessed 15 March 2015.

White, O. 1999. *Children of the French Empire: Miscegenation and Colonial Society in French West Africa 1895–1960*. Oxford: Clarendon Press.

Roy Dilley, D. Phil. (Oxon) 1984, is Professor of Social Anthropology at the University of St Andrews. Having completed over thirty years of field research in Senegal, West Africa, he now works in French colonial archives on historical ethnography, biography and photography. He was a visiting Professorial Research Fellow at the Institute for Advanced Studies, University of Konstanz, 2011–2012. His books include *Islamic and Caste Knowledge Practices among Haalpulaaren* (2004), *Nearly Native, Barely Civilized: Henri Gaden's Journey across Colonial French West Africa* (2014) and the edited volumes *Contesting Markets* (1992) and *The Problem of Context* (1999).

Chapter 7

POWER AND IGNORANCE IN BRITISH INDIA

THE NATIVE FETISH OF THE CROWN

Leo Coleman

Each time that ethnocentrism is precipitately and ostentatiously
reversed, some effort silently hides behind all the spectacular effects
to consolidate an inside and to draw from it some domestic benefit ... .
Between rationalism and mysticism there is, then, a certain complicity.
The writing of the other is each time invested with a domestic outline.

– Jacques Derrida, 'Of Grammatology as a Positive Science'

In 1911 George V, the newly crowned King of Great Britain and
Emperor of India, travelled to Delhi to proclaim his coronation and
receive the honours and obeisance of his Indian empire. This event,
organized by officials of the colonial state, was called a 'Coronation
Durbar' or an 'Imperial Durbar', in imitation of the royal rituals of
Indian sovereigns – whose courts and receptions were both called,
in Persian or Urdu, *darbār* – and it also repeated on grander scale
a common, highly ritualized form of governmental reception practised throughout India and indeed the British Empire. 'The colonial
durbars of British India were held when the viceroy went on tour or
were staged by governors', and they served as a venue for interacting with, and ritually incorporating into a quasi-feudal structure of
government, 'regional princes and chiefs' (Apter 2004: 180–81).
This ceremonious form of interaction between officials and subjects
of the British Crown was borrowed from colonial India for rituals

of suzerainty over African leaders by Lord Lugard, and by the early twentieth century the durbar was the key ritual expression of British imperial rule, in which 'the central symbol of the British state and focus of national loyalty – the Crown – was reworked ... in relation to India and the rest of the empire' (Cohn 1996: 4; see also Haynes 1990).

The Coronation Durbar of 1911, however, was an event of special grandeur and significance for the British Government of India. No monarch had ever personally visited the colony while reigning, the Viceroy, Lord Hardinge, pointed out as the durbar was being planned, and such an event provided an opportunity to project British sovereignty over India in uniquely imperial terms and to capture the imagination of the whole country with a great, sovereign act (see Frykenberg 1986). Indeed, this was quite a show: George V appeared as King-Emperor before a conclave of thousands of 'his' Indian subjects in an amphitheatre built for the occasion north of Delhi, wearing an imperial crown specially fashioned for the occasion. All of this, meanwhile, was paid for by Indian revenues, not by the Crown and its establishments in Britain.

According to the reigning imperial ideology, developed in the context of earlier such grand colonial durbars in 1877 and 1903, the event had to include a 'boon' in order to touch the 'native mind' and meet the 'special requirements of the Orient' for a dash of ceremony in government (Curzon 1925: 202; see also Trevithick 1990). The problem of finding an act of sovereign grace for the king to perform in person, moreover, granted greater political importance to this particular imperial ceremonial, for India and Britain alike. Six years earlier, an administrative reorganization had split the powerful Indian province of Bengal into two parts, in an overt attempt to sever the centre of Bengali intellectual life, Calcutta, from the rest of its region and thus quell – or perhaps simply punish – nationalist agitation. The expedient of this 'partition' had failed, however, and it had instead spurred more active opposition to the colonial order and fostered the growth of the *swadeshi* or 'our country' movement in Bengal. As the historian David Johnson has recently shown, by 1911 colonial officials very much wanted to reverse the partition, but had to find some way to do so which was palatable to Indian opinion, as they saw it, and did not offend British imperialist pride. 'British colonial policy', he writes, 'could never be seen as stemming from or influenced by nationalist demands. A new colonial policy was needed, one in which the reunification of Bengal was seen as a secondary component of a much larger colonial policy' (Johnson

2010: 96). This was not entirely cynical, however: ultimately, *raison d'état* had to be pursued in a way which would make political expediency conform with an imperial mission and sense of civilizational supremacy, as those latter were symbolized by the beneficence of the King-Emperor.

The much larger plan, as it was ultimately effected, was to transfer the imperial capital from Calcutta to Delhi, making a grand gesture by relocating the British administration to the ancient sovereign city of India. This boon was secretly agreed upon amongst a small circle comprised of the viceroy, the prime minister, select cabinet ministers and the king himself (Eustis and Zaidi 1964). Secrecy was demanded so that political carping beforehand would not ruin the effect of the boon or diminish the majesty of the king, as well as to benefit from the influence of the king in effecting the unpopular (among colonial officials) reversal of the partition of Bengal. On the day of the durbar, the king and queen 'arrived in the Imperial state in which their loyal subjects love to see them', escorted by 'a great cavalcade' of horsemen and 'clad in their superb coronation robes and [wearing] Imperial diadems', in the breathless description of a *Times of India* journalist named Stanley Reed, who covered the durbar and the whole royal tour (Reed 1912: 150). They took their place in the 'Reception Shamiana' – a sumptuous tent at the centre of the amphitheatre – and received homage from Indian rajas, nawabs and chiefs, while bands played. They then processed to the Imperial Pavilion, for speeches from the king and the viceroy. When the viceroy had read the full list of official actions to commemorate and celebrate the durbar (including grants for extension of public education and surplus pay for members of the Indian Army), and it appeared that all the ceremonies were concluded, the heralds trumpeted once again and the king stood forth to announce a further boon, 'the secret of which had been well kept' (Reed 1912: 160):

> We are pleased to announce to our people [the king read out] that on the advice of our Ministers tendered after consultation with our Governor-General in Council [the viceroy], we have decided upon the transfer of the seat of the Government of India from Calcutta to the ancient Capital of Delhi, and simultaneously, and as a consequence of that transfer, the creation at as early a date as possible of a Governorship for the Presidency of Bengal. (George 1912: 120)

The proclamation continued in this vein, and (according to Reed) it only slowly dawned on the audience what had just been announced. The transfer of the capital was surprise enough, but the reunification of Bengal was a real government action – although, as if to obscure the significance of it, the king's pronouncement was cloaked in administrative jargon and ended with the feeble flourish, 'It is our earnest desire that these changes may conduce to the better administration of India and the greater prosperity and happiness of our beloved people'. Regardless, the effect was decisive and, as everyone at the durbar knew, the really consequential change was the one announced second.

As well as marking a significant political response to Indian nationalist agitation, the personal presence of the king in India and his announcement of his Durbar Boon also raised British constitutional questions. For perhaps the last time in the history of the constitutional monarchy of Great Britain, the king was effectively able to decree legislation and to perform, personally, what were in fact the decisions of elected, responsible representatives and ministers. Because of this, the Durbar Boon presented the problem of a political decision which was unreviewable and unmodifiable: 'This is the King's will, and it is final' (Reed 1912: 166). But, more broadly, the king gained some real personal prestige and increase in his informal influence from this. By imperialists like Reed, George V's apparently personal gesture was hailed as the height of statesmanship and knowledge of the needs of India: 'His Imperial Majesty ... gauged much more correctly than many who have passed the best years of their life in [India] the real feelings of myriad people of India and their sentiments toward the Throne' (Reed 1912: 294). In this, admittedly hyperbolic, paean to royal power, the king's 'judgement' rules over all the expertise – whatever it may have consisted in – of colonial officials, and over all the proprieties of Britain's domestic parliamentary government.

The divided political goals of the durbar, aiming at both ceremonial aggrandizement and practical political manoeuvre, were thus entangled in the royal majesty of the king, his personal presence and his powers of pronouncement – all of which is hard to square with the high claims for the rationality of the colonial mission, both contemporary partisan ones and more recent theoretical ones. Stanley Reed's account of the durbar, once again, distils the tenor of the imperialist argument:

> What was signified by the presence here of His Imperial Majesty, the King, Emperor of India? ... Surely none other than this – the bond of Empire is the Crown! ... The monarchy has drawn unto itself those steel threads of sentiment and interest which knit the empire into a whole, one and indivisible. ... To India, in special degree, the Crown is the oriflamme of unity. (Reed 1912: 157)[1]

Historians and anthropologists have long analysed this special ritualism of colonial states and interrogated how performances such as the durbar, and their motivating ideologies of colonial difference and civilizational supremacy, are connected to the practical, governmental operation of colonial power: its ordering of colonial society and culture (see Cohn 1996, and below). Moreover, the political revival of the British monarchy in the context of colonial expansion has been an important aspect of studies focused on the anti-democratic impact of imperialism, both domestically and overseas (e.g., Ranger 1980; Bayly 1989; Cannadine 2001). There is no doubt that spectacular ceremonials and the more routine dignified receptions that were central to imperial statecraft together staged and motivated racial categories of understanding, fostered a position of civilizational and aristocratic privilege among colonizers and seemed to confirm Orientalist knowledge of colonized cultures and of non-European principles of political order, which were an important part of colonial control.

In this vein, much work on colonial states pursues and advances Michel Foucault's core insight into disciplinary power – that the signs of power and participation in society changed with the growth of rational, governmental institutions, as power itself became productive and intervened directly and micrologically in the scenes of entrainment and discipline rather than standing, splendidly, apart from the management of everyday social life. 'For the marks that once indicated status, privilege, and affiliation', Foucault writes, 'were increasingly replaced – or at least supplemented – by a whole range of degrees of normality indicating membership of a homogeneous social body'. This does not imply the final triumph of reason, but rather is a new configuration of disciplinary power and rational knowledge of 'norms', that combines 'the ceremony of power and the form of the experiment, the deployment of force and the establishment of truth' in locations throughout the social body, whether colonial or metropolitan (Foucault 1977: 184).

All the pomp and proclamation of the durbar is, however, hard to square with this conception of power-knowledge, particularly because it rested on no secure governmental knowledge, no assessment of the acceptability or particular meaning of such rituals to those whom they were supposed to address, and indeed was more often justified by a tissue of assumptions, assessments and personal prejudices about the effectiveness of ceremony and the appeal of royal power. Moreover, the personal presence of the king made the whole affair of the 1911 durbar a nervous one, marked by regular fears of 'anarchist' threat to the king's body. These fears arose from

worry about the very nationalist movements that demanded the revocation of the partition of Bengal. And this indicates that there was
a central paradox in the combination of ritual and political logics in
this durbar: the principal Durbar Boon, the revocation of partition,
aimed to address the demands of a movement which colonial officers
just as often dismissed as not representing 'true' Indians. The boon
itself thus aimed to communicate with urban, educated, politically
active Indians – the very stratum of the population that the durbar
form, in its logic and performance, tried to ignore and circumvent by
constituting instead a mass of awed subjects and loyal princes and
nobles.

As others have pointed out in different terms, the secrecy, fear,
doubt and anxiety that suffused colonial relations can only poorly
be accommodated in any account of rational procedure and positive
knowledge (see, for example, Cooper 1994; Prakash 2002). As Ann
Stoler has said, critically, 'much of colonial studies over the past decade has worked from the shared assumption that the mastery of reason, rationality, and the inflated claims for Enlightenment principles
have been at the political foundation of colonial regimes and should
be at the center of critical histories of them' (2009: 57). By contrast,
for Stoler the mastery of affect and the management of dangerous
intimacies should take precedence (2009: 70).

In fact, as Roy Dilley has argued (Dilley 2007, and this volume),
the progress of knowledge in colonial governmentality was always
paralleled by the production of zones of ignorance, indistinction
and obscurity, which allowed the intimacies of everyday colonial life
to continue beneath the edifice of colonial difference and distance,
while the norms and proprieties of the latter reasserted themselves
in violent refusals of recognition and engagement. Likewise, George
Steinmetz's (2007) work on German ethnography and Danilyn
Rutherford's (2009) considerations of colonial 'sympathy' trace how
systematic distortions in knowledge and relationality, characteristic
of imperial bureaucracies, were crafted in sumptuary and excessive
ritual performances – as distinct from Foucault's routinized 'rituals'
of examination and punishment – and through fantasies of both
colonial intimacy and imperial status. These studies have shown
that individuals and institutions within the colonial state worked to
constitute, and reconstitute, absences in the fabric of governmental knowledge, and pursued personal projects of status-exaltation
and a symbolics of relation through blood and honour, as much as
they pursued rational control over the processes and populations of
the colony. This is not to imply that colonial states simply or directly

repeat antique forms of power and privilege; as Steinmetz is careful to explain, the important point is that both colonial and metropolitan ritual forms and symbolic identifications were distorted, reshaped, and made to serve 'imaginary' projects of imperializing distance, status exaltation and control over others (Steinmetz 2007: 45–65). Together, these scholars show how imperial ritual performances shaped daily interactions, allowed both intimacy and disavowal, and produced anxious cross-identifications, indicating that a ritualized regime of ignorance might be as important an aspect of colonialism as its forms of knowledge.[2]

Sociologically speaking, ignorance is as productive as its better-analysed obverse, and equally integrated into social regimes of power. As Georg Simmel puts a related point in his essay on secrecy, 'reciprocal knowledge, which is the positive condition of social relationships, is not the sole condition. On the contrary, such as those relationships are, they actually presuppose also a certain nescience, a ratio, that is immeasurably variable to be sure, of reciprocal concealment' (Simmel 1906: 448). It may be clichéd, but true, to say that imperial bureaucracies were characterized by routine ignorance, disregard and simple lack of interest in knowing the colonized; it remains to be seen how such systematic ignorance was promoted and produced in rituals of display and excess like the durbar.

That is, far from Enlightenment principles and rational government, or micrological discipline and 'ceremonies' of experimentation – far even from the constitutional standards of British democracy – the secrecy surrounding the king's boon and the constant rumours and frights of a nationalist threat, as have been described above, indicate an imperial economy of knowledge and ignorance in which the Crown played a special role as a fetish. That is, both as a legal device of governmental unity and as a social role personally invested in one man, the Crown came to bear a special power; not only to symbolize the unity of the imperial state as a political body, but also to obscure real, positive governmental knowledge about the needs and interests which gathered in the other body of the colonial state, among Indians in their diverse communities and situations.

In this chapter I interpret a 'symptomatic' text of such fetishism, a pamphlet entitled *The Coronation Durbar and after* (Scotus 1911), that was published shortly before the king sailed to India – before the Durbar Boon was even known – and which, in its recapitulation (in almost satiric form) of the most hackneyed tropes of imperialist monarchism, anticipates many of the turns taken by the actual durbar and its staging of power and difference. By interpreting this

anonymous text in light of the Freudian account of fetishism, I aim
to understand the dynamics of power-ignorance in imperial contexts and to account for the sovereign meanings and forms of representation which gave the durbar and the other ritual forms of the
colonial state their evident efficacy and reach, despite their distance
from any rational routine of power. The imperial fetishism I aim to
describe and analyse, then, operates a kind of secrecy and concealment which has a real governmental efficacy and relies on a ratio
of ignorance that situates other people in proximity to power (see
Kirsch, this volume).

More broadly, I am interested in the metaphysics of the British
Crown, as they were personified and substantialized in the Coronation
Durbar, and as they contributed to the making of an imperial state.
At the height of British colonialism, the Crown's imperial titles incorporated difference into the body of the sovereign, and made the
Crown the organizing symbol and site of a fetishistic representation
of otherness within the state. This aspect of the Crown was realized
both ritually and juridically in the durbar, as is reinforced by the argument presented by the pamphlet *The Coronation Durbar and after*
(Scotus 1911). This sovereign representative function marks a limit
to theories that would dissolve all the reality of state power – colonial or liberal – into micrological, distributed knowledge-practices
(see Mitchell 1999). In short, despite what has been learned over the
past several decades about the modernity and governmentality of
colonial states, and of liberal states more generally, the operation of
even the most micrological, disciplinary and governmentalized state
power is not entirely captured by tabulated knowledge and bureaucratic routine, but also involves representations and performances
on a social scale, shaped and normed in fantasmatic scenes, which
distort and obscure just as they attract, incite participation, shape
ideas and motivate practices.[3]

By thinking through the highly particular contexts of imperial
ritual and the ways in which the British Crown was employed to
accommodate and represent colonial difference, this study further
aims to contribute to understanding of the current and ongoing operation of sovereign power in those liberal states which share the
legal and cultural inheritance of the British Empire. In closing, then,
I examine briefly how a fetishistic image of the Crown has been re-
animated in the context of First Nations' land-claims in Canada, at
once marking and perpetuating an active ignorance of cultural difference within practices of liberal recognition, and buttressing imperial relations of power.

Scotus Indigena and Native Authority

In advance of the king's departure from Britain for the Coronation Durbar, a pseudonymous pamphlet appeared in London with the title *The Coronation Durbar and after*, written by someone calling himself 'Scotus Indigena'.[4] The most immediate domestic context for Scotus' pamphlet was the British domestic democratic crisis in 1909–1911 spurred by the 'People's Budget'. David Lloyd George, the Liberal Chancellor of the Exchequer, had introduced a budget, supported by the nascent Labour Party, that introduced extensive welfare provisions and raised taxes on income and land. It met vigorous resistance from the Conservative Party and the hereditary House of Lords (full of wealthy landowners). Though the elected House of Commons easily passed Lloyd George's budget, the struggle to get it passed through the Lords raised questions about the maintenance of the hereditary principle in a democratic country, and spurred not one but two elections on the issue of the 'powers of the Lords' in 1910. Although this crisis was resolved with the Parliament Act, 1911 – which removed the Lords' ability to effectively veto certain bills – it had raised constitutional problems of which Scotus, and no doubt others, were reminded with the prospect of a great festival of monarchical privilege and imperialist propaganda in India (Thornton 1959: 264ff.). Confronted, in the political culture of his day, with a crisis of democratic legitimation, anti-democratic arguments for aristocratic and hereditary privileges and insistent pressure for maintenance of the empire and the Imperial Crown, Scotus offers a comprehensive solution that will at one stroke settle Britain's empire in a permanent political relation to the English Crown (as he calls it), and secure democracy in a Britain rid of monarchy.

In this pamphlet, Scotus first undertakes a brief review of the reign of foreign kings in India, leading to the depredations of the British East India Company, and ending with the 'dethroning' of this mercantile 'John Company' and the 'British Monarch [being] placed in the 'vacant room' of Indian sovereignty (Scotus 1911: 6). As is usual in accounts of this type, Scotus explains away the sparks of Indian anti-colonial animus, which blazed forth in the great Uprising, or Mutiny, of 1857, as the direct results of the misrule of the East India Company. The 'direct sovereignty' of the Crown in India after 1858 is said to herald the advent of a new era of beneficent imperialism. Ultimately, Scotus says, the invention some twenty years later – in 1877 – of the title 'Empress of India' for Queen Victoria by Prime Minister Benjamin Disraeli both confirmed the new role that the Queen played in Indian government through her directly appointed ministers and radically transformed the nature of the Crown itself. For Scotus, Disraeli's fantastic imperial imagination unmoored the Crown from its own proper corporate body – 'England' – and 'linked the Royal House with the great dependency [India] by a new chain which was independent of England' (ibid.: 7–8). Thus, 'When George of England takes his place on the "Peacock Throne" of Delhi it will be (in the eyes of all India) as the successor of Akbar'. Moreover, George V's visit recalls, and even repeats, the triumph of royal legitimacy and grace over the 'reign of the fraudulent merchants ... from which the Emperor has delivered his country' (ibid.: 14, parentheses in original). Scotus' collapse of a century's worth of colonial history into one moment of sovereign grace should be noted (this important passage will be discussed further below).

Immediately, Scotus asks and answers the pertinent question, from the British and democratic point of view: 'And what place is there in all this for the British House of Commons? For alternating Secretaries of State who owe their position to the voters of Peckham or Tony Pandy [*sic*]?[5] For the army of Civil Servants recruited annually in London? Very little' (Scotus 1911: 14). With the Parliament Act only recently passed, Scotus sees the access of democracy in Britain at hand, to be realized as simple majority rule and a sovereign House of Commons. But something stands in the way of this realization: the Crown – not merely as a juristic fiction for the corporate body of the state, but as a real monarchy occupied by a chain of hereditary succession. The royal prerogative – the Crown in its personal guise – was directly at issue in the two elections held in 1910 (part of the reason that the Liberals had to 'go to the people' twice was because Edward VII died and George V ascended to the throne, and it was thought impossible to commit one monarch to the compromises of his predecessor, whatever the mystical unity and imperishability of the Crown). Indeed, whether a royal power could remain at the heart of a democratic system is, as Scotus frames it, the real issue at hand in the debate over the powers of the Lords. He writes that all the attacks on the Lords were nothing more than veiled attacks on the Crown and the hereditary principle; Keir Hardie, the leader of the Labour Party, 'has told us more than once in the past year that the Crown is in danger' (ibid.: 23).

Scotus' satirical imagination projects, then, a pathway to pure democracy for Britain. Over time, 'the democracy has shewn itself the serpent of Moses and has devoured its partners', aristocracy and monarchy (1911: 15). Scotus writes that 'Nothing now can preserve the Monarchy' in England, and yet that there will be no fighting, no upheaval, for the Crown now has a place to go where it is needed and can retain its imperial titles (ibid.: 27). 'India needs ... strong personal government', he says, trotting out one of the oldest fictions of the Oriental need for despotism: 'It is one of the beneficent coincidences of history that at the very moment when the East is clamouring for the King the West has ceased to desire his presence' (ibid.: 28). Scotus' image of an imperial future for the Crown deserves to be quoted at length:

> The loss of his island-home will set the [English] Emperor of India free to devote his whole energies to his vast eastern dominions ... [.] Egypt, the Sudan, Uganda, and British East Africa will naturally throw in their lot with India. The People [of England] have no wish to administer any of them and they are far too feeble to stand alone. Provincial autonomy under the Kaisar-i-Hind will settle the Egyptian question for a century at least. Southern Persia and Arabia will inevitably form part of the Emperor's dominions ... . In this way that portion of the world that lies between China and the Sahara, and between the Himalayas and the African Lakes will form a single independent Empire.
>
> What all this means for the world's history can only be guessed at yet. But it is evident that the ancient homes of civilization will have their chance to win back all the glory of their past. No longer under the obsession of cheap western atheistic 'science' they will develop freely on their own lines. From the Irrawaddy [in Burma] to the Nile, art, literature and philosophy will enter a new course, destined in all human probability to eclipse the splendours of antiquity. (Scotus Indigena 1911: 28–30, paragraphing altered)

Scotus magnanimously envisions Britain surrendering the Crown in order to concentrate on democracy and industry. Meanwhile, he suggests, the Crown will work to unify a vast, polytheistic dominion of arts and beauty. What a dream! He asserts that the one thing the East needs to realize its desire for independence – Scotus acknowledges that calls for home rule are already in his time a feature of Indian politics – is an English king, and by granting that wish Britain will secure democracy at home, while retaining the prestige and goodwill built up by its empire abroad.

Ironically, given that this is at least on the surface a republican argument, what is preserved in this solution is the aura of potency and majesty around the Crown. The Crown is in danger, Scotus declares – indeed, the crux of his argument is that the recent constitutional crisis focused on the Lords in fact imperilled the Crown. At first, it is not clear why that should be a problem in an argument that explicitly aims at a non-monarchical constitution for Britain. Indeed, what Scotus Indigena saw as a solution to differential political needs of West and East was plainly impossible: neither imperialists nor Indian nationalists could accept the sundering of the Crown's connection with Britain only to install an English emperor on the throne of Delhi (though perhaps a Scot could). But in what he offers up as a solution and what he protects and maintains, Scotus' odd diagnosis of the political ills and prospects of the English Emperor in India reveals a more comprehensive logic structuring the practice of imperial ritual, and more generally characteristic of the operation of imperial power-ignorance. In the fetishistic logic of this argument, moreover, the Crown will continue in India to incite loyalty and secure the benefices of civilization through grace and majesty. What the nineteenth century constitutional thinker Walter Bagehot (1966) called the 'dignified' aspect of the constitution, as opposed to its 'efficient' machinery of parliamentary democracy and Cabinet rule, can be both destroyed and preserved, both disavowed and kept alive, by the simple expedient of displacing this prime symbol and all its ritual onto some other people in India.

Beyond Power-Knowledge

Imperial rituals like the durbar have long been understood to be performances where notions of political and cultural difference were ratified and rationalized and the 'native subject' was recruited into a dramaturgy of colonial knowledge and meaning (Gluckman 1940; Cohn 1983; Haynes 1990). As Caduff (this volume) stresses in a different context, however, it is important neither to overstate the rationality of these processes that link power and interest to an economy of knowledge, nor to assume that these processes contribute to the reproduction of a stable hierarchy of power. In this regard, Andrew Apter's (2004: 121–200) account of the uses of colonial ritual in Nigeria is very useful, for clearing some ground and in the description it offers of a distinctively colonial culture revealed in such rituals. Further, Apter traces the often unexpected uses of ceremonialized tradition within diverse governing programmes in postcolonial Nigeria, from the crafting of a unitary 'national' culture to the extractive programme of the contemporary oil economy.

Apter starts from the well-known abstractions and ethnocentrism of colonial knowledge and the reification of culture in the form of governmentalized tradition, processes which he locates in the ritual machinery of indirect rule. But Apter goes on to demonstrate that just because the durbar-form – which was deployed in Africa, Fiji and throughout the British Empire – offered objectified performances of cultural difference, this does not mitigate the alternative uses to which such durbars could be put, even now, in service of different forms of government, different claims of power. That is, the durbar-form never lapses, in Apter's account, into purely stereotyped and repetitive action, but rather is reproduced under new regimes with all its representational force and cultural and political power intact.

Apter thus demonstrates the incredible productivity of such spectacles and rituals, creating representations of culture and interweaving them with power and meaning in ways which ultimately lie beyond truth or falsity, and certainly have little to do with the inculcation of their representations of culture, as subjective truth, through discipline or entrainment. Apter demonstrates how historical myths and claims of status forcefully operate to bar a more embracing collective consciousness of political interdependency, while at the same time returning as uncanny and artificial doubles of a 'true' shared culture in later performances. His account, like the Comaroffs' recent study of the ongoing commercialization of 'traditional' forms of rule in South Africa as 'brands' and corporate structures, indicates that in colonial and postcolonial royal rites alike new sites and opportunities for power are created exactly at the point where the obscurity of real, positive knowledge is at its greatest – where cultural meaning is most condensed into representations and symbols of 'custom' (Apter 2004: 187; Comaroff and Comaroff 2009). The problem with all the colonial misrecognitions deployed in the durbars he studies is not, for Apter, the fact that they obscure some hidden, true, 'native' culture residing behind all the abusive stereotypes. That is, colonial durbars did not only reflect and ratify stereotypes and alibis of culture, covering over a real power exercised elsewhere; they also promised intimacy with, even incorporation of, difference and a mode of rule which could commensurate between distinct political rationalities and traditions. This imperial logic could be appropriated and reproduced under different regimes, but at the cost of also reproducing the general economy of colonial representations which first structured it: a kind of governmental intimacy and control are both won at the cost a more extensive knowledge of, and relational engagement with, others, in a cycle of repetitions (with a difference) in which representations, and aspects of the imperial subject, are continuously detached, estranged and awkwardly attached to others (Derrida 1976: 80).

To trace the substitutions and reifications that matter to him, Apter uses a Marxian vocabulary, based in the notion of the commodity fetish. My analysis of the durbar-form and its symbolic potency in colonial India and imperial Britain, by contrast, turns on the Freudian account of fetishism, which offers a different way to account for a general economy of representations that is centred on a symbol of power – the Crown – that 'itself' actively distributes rights and obligations and situates subjects in relation to its ritualized force. Though the Freudian and the Marxian accounts of fetishism are thoroughly entangled in most modern thought, and both offer insights into the production of meaning and difference (see Apter and Peitz 1993), the Freudian model offers a more fruitful analytic contrast to the notion of 'power-knowledge' which might otherwise be employed in the task of understanding imperial rituals and their orchestration of wider relations of authority, intimacy and control.

Fetishism and the Maintenance of Ignorance

One standard avenue of critique of Orientalist schemas like those offered by Scotus, with their attribution of a feminine lack or need to the colonized and a masculine potency and presence – of democracy, of reason – to the colonizer, aims to show that the 'native subject' is 'fetishized' in a quite particular, and erroneous, sense: abstract knowledge is reified or fixed at the site where difference and relationality *really* are. The sexual fetishist cannot see what 'the woman' is, which is simply *different* (Bernheimer 1993: 81), and that difference is obscured by the powerful invention of the fetish. The fetish, then, is pure representation – 'not an atom of matter' makes its way into the completed and mystifying commodity fetish in Marx's much quoted, and often misunderstood, terms from *Capital*, Volume I.[6] The analyst's task is purely investigative: to get behind these misrepresentations to the true person or relation covered over by them. The key assumption in such deployments of fetishism in service of critique is that new positive knowledge can then act against unreal and occluding fantasies.

However, in any close reading of fetishism, the relations of occlusion and mutual dependence between (abstract, misrecognized) knowledge and material symbol or body are more intimate and complex than such a critique, with its faith in knowledge, can encompass – the fetish is productive and it gains a power over those who fetishize it, in part precisely because of the way it materially stands in the place of disavowed relations and obscures a real aporia, a permanent doubt and worry, about the source of power (Taussig 1993). In Freud's account, specifically, the fetish is constructed to displace an initially disavowed (and false) knowledge of difference, and fetishism thus produces a real presence to maintain the occlusion of an erroneous, but persecutory, knowledge of power and difference.

Most importantly for a Freudian critique of colonial knowledge relations, the fetish and what it preserves and disavows are all bound by their prior formation in an experience of power – not only by desire or symbolic processes of displacement. Briefly, the Freudian account – complete with a one-sided focus on the male child – goes thus: the male child has a sexual theory, in which all people have a penis just like his (see Freud 1959 [1908]: 215); his theory – since it is erroneous – is threatened when he catches a glimpse of female genitals; finally, his interpretation of what he thinks he sees (an absence), and his consequent panicked anxiety about his own genitals, forces him to construct a fictive replacement for this apparent absence – the maternal phallus results. In a secondary step, this maternal phallus – the thought of the sight of which is equally terrifying and enticing – provides the energy for investing incredible sexual power in the most mundane of objects, which stand as replacements and imitations of it (I leave aside Freud's own unconvincing narrative of how this second step happens) (Freud 1961).

It is essential for the logical coherence of this account that the child has already entered the castration complex, which only flowers fully in this moment of anatomical curiosity. His innocent pleasure in his own penis must already have been threatened by the sanction of paternal power: 'He *will have been* detected in [autoerotic play] by his parents or nurse and terrorized by the threat of having his penis cut off', Freud writes (1959: 215, emphasis mine). It is the (male) child's narcissistic attachment to his own penis that motivates the formation and projection of the maternal phallus as a terrifying, ghostly image of what he thinks he saw. When he discerns what, from his point of view, is the absence of a penis, he seeks some cause for this lack in the real world that he, so far, knows; the cause he finds is a political one, having to do with paternal power. The mother, the boy thinks, must have had her penis removed at some point, and the only person in his social world with the power to do this is the father. The boy hypostatizes a social power as physical violence – and according to Freud, he develops a 'sadistic view of coition' to go along with the fully fledged castration complex (1959: 220). It could be said that Freud begs the question of paternal power – he assumes it as a sociological reality. Or rather, it might be said (more in the spirit of the hypothetical narrative as Freud offers it) that the child is already possessed of a political theory against which he tests his erroneous theory of sexual difference, and in which he finds the latter's confirmation.

In short, the Freudian fetish helps the subject remain in a state of ignorance or infantile refusal to see difference. For Freud, the 'unwelcome fact' (as he calls it) of the mother's castration is what must be obscured, and no amount of insistence that the mother is simply different will challenge that need, for the subject's allegiance to the truth of his theory – his positive ignorance – is sustained by a wider economy of substitutions, displacements and representations, satisfying his insatiable emotional demands. On this account, what matters is not what lies behind the fetish (since there is nothing there) but what it productively obscures about the subject's own, more fundamental relation to power.

Further, the fetishist operates a powerful network of things that stand for what he thinks he knows and obscure what he has only glimpsed, and this economy of meaningful things affects not only himself but also all those who are in relation to him. Thus, read in a certain way, the Freudian account of sexual fetishization offers another avenue of critique of imperial and colonial forms of knowledge and the state power which they buttress. Read through Freud, imperial fetishism is not only a matter of misplaced concreteness – reifying that which was originally flexible and relational (see, for example, Dirks 2001). Rather, a fetishized state power, invested in a material symbol which is itself a displacement of political relations (the Crown, the King), fills a space carved out by the refusal to recognize any difference.

A theory of power, an imagined threat and a fantasied presence result in the displacement of positive knowledge of (sexual) difference and through this, the symbolization of (paternal) power in the phallus. The phallus, moreover, which is the kernel of the achieved fetish, is a construct that is fully detachable and mobile, and condenses an understanding of power, an experience of difference and an anxious assumption of threat. This phallic complex, of which the fetish is only one particularly powerful condensation, filters all later positive knowledge, giving especially but not exclusively sexual knowledge its particular affective colouring and, in the extreme, maintaining a positive ignorance in the face of all contrary evidence.

In all Freud's examples, the fetish withstands the test of reality, and the fetishist's fixation on a substitute for the (non-existent) maternal phallus is only reinforced by later, actual knowledge about anatomy. Freud goes so far as to say – and the point is a good one – that when the young fetishist learns at school that the clitoris and the penis derive from the same fundamental embryonic structure, his notion of the maternal phallus is confirmed by that scientific, positive knowledge (Freud 1959: 217). Fetishism remains as a screen and an interpretive guide, even to later, positive knowledge, which, however detailed it may be, can only reaffirm the fantasied power relations that have taken up residence in this special symbol.

As Freud later puts it, the 'horror of castration sets up a sort of permanent memorial to itself by creating this substitute'. The fetish 'remains a token of triumph over the threat of castration and a safeguard against it' (Freud 1961: 154). And he also points out here the political power of this complex quite exactly: 'In later life a grown man may perhaps experience a similar panic when the cry goes up that Throne and Altar are in danger, and similar illogical consequences will ensue' (ibid.: 153).

Freud's account of fetishism, then, provides one answer to the question of how power and non-knowledge are put together, as ignorance. He links the occlusion of knowledge of difference to the subject's dawning understanding of paternal power, and proposes one pathway by which a positively maintained ignorance and power together take form and circulate in a persecutory symbol of difference. If this account is taken as the germ of a theory of the formation of representations of social differences – such as were staged and reinforced in the performance of the Coronation Durbar – then the way out of this fetishistic ignorance is not education or information, more and better knowledge of difference, but rather analysis of the distorted representations and material symbols in which difference and power are put together in the first place. Moreover, the central importance for critique of the colonial fetish no longer rests on its reification and misrepresentation of 'native' society, but lies within a theory of sovereignty which structures relations with the colonized society in the first place. The idea that the Crown and its powers can most immediately and best be employed overseas, then, represents the symptom of a more comprehensive imperial fetishism, around which is organized a whole structure of relations of displacement and representation, displayed and strengthened in rituals like the Durbar.

The Crown in India

Scotus' solution to the problem of democracy at home and empire abroad, in which the Hanoverian king will take his place on the throne of Delhi and British democracy can continue on its productive path, is probably more than half-satiric, although there are some very intently argued passages. But precisely because of this note of satire, of withholding of real investment – I would venture – it reveals an anxious desire to ignore the more deeply rooted violence and inequity of empire. This pamphlet thus offers the possibility of interpreting, in new ways, the more vivid, and perhaps more successful, fixed and fetishistic disavowals and displacements in the Coronation Durbar, and in imperial rule more generally. For Scotus helps to define how these rituals licensed a deep incuriosity and ignorance about the real political processes of India, while buttressing imperial relations of authority and evading the complexities of representation 'at home'.

In her *Critique of Postcolonial Reason*, Gayatri Spivak points out that the Foucauldian account of micrological power operating in knowledge-institutions and in disciplinary relations, for all of its theoretical and political strengths, is inadequate for understanding imperialism and its incorporation of bodies and territories into a 'monstrous and misshapen' state (Spivak 1999: 279). She argues that the anatomist of power in miniature is so focused on schools, workhouses, prisons and asylums that he misses the colonial 'theaters' (her word) where sovereignty operated on the gross anatomy of the world as a whole through the medium of spectacular (mis)representations. According to Spivak, the Foucauldian account of power-knowledge, in its focus on positive knowledge-claims and the silent elicitation of mimetic obedience, only perpetuates 'the sanctioned ignorance that every critic of imperialism must chart' (ibid.: 279), and she recommends instead that we examine again the 'double session' of political representation in colonial contexts – the mutual implication in any act of representation, aesthetic or political, of both 'portrait', or imitation, and 'proxy', or substitution. Spivak's analysis of the aporetic relation between proxy and portrait in colonial representations further supports the usefulness of the Freudian fetish, with its own structure of anxiety, mimesis and displacement, for interpreting the power of imperial rituals.

In his account of domestic struggles over the Parliament Act and the power of the House of Lords, Scotus Indigena indicates that the British attachment to their own king was, indeed, threatened in this period. Scotus saw a republic in the offing: he wrote, 'Democracy has shewn itself the serpent of Moses', a magical beast that devoured its partners, 'aristocracy and monarchy' (Scotus Indigena 1911: 15). Later he says that 'Keir Hardie', the Labour leader, 'is the Marat of the Liberals ... . Keir Hardie has told us more than once in the past year that the Crown is in danger' (ibid.: 23). Finally, he says, 'Nothing can now preserve the Monarchy' (ibid.: 27) – except, he finally insists, that the king leave England with his imperial crown and form a new and even broader empire, away from Britain. And yet, reciprocally, if the

British people now want only to represent themselves democratically, and to invest in industry and progress (as Scotus defines the goal), they still need the imperial crown elsewhere, disavowed and banished but retaining its full sovereign potency, to contain and control difference – to sequester arts and civilization on the banks of the Indus, as it were. This phallic fantasy thus composes a global political order without lack, absence, exclusion or any trace of violence.

Meanwhile, in the history of Indian rulers that Scotus sketches, though 'Hindu and Musselman' were 'welded into a single constitution' at a very early date, this too is the heroic achievement of kings and emperors (Scotus 1911: 4–5). He credits Akbar with a signal act of unification, which was simply repeated by the British Crown when it assumed the imperial title over India in 1877. As has been discussed above, Scotus marks the adoption by Queen Victoria of the royal style 'Empress of India' as the real moment of importance in the 'chain' of events linking the British Crown to India, rather than either the arrival of commercial adventurers more than a century earlier or the 'dethroning' of John Company after the disruptive and violent political events of 1857–1858. Further, Scotus' displacement of the beginning of the relation between Crown and India to 1877 – although royal charters and noble titles were part of the colonial government of India from the start – establishes that, perhaps unsurprisingly, the problems of colonial legitimacy – not least as they were posed by company rule and then by the Indian Mutiny – stand as the disavowed content of the imperial fetish. Indeed, Scotus introduces his whole discussion of what ties Britain to India with the revealing comment, 'over the doings of the East India Company ... the patriotic Englishman would gladly draw a veil' (ibid.: 6) – the Crown, precisely, is the veil which hides the imperial history of violence, and the ongoing maintenance of this fiction requires that this very part of the 'English' political structure be imaginarily surrendered to the colonial Other.

As was discussed at the start of this chapter, the whole ceremony of the Durbar was orchestrated to aggrandize imperial power and place it serenely above the scene of nationalist politics in India, while at the same time serving the policy needs of the colonial government. Following the accepted protocols of constitutional monarchy, the king's proclamation was carefully drafted to include acknowledgement of these complexities: 'We are pleased to announce to our people that *on the advice of our Ministers* ... we have decided upon the transfer of the seat of the Government of India', the proclamation began (George 1912: 120, emphasis mine). But a crucial problem was thus dissimulated – in order to secure the political effect desired from his proclamation, the king himself had to assume in his own person the constituted power of democratic British government, to personally decide on and proclaim his Durbar Boon, and in so doing to summarize and represent the interests of his colonial subjects, thus collapsing the proxy and the portrait in the double session of representation and obscuring any real difference between India's interests and those of a British constitutional monarch.

Scotus solves simultaneously both of the problems of knowledge and responsibility implicated in this double session of colonial representation: both political representation, or 'proxy', and the arduous procedures of compiling intimate and detailed knowledge of the colonial political body, or 'portrait', are – in his account – routed through a theory of the power of the Crown, supplemented by his imagination of what the personal presence of the king will achieve, once he finds his proper home in India. The problem of how to secure democracy at home and empire abroad is resolved in a fetishistic disavowal and displacement – and not only the primal violence of conquest, but also the threat of revolution and violence at home are thus warded off. 'There will be no fighting', Scotus says, as he imagines the Crown travelling, with the king, away to India (Scotus 1911: 27–28). Most centrally, this solution – whether in the durbar's resolution of a sticky problem of 'Indian statesmanship', or in Scotus' answer to the future of the empire – involves no knowledge, curiosity or inquiry into what Indians may, historically and collectively, desire, what future they may shape for themselves. When it comes to positive knowledge and governmental efficacy, all one needs to know is that the Crown is the problem at home (too present) and the solution abroad – covering over a problematic lack of sovereign self-representation – and hence it need only be removed from one site and affixed to another to make all complexities disappear.

This path of ignorance comports, as a political solution to a vexed problem of knowledge and representation, with the prevarications of liberal discourse about the imperial mission. Many eminent liberal theorists – notably John Stuart Mill and Henry Maine – had addressed themselves to what Scotus likewise saw as the contradiction between the (increasingly) liberal constitution of England, grounded in theories of natural rights to political self-representation, and the maintenance of monarchical power in Britain's colonial possessions. The characteristic theoretical resolution was developed by Mill, for whom political rights were the gift of civilization, not of nature, and India's political freedoms therefore were to be deferred until India was trained up, had become a mature political community capable of self-government, a process of which colonialism was in fact the handmaiden. According to Uday Singh Mehta, this liberal tradition – in its relation to India, and before the later imperialist theorization of 'indirect rule' as a basis of colonial legitimacy – 'is virtually unified in its view regarding the absence of political community in India and, more generally, in the colonies. This absence and the redress that the empire purportedly supplies for it is the mainstay of the liberal justification of the empire: India is in a condition of tutelage' (Mehta 1999: 162). While few political theorists followed the path of Scotus, recommending the ultimate disjuncture of liberal constitutionalism from the Crown, and Empire, in order to preserve both, his pamphlet nevertheless represents the fullest working out of a logic of an imperial fetishism that is implicit in the liberal theorization of empire. As Mehta puts it, 'the will to power that liberals ... express[ed] for the empire [was] always as a beneficent compensation for someone else's powerlessness relative to a more elevated order' (Mehta 1999: 191). The Crown came to represent the fetishistic resolution to the problems of the putative political difference of the colonized, and the vexed issues of similitude and difference that the liberal theory raised were thus resolved – not solely by pedagogical deferral, but also by entrusting all colonial beneficence to the Crown itself.

The reading that is offered here of the Freudian account of fetishism and of Scotus Indigena helps us understand this last claim about the relation of liberal power to knowledge of someone else's powerlessness. For Scotus, the fantastic political theory which links the Crown to India absolves Britain of its own remaining (undemocratic) tie to monarchy, at the same moment as it situates India in permanent subservience to a British king. It is not the abusive account of India's lack of autonomous history that matters here, but the insertion of a fictive 'chain ... independent of England' which links the British Crown with India, for it allows Scotus to acknowledge both India's powerlessness in the imperial structure and the ways in which this was produced, while absolving British democracy of all responsibility, past or future – even, indeed, situating direct, imperial control over India as the salvation of India's own powers. This disregard of the ethical problems presented by any imperial power, in favour of a narcissistic pursuit of democracy at home, underscores the fetishistic structure of colonial rule. As Freud (1961) makes clear, the medical and ethical problem of fetishism is not to be found in the devious route by which the fetishist's satisfaction is achieved; rather, the need for treatment comes from the fact that such satisfaction comes at the expense of the conscious participation of others, who are reduced to mere possessors, or

wearers, of displaced sexual attributes over the use of which they have
no control. The fetishist denies the subjects of his sexual fantasies any
of their own autonomy or personhood.

However, the fetish itself retains immense and persecutory power
over the fetishist, if actual women (and men) are left as mute objects.
It need only be noted that Queen Victoria was styled 'Empress of
India' – not 'British Empress', a conjunction of democratic Britishness
and imperial titles that Scotus admits was 'unthinkable' (1911: 12)
– to see the fetishistic reversals in play in actual British imperialism.
Materially speaking, the imperial crown – the physical object – is as
much India's possession as is, imaginarily, the legal and notional
'Imperial Crown' (it should be recalled that Indian revenues paid to
fabricate the bejewelled Imperial Crown worn by George V in Delhi).
This accords precisely with the fetishistic reversal in which the boy's
own threatened phallus is attributed to the newly punishing and
super-powerful Mother to cover the absence he thinks he sees – the
fearsome and repulsive power invested in this fantasied 'phallus-out-
of-place' is contained and domesticated in the fetish, which then the
boy holds onto and cherishes (George V's Indian crown was returned
to Britain, for safekeeping, after the Coronation Durbar).

Was domestic democracy actually threatened in Georgian Britain?
Perhaps. Was imperial power less secure than it seemed? Certainly.
What is Scotus' solution? Grant the Crown to India and avert your gaze
from the consequences! In place of knowledge of the colonial other
and of the colonized society's relation of subordination to Britain's
domestic democracy, a debased self-image, a distorted reflection of the
British subject's own anxious relation to monarchical power, is put
in its place. Thus, just as the sexual fetish is not primarily the result
of any engagement with difference, but rather the contentless material sign of disavowal and displacement, so too is the imperial fetish
empty. There is no proper body behind the maternal phallus, just as
there is no political body behind Scotus' notion of the Imperial Crown.
Because it is rooted in the castration complex, fetishism is first a result of power and a displacement of the fetishist's own panicked response to the threat of violence. What satisfies the fetishist is the way
in which the fetish allows him both to maintain the theory that the
violence which threatens him has already been expended elsewhere
and to deny the consequences of that theory; ultimately, he is enabled
by his fetishistic disavowal to order relations in such a way that paternal authority and his own emergent social power are both preserved,
while knowledge of difference, and of a differently constituted world
of social power, are each set beyond reach, endlessly obscured by the

false positivity of the maternal phallus and its persecutory powers of attraction.

Coda: The Afterlife of the Crown in Postcolonial Sovereignty

The fetishistic structure of ceremonies like the Coronation Durbar not only projected the incompletion of the Indian body-politic which was the prime liberal justification for empire, but also licensed the exercise of personal power and decision, as seen in the king's pronouncement at the durbar. Finally, as later political theorists such as Harold Laski (1938) would point out, the modes of imperial administration rooted in such fetishistic love of power would rebound negatively on domestic politics. For Laski, witnessing the development of the administrative state in the 1930s and its suppression of political difference in the name of order, the 'habits of imperialism' threatened to overwrite the 'habits of democracy' in everyday governance (see Morefield 2009). In this, Laski's assessment of the consequences of the imperial monarchy was less happy, but perhaps more truthful, than Scotus Indigena's enthusiastic embrace of the imperial adventures of the Crown. Laski's diagnosis of the domestic perils of the Imperial Crown leads to a final analytic point of some relevance to the afterlife of the Crown in contemporary states: governmental administration is most powerfully productive, and most culpably ignorant of variety and difference within the political body, when it is joined, ritually and customarily, to a sovereign claim of total representation.

There is some evidence that the specific fetishistic and representative function of the British crown that has been examined here is now being revived in the internal colonial politics of settler societies like Canada and Australia. Or, at least, a similarly fetishistic fixation on the Crown as a political solution to problems of knowledge and difference can be discerned in recent Canadian jurisprudence of indigenous land claims, in which a medieval principle of the 'inherent honour of the Crown' has been revived so courts may more easily recognize the customary or traditional forms of belief and title which underlie First Nations' claims of rights.

The systematic misunderstanding and misinterpretation of indigenous notions of the sacred, of possession, and of rights in land in liberal law and political theory have been major topics of recent anthropological studies (see Kuppe 2009). Anthropologists are now well equipped, theoretically, to critique the positivism and powerful productivity of legal knowledge (Povinelli 2002). In Canadian courts, this anthropological critique has been incorporated into ongoing legal reforms and creative jurisprudence around indigenous land claims. The kinds of documents and positive, expert knowledge previously demanded to support a land claim are now increasingly seen as perpetuating a form of legal violence, since such evidentiary procedures actually rest on the very treaties and legal forms of expropriation which sundered indigenous people from their land in the first place.

Marianna Valverde (2012) has explored some of the paradoxes of this appropriation of anthropological critique into Canadian jurisprudence. She emphasizes that the critique has perhaps gone too far, and while courts have stopped requiring certain forms of evidentiary procedure in order to take a less time-consuming legal route to recognition and redress, they have had recourse to legal technicalities that may not have the desired effects. Resting their decisions on the doctrine of the 'honour of the Crown', judges can now impose duties on the state to administer land claims in the interests of indigenous people (however these interests may be defined) and can empower officials to exclude certain kinds of alternative uses of protected land, while avoiding the epistemic work of adjudicating between plural, different claims over land and finding points of comparison between radically different systems of tenure and rights. The Crown in this legal theory is at once necessarily higher and more authoritative than any actually existing government, and it is 'self-acting' – in the name of the Crown's honour, judges can impel and reconfigure relations between the state and its subjects, and evade the problems of commensuration internal to liberalism.

However appealing the use of this old legal doctrine for benevolent inclusion may be, the thrust of Valverde's critique is that such recourse to vague legal theories of metaphysical honour actually abrogates the very principles by which any limitation to power could be secured. When a jurist uses the 'inherent honour of the Crown' – the mystical and ever-present power of the Crown to fulfil its duties and act always rightly – in ordering consultation, recompense or other legal action, consequential constitutional divisions of powers, real histories of expropriation and violence and concrete claims for redress are all equally made impossible to cognize within the ambit of the law. In place of a careful acknowledgement of historical relations of unequal power and violence – with whatever, necessarily insufficient, evidence could be brought to bear to support this new form of recognition – there is instead an imaginary and self-acting duty to do right not only symbolized by but inherent to the sovereign. Thus, in new but very familiar ways, juridical and democratic procedure and epistemological rigour are subsumed under a 'royal' fiat. Of course, in this case, it is not Queen Elizabeth or any of her successors who will have the power to invoke the Crown in this way; but who, personally, exercises the Crown's power is less important than the Crown's continued presence as a legal site for unaccountable, unquestionable actions.

As in the Durbar Boon, which reversed a colonial policy, the Crown has been invoked in these Canadian cases in order to cover over real arguments, differences and political struggles, and to make colonial Others reachable by a state power not bound by the niceties of liberal constitutionalism. This legal manoeuvre perpetuates an imaginary dream of total knowledge of the Other at the same moment as it obscures the workings of power. And whatever are the ethnocentric fantasies or abusive fictions on which this recourse to the Crown is based, it is an effective move in the maintenance of a larger economy of imperial political relations. Just at the point where liberalism expands its jurisdiction to others through such grants of super-ordinary recognition, at this same moment they are reconstituted as subjects of a direct and administrative power, awaiting incorporation into the privileges of procedure only once they reach their full majority. The honour of the Crown puts claimants in a position of quasi-filial dependence, rather than granting them the status of fully fledged subjects of law.

This is what makes the recourse to the 'honour of the Crown' an instance of imperial fetishism: it resolves the problems of knowledge and commensuration raised by liberalism, but only by situating others in the same subordinate position to power that the liberal subject fears and seeks to escape through procedure; furthermore, it licenses a real ignorance of, and disregard for, the fate of others at the hands of this sovereign power. The only way to escape this imperial consequence is by struggling with the truth of other claims on power and in so doing claiming our own maturity, as political subjects, on terms of equality – which is neither pure identity nor difference – with other subjects. As Borneman points out (in this volume), the passage to knowledge of self and other does not pass solely through the gate of information, but involves a relational process of becoming knowledgeable. This is certainly harder than it might at first sound, given the durable political effects of fetishistic and imperial ignorance. This, at least, is the monitory lesson of Scotus' imaginary and decadent empire, from the Irrawaddy to the Nile, in which the inscription of the Other was invested with a domestic political benefit.

Notes

1. According to the Oxford English Dictionary, an oriflamme is 'an object, principle, or ideal that serves as a rallying point in a struggle'. As will become clear, this imputed, attractive power of the Crown is a decisive part of its meaning in these contexts.
2. See Kerr (2003), who has similarly discussed the literary tropes of ignorance and obscurity as an essential component of the imperial claim to legitimate power over others.
3. It should be added that the insufficiency of rational, materialist accounts of state power, as residing in concrete relations between actors differently situated in relation to rights and resources, was long ago argued – with similar intent, if in different terms – by Clifford Geertz (1980).
4. As far as I can ascertain, there is only one copy of this pamphlet extant, in the Ames Library of South Asia at the University of Minnesota. All the publisher's records from before 1940 were destroyed during World War II (personal communication from A.H. Stockwell, publishers), and without further analysis of the pamphlet and related works it is not possible to ascertain who the author was. Scotus Indigena could be translated 'A Native Scot'; the phrase is most likely to be simply a clever play on the name of the medieval Irish monk Scotus Eriugena, and there is no explicit reference to any non-English British identity in the text at hand. However, it is probably not accidental that Scotus Indigena is alert to the cross-national representative function of the Crown in British life, and on that basis embraces a pluri-national constitution for a future British Empire beyond the Atlantic archipelago (see Pocock 2005).
5. The choice of these constituencies to represent the democratic genius of Britain is not accidental: Peckham was a working-class district of London; Tonypandy (in Wales) was the site of important riots by striking mineworkers in 1909–1910, and was an area associated with Lloyd George himself.
6. See Peitz (1993) for an account of how Marx draws upon, transforms and exceeds binaries between matter and ideas, and theories of primitive religion as simple mystification and error, in his elaboration of commodity-fetishism.

References

Apter, A. 2004. *The Pan-African Nation: Oil and the Spectacle of Culture in Nigeria*. Chicago, IL: University of Chicago Press.

Apter, E. and W. Peitz (eds) 1993. *Fetishism as Cultural Discourse*. Ithaca, NY: Cornell University Press.

Bagehot, W. 1966. *The English Constitution*. Ithaca, NY: Cornell University Press.

Bayly, C.A. 1989. *Imperial Meridian: The British Empire and the World, 1780–1830*. New York: Longman.

Bernheimer, C. 1993. 'Fetishism and Decadence: Salome's Severed Heads'. In *Fetishism as Cultural Discourse*, ed. E. Apter and W. Peitz. Ithaca, NY: Cornell University Press, 62–83.

Cannadine, D. 2001. *Ornamentalism: How the British Saw Their Empire*. New York: Oxford University Press.

Cohn, B.S. 1983. 'Representing Authority in Victorian India'. In *The Invention of Tradition*, ed. E.J. Hobsbawm and T.O. Ranger. New York: Cambridge University Press, 165–209.

———. 1996. *Colonialism and its Forms of Knowledge: The British in India*. Princeton, NJ: Princeton University Press.

Comaroff, J. and J. Comaroff 2009. *Ethnicity, Inc*. Chicago. IL: University of Chicago Press.

Cooper, F. 1994. 'Conflict and Connection: Rethinking Colonial African History'. *American Historical Review* 99, 1516–45.

Curzon, G.N. 1925. *British Government in India, Volume 1*. London: Cassell.

Derrida, J. 1976. *Of Grammatology*, trans. G. Chakravorty Spivak. Baltimore, MD: Johns Hopkins.

Dilley, R.M. 2007. 'The Construction of Colonial Knowledge Practices: The Case of Henri Gaden'. In *Ways of Knowing: New Approaches in the Anthropology of Knowledge and Learning*, ed. M. Harris. Oxford: Berghahn, 139–57.

Dirks, N. 2001. *Castes of Mind: Colonialism and the Making of Modern India*. Princeton, NJ: Princeton University Press.

Eustis, F.A. and Z.H. Zaidi 1964. 'King, Viceroy, and Cabinet: The Modification of the Partition of Bengal, 1911'. *History* 49, 171–84.

Foucault, M. 1977. *Discipline and Punish: The Birth of the Prison*, trans. Alan Sheridan. New York: Vintage.

Freud, S. 1959 [1908]. 'The Sexual Theories of Children'. In *The Standard Edition of the Psychological Works of Sigmund Freud, vol. 9*, ed. J. Strachey. London: Hogarth, 210–26.

———. 1961 [1927]. 'Fetishism'. In *The Standard Edition of the Psychological Works of Sigmund Freud, vol. 21*, ed. J. Strachey. London: Hogarth, 152–57.

Frykenberg, R.E. 1986. 'The Coronation Durbar of 1911: Some Implications'. In *Delhi through the Ages: Selected Essays in Urban History, Culture, and Society*, ed. R.E. Frykenberg. Delhi: Oxford University Press, 225–46.

Geertz, C. 1980. *Negara: The Theatre-State in Nineteenth-Century Bali*. Princeton, NJ: Princeton University Press.

George, King of Great Britain 1912. *The Speeches of His Majesty King George in India*, 2nd edition. Madras: G.A. Natesan.

Gluckman, M. 1940. 'Analysis of a Social Situation in Modern Zululand'. *Bantu Affairs* 14, 1–30.

Haynes, D. 1990. *Rhetoric and Ritual in Colonial India: The Shaping of a Public Culture in Surat City, 1852–1928*. Berkeley: University of California Press.

Johnson, D. 2010. 'Land Acquisition, Landlessness, and the Building of New Delhi'. *Radical History Review* 108, 91–116.

Kerr, D. 2003. 'Not Knowing the Oriental'. *New Zealand Journal of Asian Studies* 5, 33–46.

Kuppe, R. 2009. 'Religious Freedom Law and the Protection of Sacred Sites'. In *Permutations of Order: Religion and Law as Contested Sovereignties*, ed. T. Kirsch and B. Turner. Farnham: Ashgate, 49–66.

Laski, H. 1938. *Parliamentary Government in England: A Commentary*. New York: Viking.

Mehta, U.S. 1999. *Liberalism and Empire: A Study in Nineteenth-Century British Liberal Thought*. Chicago, IL: University of Chicago Press.

Mitchell, T. 1999. 'Society, Economy, and the State Effect'. In *State/Culture: State Formation after the Cultural Turn*, ed. G. Steinmetz. Ithaca, NY: Cornell University Press, 76–97.

Morefield, J. 2009. 'Harold Laski on the Habits of Imperialism'. In *Lineages of Empire*, ed. D. Kelly. London: British Academy, 213–37.

Peitz, W. 1993. 'Fetishism and Materialism: The Limits of Theory in Marx'. In *Fetishism as Cultural Discourse*, ed. W.A. Peitz and E. Apter. Ithaca, NY: Cornell University Press, 119–51.

Pocock, J.G.A. 2005. 'Two Kingdoms and Three Histories? Political Thought in British Contexts'. In *The Discovery of Islands: Essays in British History*, ed. J.G.A. Pocock. Cambridge: Cambridge University Press, 58–76.

Povinelli, E.A. 2002. *The Cunning of Recognition: Indigenous Alterities and the Making of Australian Multiculturalism*. Durham, NC: Duke University Press.

Prakash, G. 2002. 'The Colonial Genealogy of Society: Community and Political Modernity in India'. In *The Social in Question: New Bearings in History and the Social Sciences*, ed. P. Joyce. New York: Routledge, 81–96.

Ranger, T.O. 1980. 'Making Northern Rhodesia Imperial: Variations on a Royal Theme, 1924–1938'. *African Affairs* 79, 349–73.

Reed, S. 1912. *The King and Queen in India*. Bombay [Mumbai]: Bennett, Coleman & Co.

Rutherford, D. 2009. 'Sympathy, State Building, and the Experience of Empire'. *Cultural Anthropology* 24, 1–32.

Scotus Indigena [Pseud.] 1911. *The Coronation Durbar and after.* London: Arthur H. Stockwell.

Simmel, G. 1906. 'The Sociology of Secrecy and Secret Societies'. *American Journal of Sociology* 11, 441–98.

Spivak, G.C. 1999. *A Critique of Postcolonial Reason: Toward a History of the Vanishing Present*. Cambridge, MA: Harvard University Press.

Steinmetz, G. 2007. *The Devil's Handwriting: Precoloniality and the German Colonial State in Qingdao, Samoa, and Southwest Africa*. Chicago, IL: University of Chicago Press.

Stoler, A. 2009. *Along the Archival Grain: Epistemic Anxieties and Colonial Common Sense*. Princeton, NJ: Princeton University Press.

Taussig, M. 1993. 'Maleficium: State Fetishism'. In *Fetishism as Cultural Discourse*, ed. W.A. Peitz and E. Apter. Ithaca, NY: Cornell University Press, 217–49.

Thornton, A.P. 1959. *The Imperial Idea and Its Enemies: A Study in British Power*. London: Macmillan.

Trevithick, A. 1990. 'Some Structural and Sequential Aspects of the British Imperial Assemblages at Delhi: 1877–1911'. *Modern Asian Studies* 24, 561–78.

Valverde, M. 2012. 'The Crown in a Multicultural Age: The Changing Epistemology of (Post)colonial Sovereignty'. *Social & Legal Studies* 21, 3–21.

Leo Coleman is Associate Professor of Anthropology at Hunter College, City University of New York. He is the editor of *Food: Ethnographic Encounters* (2011) and has published several articles on ethnographic method and on urbanism, infrastructure and legal knowledge in India and the British Empire. He is working on an historical ethnography of electrification, ritual and state power in twentieth-century Delhi.

Chapter 8

SECRECY AND THE EPISTEMOPHILIC OTHER

Thomas G. Kirsch

It is often taken for granted that human beings are epistemophilics; that is, that they have 'a natural desire to know'. Georg Simmel, for instance, in his celebrated work on secrecy and secret societies makes the universalist claim that, 'In general, men credit themselves with the right to know everything which, without application of external illegal means, through purely psychological observation and reflection, it is possible to ascertain' (1906: 455). However, as the present chapter aims to show, this naturalizing emphasis on epistemophilia produces its own blind spot, namely the fact that the assumption that humans are epistemophilics is itself a cultural construction. Suspending this assumption allows a reconsideration of basic categories of social scientific thought, such as 'the secret'.

Of all things unknown, those that have received the most attention are unbeknown to some because they have been wilfully concealed by others. In turn, the advisability of this heightened attention is generally accounted for by equating acts of concealment with acts of secretiveness. Take, for example, Sissela Bok's renowned definition of 'secrecy':

> A path, a riddle, a jewel, an oath – anything can be secret as long as it is kept intentionally hidden, set apart in the mind of its keeper as requiring concealment. ... To keep a secret from someone, then, is to block information about it or evidence of it from reaching that person, and to do so intentionally: to prevent him from learning it, and thus from possessing it, making use of it; or revealing it. The word

'secrecy' refers to the resulting concealment. It also denotes the methods used to conceal, such as codes or disguises or camouflage, and the practices of concealment, as in trade secrecy or professional confidentiality. Accordingly I shall take concealment ... to be the defining trait of secrecy. It presupposes separation, a setting apart of the secret from the non-secret, and of keepers of a secret from those excluded. ... The separation between insider and outsider is inherent in secrecy; and to think something secret is already to envisage potential conflict between what insiders conceal and outsiders want to inspect or lay bare. (Bok 1984: 5–6)

Yet, this understanding of secrecy as 'consciously willed concealment' (Simmel 1906: 449), widely held in both popular culture and scholarly thought, falls short of analytical purview in one important aspect that becomes apparent when 'the secret' is correlated not with common-sense antonyms of 'concealment' – such as 'disclosure', 'transparency' and, increasingly, 'leakage' – but with 'the private'.[1] Correlating these two notions with respect to their semantic overlaps and differences reveals that the defining features of secrecy might lie not just in the act of concealment but in another aspect whose pertinence for theorizing 'the secret' will be elaborated in this chapter and which is aptly illustrated by examples from my fieldwork in Zambia.[2]

Imagine a house in rural Zambia, grass-thatched and made of mud bricks. In this region, people spend most of their time outside their homes with hardly any social event taking place inside of them. Doors or curtains at the house entrance restrict access and fend off unwanted gazes, and it is exceptional for a non-family member to be invited to enter another person's home. In this context, home is an exclusionary space, confined to a very limited number of persons whose interactions inside the house are characterized by an air of privacy. Yet, the efforts employed to ensure this air of privacy at times give rise to others' suspicions that the activities undertaken inside a given home might not be just private affairs, but might be malign in nature and secretively harmful to others, for example in the form of witchcraft or crime.

In this chapter, I am not specifically interested in the classificatory ambiguity between 'privacy' and 'secrecy' that is typical of the ethnographic constellation sketched above. Nor do I aim to examine whether or in what ways it is the particular nature of an activity, an object or a stock of knowledge that, according to the understandings of the social actors involved, makes it a private or a secret affair. Instead, I want to call attention to a peculiar difference between privacy and secrecy that promises to provide interesting new insights into the secret as a cultural category and a discursive operation reliant on the non-knowledge of some people in contradistinction to others (see also Lochrie 1999: 4). To put it in a nutshell, I surmise that these two notions, while having several features in common, such as concealment and social exclusivism, differ in the fact that the category of 'the secret' – in contrast to 'the private' and its semiotic extensions like 'privacy' – presupposes the existence of (real or imagined) Others who are concerned and consequently have an interest in the disclosure of what is concealed from them.[3] On top of that, I argue that these epistemophilic Others are not already out there prior to acts of secretiveness, but are performatively constituted and thus brought into existence through acts that are classified in that way.

To clarify what I mean by this, let me return to the example above. No different than what can be found on a daily basis in billions of homes around the world, activities, conversations and interactions take place in people's homes in Zambia that are wilfully concealed from others who are considered to be part of the wider public. It is crucial to note that, in many or even the majority of such concealments, these very others are not particularly interested in gaining knowledge about the nature, attributes or contents of these activities, conversations and interactions; all too often, they simply do not care about what is being kept from them (cf. Tefft 1980: 320; Nippert-Eng 2010: 24). In other instances, however, these others are concerned that what is being concealed from them might be personally relevant for themselves and/or for the wider public or some specific section of it. In the example above, such concerns are triggered by the fear that others may be engaging in witchcraft or crime. Knowing what activities, conversations and interactions are taking place in the homes of certain people thus seems vital for preserving the interests of those who might be concerned or affected by them.

This wanting-to-know makes a difference to how 'consciously willed concealment' is interpreted and evaluated, in the cases above transmuting it from being considered a morally blameless aspect of 'privacy' into an aspect of 'secrecy' associated with immorality (see also Warren and Laslett 1980: 26). One could give many examples of classificatory transmutations of this kind, such as when a nightly gathering of friends is reinterpreted from being regarded as a private party to being classified as a conspiratorial meeting of criminals, or when the private handling of herbal medication is no longer believed to serve the curative treatment of a bedridden patient but is instead thought to represent a secretive enactment of black magic harming others. In cases like these, the activities, conversations and interactions themselves may not have changed. It is therefore not necessarily an alteration in their specific nature that causes the reclassification from 'private' to 'secret'. Instead, what underlies such reclassification is a shift in people's presumptions concerning the question of whether it is important for some to know what others are concealing from them – presumptions that can be connected to issues of im/morality, but also to questions of power in its various forms. The latter point makes it clear that people's concern often relates to 'the secret as an aspect of the sacred' (de Jong 2007: 9; see also Johnson 2002: 3).

Up to this point, my argument has been developed relative to the point of view of people who presume that certain others have secrets. However, it is also possible to approach this issue from the perspective of people who, implicitly or explicitly, frame some of their own activities, conversations or interactions in terms of secrecy. Nonetheless, the argument remains the same. No different from what has been explicated above, use of the notion of 'the secret' as a self-descriptive category presupposes the idea that there exist people who have an interest in gaining knowledge about what is concealed from them. Take the example of a diary privately stowed away in a chest of drawers. There is nothing secretive about this diary unless it is taken for granted that there is someone who wants to find it and read it. In other words, merely hiding the diary does not make it a secret.

On the face of it, this argument states the obvious. Upon closer inspection, however, it becomes clear that, despite their general sophistication, scientific definitions of secrecy tend to be based on an implicit and highly debatable assumption, namely that people around the world and throughout time are characterized by some sort of natural epistemophilic impulse in relation to whatever is concealed from them. For example, as mentioned above, Simmel claims that 'men credit themselves with the right to know everything' (1906: 455). In a similar vein, when trying to come up with an explanation for why an 'individual's attempt to make something accessible to others rarely seems to be as much of a problem as an attempt to make it inaccessible to them' (Nippert-Eng 2010: 8), Christina Nippert-Eng takes recourse to biological determinism: 'The curiosity of our species seems to play a large role in this. Humans are constantly scanning, constantly receptive to and looking for whatever they can perceive about each other, for whatever is put out there' (ibid.).

Against this backdrop, while people's wanting-to-know in questionable ways often appears to be a self-explanatory trait of 'the
secret', this chapter examines what happens to our understanding
of this notion once we recognize the importance of another truism,
namely that people do not always and necessarily feel concerned by
what others may be concealing from them. After all, 'strategies of
concealment permeate multiple levels of discursive and social practice, from the realm of ... politics to the more mundane realms of
domesticity and productive activities' (Ferme 2001: 1). Given this
ubiquity of concealment (cf. Piot 1993), people often simply do not
care. Taking account of this crucial point allows us to problematize
simplistic equations of 'concealment' and 'secrecy' and to denatu-
ralize the idea of the epistemophilic impulse, thus making the performative constitution of epistemophilic Others through secrecy the
focus of analysis.[4]

In what follows, this argument about 'secrecy' as a social practice
of constituting (real or imagined) epistemophilic Others will be elaborated by, in the first step, relating it to social-scientific debates on secrecy in order to contextualize it in terms of anthropological theory.
Thus, 'secrecy' is conceptualized here as a cultural category and discursive operation (cf. Gal 2002, 2005). It is argued that it has a peculiar social form (cf. Simmel 1906) that encompasses two spheres
of sociality that are disconnected as regards certain communicational transactions but interconnected in terms of their structural
relationship. Following that, ethnographic data from my research
on African Christianity in Zambia will be presented to illustrate and
analyse how the performative constitution of epistemophilic Others
through secrecy is played out in social practice.

Perspectives on Secrecy

In anthropology, the notion of 'the secret' has played an important
role in analyses of political and religious power (e.g., Cohen 1971;
Luhrmann 1989; Gusterson 1996; Geschiere 1997; Keen 1998;
Lattas 1998; Ferme 2001; Meyer and Pels 2003; Whitehead and
Wright 2004; Duncan 2006; Masco 2006; de Jong 2007; Nuijten
and Anders 2007), studies of secret societies in different parts of
the world (e.g., Boas 1897; Butt-Thompson 1929; Fortune 1932;
Murphy 1980; Bellman 1984; La Fontaine 1986; Johnson 1991;
Herdt 2003) and discussions problematizing the methodological as-
sumption in ethnography that it is 'by peering behind the facade that

we see things as insiders rather than as outsiders and thereby discover the truth' (Gable 1997: 215). More recently, anthropologists have also been concerned with the ethics and politics of keeping and/or disclosing the secrets of others – be it subaltern sections of society engaged in acts of resistance or Western intelligence agencies pursuing counterinsurgency operations (e.g., Fluehr-Lobban 2003; Price 2004; Besteman and Gusterson 2005; Wax 2008; Besteman 2009; Kelly, Jauregui and Mitchell 2010; Mahmud 2012).

Broadly speaking, it is possible to distinguish two different attitudes of anthropologists towards 'secrecy' as an object of scientific inquiry. There are those who seek reflexively to degrade the secrecy claims of those studied, to establish that there is no substance to them, to uncover that what is concealed is nothing other than emptiness. As a consequence of this attitude, what remains of secretiveness in terms of its analysis is nothing but a sense of indecent strategizing, pretence and delusion. Michael Taussig has argued along these lines that the unveiling of a secret always reveals the existence of another one and that 'to the extent that the secret can be and is revealed ... revelation is precisely what the secret intends' (Taussig 2003: 297; see also Taussig 1999).

On the other hand, there are anthropologists who feel drawn to dig into secrets, thus putting the rigour of scientific enquiry to use for the disclosure of aspects of reality that had previously been concealed from the wider public. This attitude is usually driven by a sense of the scientist's sociopolitical responsibility in making the unknown known. Most important for the argument of this chapter is that this attitude generally invokes the idea that certain others – in most cases, readers of the ethnographic study and (some section of) the wider public – would be well advised to be concerned about it as well. It is in this sense that, no different from people in the non-academic world, scholars in the social sciences at times take part in the constitution of epistemophilic Others through using the category of 'the secret'.

Yet, despite this long preoccupation with 'the secret', the all-important question of which particular forms of sociality are constituted through secrecy has remained surprisingly underexplored in anthropology. One could claim that this relative neglect is a consequence of 'the exoticism inherent in secrecy' (Herdt 2003: xii), the stereotypical ascription of anti-social and dissociative characteristics, and secrecy's morally problematic propensity to inhibit free communication. However, one should recall Georg Simmel's influential insight that secrecy is nothing exceptional but a 'universal sociological form' (1906: 463) which ought be studied without moral evaluation and which can serve social integration because, as Simmel points out, 'with publicity many sorts of purposes could never arrive at realization' (1906: 462; see also Barth 1975). For instance, while Simmel's approach stands in contrast to the critique of secrecy as formulated in the historical Enlightenment and by proponents of participatory democracy (see also Paley 2002), there are good reasons to assume that the latter type of democracy requires the existence of a system of secret voting (Bertrand, Briquet and Pels 2007). Similarly, there is a sense in which certain empirical phenomena, such as crime prevention, can be said to be based on a certain functional necessity of secretiveness: if you want to succeed in preventing crime – for example, as a member of the police force – you need to make sure that certain types of information are concealed from certain other people.

These insights into the productiveness of secrecy point to the fact that, in focusing on the question of the sociality of secrecy, scholars face troubling complexities. After all, in secret-service agencies no less than in secret societies, it is secretiveness which institutes and symbolizes the boundary between the social inside and outside. But since 'the secret' in a paradoxical way expresses the presence of an absence, there remains something puzzling and enigmatic about it which defies easy description. Given this complexity, it is interesting to note that scientists have tended to rely on a quite elementary model in dealing with the question of how social inclusion and exclusion are organized through secretiveness. Broadly speaking, the sharing of a secret is conventionally depicted as 'a social technique of boundary formation' (Johnson 2002: 8) that creates bonds of inclusivity between those who share it and that marks a powerful distinction from others who are wilfully excluded from this secrecy transaction. What is more, in scientific descriptions of asymmetrical configurations like these, secrecy boundaries can be drawn from both sides, and they can mutually reinforce themselves because, when reacting to the secretiveness of others, social actors sometimes resort to 'counter-secrecies', for instance in the form of 'hidden agendas' (Scott 1990).

It is crucial to note that, as mentioned above, studies of secrecy that make use of this model tend to take it for granted that social actors who are excluded through secretiveness have an intrinsic interest in reaching out into the social sphere of the secret holders in order to bring about disclosure of or participation in what has been barred from them. If successful, so the conventional argument implies, this endeavour leads to a sort of knowledge osmosis between the two social spheres and eventually to the dissolution of the secrecy boundary separating them.

However, while this approach has been very helpful in exploring various aspects of the role of secrecy in social life, it becomes evident on closer examination that there is something more complex involved in trying to account for the sociality of secrecy. One can gain a sense of a more nuanced account in Paul Johnson's work on the role of secretiveness in religious practices in Brazil and Haiti, where he draws attention to 'secretism' – that is, the active and performative 'invocation of secrecy as a source of a group's identity, the promotion of the reputation of special access to restricted knowledge ... and the successful performance or staging of such access' (Johnson 2006: 420; see also Johnson 2002).

In my reading of Johnson's argument, the sociality of 'secretism' represents a two-pronged process. By claiming to be in possession of a secret, social actors in the one sphere are drawing an exclusivist boundary in relation to others. However, by simultaneously communicating to the wider public that knowledge of the contents of this secret is desirable and – at least in principle – attainable not only for the people within their own socioreligious sphere but also for people outside of it, 'secretism' is also structurally integrative across the boundaries of social spheres.

I would submit that, not only can the latter mechanism be found in 'secretism'; it also plays an important role in 'secrecy' in general. In order to understand why this is the case, one needs to bear in mind, as noted above, that there is nothing essential about a secret that naturally makes it 'a secret'. Instead, a secret becomes 'a secret' by being labelled as such. In many instances, this labelling is realized in acts of interpersonal communication which, as Beryl Bellman has pointed out, entail an essential contradiction because the person 'who is telling a secret either directly or tacitly makes the claim that the information he or she speaks is not to be spoken' (Bellman 1981: 10; see also Bellman 1984). However, secrecy does not necessarily need to be communicated linguistically, but can also be a cultural category that *implicitly* informs social practice, for example when cipher language is used in a private diary in order to render it unreadable for unauthorized people who are presumed to be interested in it.

That said, I argue that secrecy pertains to two spheres of sociality that are disconnected as regards certain communicational transactions and yet at the same time interconnected in terms of their structural relationship. In exerting this role, secrecy structurally integrates the spheres into a consociated social entity that encompasses both the secret holders and a (real or imagined) group of social actors who claim and/or are presumed to be concerned by what the former are concealing from them.

This form of sociality through secrecy is characterized by strained relationality. On the one hand, secrecy is attributed a certain force of attraction that is nourished, for example, by the association of secrecy with the mysteries of the sacred (see, for example, Barth 1975: 217–222) or by the perception that secrecy 'lies at the very core of power' (Canetti 1962: 290), whatever its concrete nature. One of the most prominent proponents of the latter view is Max Weber, who claims, for instance, that 'bureaucracy seeks to increase the superiority of the professionally informed by keeping their knowledge and intentions secret' (Weber 1948: 233) and that 'every domination established as a continuing one must in some decisive point be secret rule' (Weber 1978: 952).[5]

On the other hand, and related to the preceding point, the relational sociality of secrecy is premised on the aforementioned presumption that certain (real or imagined) people have an interest in learning about certain concealments of others. Depending on the context and the viewpoint, this presumption can either be substantiated by way of induction – that is, with reference to empirical cases of specific people who manifestly strive to overcome secrecy boundaries – or it can involve acts of deduction involving the normative supposition that one group of social actors (for example, the ruled) has a moral and/or structural right to know, or even the political responsibility of wanting to know, what is being concealed from them by others (for example, the rulers).

Such acts of deduction and the accompanying projection of epistemophilic Others are not only common to much of what is being written by political commentators and politically concerned scientists that serves the disclosure of aspects of reality that had previously been concealed from the wider public. It also represents a widespread and very effective political strategy to recruit support against what one perceives to be one's adversaries. Take the so-called 'war on terror' that is currently being waged against Muslims in different parts of the world. In empirical constellations like these, much emphasis is placed on the claim that one's adversary has secrets which are a matter of vital concern for the wider public or a certain section of it. At the same time, by suggesting that the wider public has or should have an interest in having these secrets disclosed to them, an interpellative act is performed that constitutes what purportedly precedes this very act: the epistemophilic Other. As a consequence, if it is performed – in speech act terminology – 'felicitously', an accusation of secretiveness raised by one group of people is not only conducive to boundary making vis-à-vis another group of people; it also sparks off the enrolment of certain others claiming to be systematically implicated in the respective configuration of secretiveness. In turn, which particular section of the wider public can be enrolled through such accusations depends on what is taken to be the specific nature, attributes and/or contents of the alleged secret. Thus, taken together, the performative constitution of epistemophilic Others through secrecy represents a dialectical process with the social composition and scale of the interpellated Others being relative to what in particular is claimed to be the adversary's 'secret', and the other way round.

Configuring Epistemophilia

The empirical examples that will substantiate and illustrate the argument above come from my research on African-initiated Christianity in Zambia, especially the Gwembe Valley (see also Colson 1960; Scudder 1962). In the Gwembe Valley – for a long time one of the most remote regions of sub-Saharan Africa – Christianity was introduced by Western missionary societies at around the turn of the twentieth century (Luig 1997). Yet it was only after the mid-1950s that it began to increase its impact in this area, which is predominantly inhabited by the Tonga, a Bantu-speaking people with a matrilineal and formerly acephalous form of social organization. The construction of the Kariba Dam and coal mining created a new infrastructure (Colson 1971), which opened up the Gwembe Valley to the Central African Plateau and thus cleared the way for both new Western and African-initiated churches to enter the area.

Some forty years later, most Tonga of the younger generation and many of the middle generation are associated with a Christian congregation. A considerable number of Western and African-initiated churches coexist in mutual competition for members. In 1999, for instance, eighteen different denominations could be found within an hour's walk from the small market town of Sinazeze, the main area of my field research. Of these, eleven were African-initiated Pentecostal-charismatic churches – that is, churches where the divination and healing of afflictions played a pivotal role. Since these churches also work alongside different 'traditional' religious forms, my research area is marked by a high degree of religious pluralism.

On top of that, Christian practices in the Gwembe Valley are characterized by a marked selectivity in that changing one's church affiliation repeatedly (although sometimes only temporarily) represents the rule rather than the exception. To a large extent people are free to attend the church of their choice, and even after making a selection, they often tend to be sceptical of absolute claims to religious authority. This marked degree of affiliational mobility and selectivity also means that nobody can be forced to attend a certain denomination by either their relatives or the church authorities. Given this background, it is clear that the various denominations have to struggle to maintain a following. Their authority is not fixed, but has to be continuously confirmed or even constituted anew. Being embedded in a highly competitive religious context, church leaders are thus at pains to demonstrate that their own denomination has been divinely ordained. If they fail to make their claims plausible, their congregations slowly drift away.

Visibility, Disclosure, Secrecy

In the context of this pluralist and competitive religious field, many Christian denominations stress that, to an important extent, the power of Christianity lies in its programmatic visibility. For example, the quoting of Bible verses and the visible displaying of the Bible signals church membership and devotion to Christianity. But it simultaneously entails connotations that go beyond this identificatory dimension: the central basis of Christian worship and practice openly displayed in this way contrasts with the occult paraphernalia of 'traditional' herbalists and witches.

It has repeatedly been pointed out that 'traditional' herbalists (*bang'anga*) are generally regarded in southern Africa as having magical powers that can be used in either a beneficent or malevolent manner (e.g., Luig 2000: 17). In southern Zambia, there is widespread agreement that becoming a *mung'anga* (singular of *bang'anga*) often requires killing someone in order to use the spirit of the deceased henceforth for divinations and in the procuring of herbalist medicines. Other *bang'anga* are said to have inherited empowering ancestral spirits from a relative.

Nonetheless, since witches (*balozi*) are assumed to follow similar procedures of self-empowerment, *bang'anga* are not always distinguishable from *balozi*. The term for medicine, *musamu*, denotes the herbs and roots used by a *mung'anga*, as well as some of the magical items used by witches. Those who attend a 'traditional' herbalist because of an affliction are thus occasionally suspected of having become witches during their treatment. This assessment is based on the idea that healing by a *mung'anga* actually involves initiation into witchcraft.

Balozi and most *bang'anga* also have in common the fact that their practices entail the handling of occult paraphernalia. Herbalists store medicines and objects for divination and treatment in their houses; that is, in a private space that usually only close relatives are allowed to enter. Such clandestineness is even more pronounced in the case of witchcraft. For example, witches are said secretly to raise *ilomba* (spirit familiars; often a snake with a human head) within their houses; it is assumed that they possess *katobolo* (magic guns made, for example, out of a dead child's bones); and they are believed to hide *insengo* or *chifunda* (horns or small containers filled with destructive medicine) in the thatched roof of their victim's home, as well as *chinaile* (needles with magical powers) in dirt roads, so that the victims will die when stepping on them. The magical items used by witches are thus all associated with surreptitious concealment. Furthermore the dark night is assumed to be the preferred time for witchcraft activities.

Some of my observations suggest that secrecy is even essential to the magical power of witchcraft items. One morning in June 1999, a building belonging to Sinazongwe District Council in Sinazeze was found to have been sprinkled with a brown liquid the night before. A small capsule wrapped in a cloth and smeared with an unknown substance had been placed in front of the door. It was widely agreed that the liquid was witchcraft medicine (*musamu*) and that the capsule was a *chifunda*. The clerk, who was a member of the New Apostolic Church, consequently refused to enter the building unless a witch finder provided some counter-magic. However, since nobody was in a position to pay money for a witch finder – the district's bookkeeping had no provision for such expenses, and the clerk did not want to pay them himself – the *chifunda* remained in front of the council building. Nobody dared to touch it. After some weeks, however, several people told me that this magical object could soon be removed by any ordinary person at any time: the *chifunda* would gradually lose its destructive power because it was visible to everybody. Prolonged visibility was thus assumed to make witchcraft powerless.

In view of the suspicious nature of the witches' secrecy, the commonly practised public display of the Bible by Christians is a clear indication that they have nothing to hide and that they are in some way accountable to the public. For example, divinatory sessions in African-initiated Pentecostal-charismatic churches are pursued in a more or less public social space, and if an object is used for them, it is one that is visible and potentially available to everybody, namely the Bible.

However, despite Christianity's programmatic visibility and the fact that one of the main attractions of Pentecostal-charismatic churches in this area lies in their promise to bring out previously hidden truths about God's will and the malign workings of the devil, there is a sense in which, as Taussig has rightly pointed out in another context, 'the secret is not destroyed by exposure' (1999: 3). Instead, Pentecostal-charismatic divination, prophecy and witch finding all represent means to implicitly 'animate the thing defaced' (ibid.), in so doing lending secrecy a form of reality that it did not have previous to the act of disclosure. In that sense, the Pentecostal-charismatic act of revelation can be said to *make* the secret, to present the prospect of momentous spiritual knowledge to be gained in future and – most important for the argument in this chapter – concurrently to constitute the community of believers as a community of epistemophilics.

Ambiguities of Secretiveness

However, the secret is not merely an epiphenomenon of acts of revelation. As the following shows, secrecy is also actively employed in Pentecostal-charismatic churches to counter competition in this pluralist religious field – a strategy of self-authorization that, as will be illustrated below, produces ambiguities of its own.

When starting research on African-initiated Christianity in Zambia in 1993, one of the first churches I came into contact with was the St. Moses God's Holy Spirit Church in Siankumba village in the Gwembe Valley (see Kirsch 1998). This church belongs to the so-called *mutumwa* movement, which originated in the 1930s in the northeast of Zambia and has established itself since in many parts of the country. The movement started when, in the course of his career, a 'traditional' diviner started invoking Christian spiritual entities instead of ancestors when invoking spiritual powers (Dillon-Malone 1983). At present, a common element in most of the movement's churches is an emphasis on herbalist and spiritual healing that is dominated by a holistic concept of illness and what Jean Comaroff has called a 'polyvalent metaphor of healing' (1985: 197).

In the St. Moses God's Holy Spirit Church, curative treatment relates to bodily afflictions, mentally or socially odd behaviour and cases of sterility. As in most African-initiated churches in the area of my fieldwork and in other parts of southern Africa, witchcraft is considered to be the main cause of human afflictions. With respect to individually manifesting afflictions, hidden causes are sought during church services through mediumistic divinations (Devisch 1985) based on processually unfolding prophetic revelations that are occasionally confirmed or rejected by the patient. If the revelations of one prophet are repeatedly rejected by the patient, another prophet takes over. The treatment of patients relies on spiritualist and herbalist methods, including the use of medical roots (*musamu*). Yet, while spiritualist healing is usually performed during publicly accessible rituals, especially church services, the herbalist treatment of patients by church elders takes place after these rituals and without much publicity.

Most herbalist healing sessions I was able to witness over the course of my fieldwork followed a similar pattern of interaction and were quite unspectacular. In fact, much of it resembled the dispensation of medication in a Western pharmacy. The patient was asked to sit down in front of the healer's house; the healer went behind the building where the herbal medicine was stored; when he returned, the medication was handed over to the patient along with instructions for how to use it.

I would like to draw attention to a seemingly trivial detail in this interaction, namely the location where the herbal medicine is stored: at the *rear* of the healer's house. In and by itself, there is nothing mysterious about the back of a residential house in the Gwembe Valley. Most Tonga would agree that it is possible to go there in everyday life, but they are normally hesitant to do so in the case of less familiar people because doing so would be considered an infringement of the house-owner's privacy. The same holds true for the back of the home of a Christian herbalist healer – by and large, this space is treated as part of the healer's private sphere, and the interactional setting of the healing sessions described above is no exception to that.

However, it is important to note that, when I asked the *mutumwa* healers why they stored the herbal medicine where they did, they told me that it is necessary to hide the herbs and roots from the eyes of 'quack doctors' who would try to compete with them and were keen to steal what were, they claimed, widely known to be effective curative methods. This is an interesting explanation because, ironically, at the time of the research in the mid-1990s, the healers of the St. Moses God's Holy Spirit Church were themselves suspected of being charlatans by many people I talked to in the Sinazeze area. As a consequence, assuming that *mutumwa* healing sessions represented nothing but mumbo-jumbo involving ineffective substances, these others were – despite claims to the contrary – in fact not interested in what was stored behind the healers' homes. All the same, by treating the medicine as a 'secret' and by emphasizing that there exist many people who are interested in having it revealed to them, the healers of the St. Moses God's Holy Spirit Church discursively transformed 'privacy' into 'secrecy' and – most telling for the present argument – in an act of self-aggrandisement insinuated the existence of epistemophilic Others in relation to the 'secret lore' of their own religious expertise.

Yet, besides this (probably imagined) group of epistemophilic Others, which was said to be composed of jealous and curious quack doctors, there existed another group of epistemophilic Others in relation to the St. Moses God's Holy Spirit Church which was much more substantial and posed serious problems to its leadership. Since the herbalist practice of this church shows striking similarities to the practices of traditional healers (*bang'anga*), there was a time during the fieldwork when local observers of the congregation's religious activities started to doubt its claim to be Christian and suspected the elders of the St. Moses God's Holy Spirit Church of being witches themselves. Importantly, from the perspective of those voicing this suspicion, the herbal substances stored behind the healers' houses were not considered to consist of beneficial medications but items with potentially harmful effects for different sorts of people. This shift in classification implied that the backs of the *mutumwa* houses were no longer categorized as a sphere of the healers' privacy but as a sphere of secrecy. What is more, alongside this shift in classification, an increasing number of people in the Sinazeze area started to develop an interest in what in particular was stored there. Thus, whereas the classification of the herbal substances as 'curative medicine' restricted the group of people interested in them to patients (and, supposedly, competing healers), categorizing these substances as 'witchcraft items' enlarged this group and interpellated epistemophilic Others, encompassing all those people who suspected that they might become victims of witchcraft carried out by the church elders of the St. Moses God's Holy Spirit Church.

Some Words in Conclusion

This chapter started out from the premise that there is nothing essential about a secret that naturally makes it 'a secret'. Instead, secrecy has been approached as a discursive phenomenon that can be used to characterize, categorize and organize virtually any kind of social fact. It has been suggested here that, in contrast to 'the private', making use of the category of 'the secret' is based on the presumption that there is someone – be it an individual or a group of people – who is concerned and thus has an interest in the disclosure of what others have wilfully concealed from him or her. What is more, it has been argued and demonstrated here by way of ethnographic examples that epistemophilic Others do not already exist out there prior to acts of secretiveness. Instead, they are performatively constituted and thus brought into existence through acts that are classified in that way.

Through the example of African-initiated Christianity in Zambia, three modalities and social contexts of constituting epistemophilic Others through secrecy have been outlined above. First, Pentecostal-charismatic acts of revelation lend secrets a form of reality that they did not have previous to the disclosure, thus holding out the prospect of desirable knowledge to be gained in future. In this way, divination, prophecy and witch finding take part in constituting the community of believers as a community of epistemophilics – that is, as a group of religious practitioners seeking to transform non-knowledge into knowledge. Second, by concealing and declaring 'secret' the herbal medicines they employ, African Christian healers insinuate the existence of competitors in the religious field who are keen to appropriate their spiritual knowledge fraudulently. These two cases have in common the fact that the existence of epistemophilic Others is performatively projected onto the world in an attempt by religious leaders to legitimize and self-aggrandize themselves and their spiritual capacities. Third, and in contrast to the above, the categorization of the concealed herbal substances not as white magic but as black magic represents a delegitimizing move by outsiders to the church and interpellates as epistemophilic Others those people who feel endangered by what is wilfully concealed from them by others.

As these examples show, secrecy – as ascription or self-description – presumes the existence of epistemophilic Others, thus giving rise to a specific form of asymmetrical sociality that encompasses two social spheres, both of which are disconnected as regards certain communicational transactions, but interconnected in terms of their structural relationship. When making the claim that oneself or someone else has a secret, this social configuration is either taken for granted (that is, already exists) or enacted (that is, brought into existence by the claim). In both instances, what is enacted through secrecy is an interpellative politics of epistemophilia – the performative constitution not just of 'the secret', but, more importantly, of (real or imagined) Others who are desperate to know. When seen in this light, an important difference between 'privacy' and 'secrecy' thus lies in the fact that the latter entails the production of an absence, a zone of not-knowing, that is constructed as the target to be overcome for the epistemophilics.

Notes

1. The use of the term 'privacy' in this chapter, with regard to examples from the fieldwork, follows Michael McKeon's suggestion that the categories 'private' and 'public' are not just a modern phenomenon but 'a fundamental feature of traditional societies as well' (McKeon 2006: xvii). According to McKeon, in '"traditional" societies, the differential relationship between public and private modes of experience is conceived as a *distinction* that does not admit of *separation*. In "modernity" the public and the private are separated out from each other, a condition that both sustains the sense of traditional distinction and, axiomatically, reconstitutes the public and the private as categories that are susceptible to separation' (ibid.: xix; italics in the original).
2. Fieldwork in Zambia was conducted intermittently over seventeen months in 1993, 1995, 1999 and 2001. In different versions, the arguments put forward in this chapter were previously shared at the University of Konstanz (Germany), at the Anthropology of Africa Seminar of the London School of Economics and Political Science (U.K.), at the Department of Social Anthropology, University of Bern (Switzerland), and at the Department of Social and Cultural Anthropology, University of Zürich (Switzerland). I thank the participants for their helpful comments. Any errors are my own.
3. Stanton Tefft makes the brief remark that 'The prevailing rationale of secret keepers, whether the secrets concern legal or illegal acts, or relationships, is that *outsiders surely have some motive to discover the secrets*; and, that, without security, could indeed discover them' (1980: 322; italics added). However, he does not further explicate the importance of this point for conceptualizing 'the secret'.
4. The use of the word 'performative' in this context takes inspiration from speech act theory, meaning that categorizing something as a secret performs an action, namely the action of invoking the existence of epistemophilic Others.
5. However, as Elisheva Carlebach rightly points out, secrecy is not restricted to the internal workings of dominant groups or institutions because the 'attribution of concealed qualities to *any* group of people within a society has served throughout history to create difference and hierarchy' (1996: 115; italics added).

References

Barth, F. 1975. *Ritual and Knowledge among the Baktaman in New Guinea*. New Haven, CT: Yale University Press.

Bellman, B.L. 1981. 'The Paradox of Secrecy'. *Human Studies* 4, 1–24.

———. 1984. *The Language of Secrecy: Symbols & Metaphors in Poro Ritual*. New Brunswick: Rutgers University Press.

Bertrand, R., J.-L. Briquet and P. Pels (eds) 2007. *The Hidden History of the Secret Ballot*. Bloomington: Indiana University Press.

Besteman, C. 2009. *The Counter-Counterinsurgency Manual: Or, Notes on Demilitarizing American Society*. Chicago: The Prickly Paradigm Press.

Besteman, C. and H. Gusterson (eds) 2005. *Why America's Top Pundits Are Wrong: Anthropologists Talk Back*. Berkeley: University of California Press.

Boas, F. 1897. *The Social Organization and the Secret Societies of the Kwakiutl Indians*. Washington, DC: U.S. National Museum.

Bok, S. 1984. *Secrets: On the Ethics of Concealment and Revelation*. Oxford: Oxford University Press.

Butt-Thompson, F.W. 1929. *West African Secret Societies*. London: H.F. & G. Witherby.

Canetti, E. 1962. *Crowds and Power*. New York: Continuum.

Carlebach, E. 1996. 'Attribution of Secrecy and Perceptions of Jewry'. *Jewish Social Studies* 2, 115–36.

Cohen, A. 1971. 'The Politics of Ritual Secrecy'. *Man* 6, 427–48.

Colson, E. 1960. *The Social Organisation of the Gwembe Tonga*. Manchester: Manchester University Press.

———. 1971. *The Social Consequences of Resettlement*. Manchester: Manchester University Press.

Comaroff, J. 1985. *Body of Power, Spirit of Resistance: The Culture and History of a South African People*. Chicago: University of Chicago Press.

De Jong, F. 2007. *Masquerades of Modernity: Power and Secrecy in Casamance, Senegal*. Bloomington: Indiana University Press.

Devisch, R. 1985. 'Perspectives on Divination in Contemporary Sub-Saharan Africa'. In *Theoretical Explorations in African Religions*, ed. W. Van Binsbergen and M. Schoffeleers. London: Routledge and Kegan Paul, 50–83.

Dillon-Malone, C. 1983. 'Indigenous Medico-Religious Movements in Zambia: A Study of nchimi and mutumwa "Churches"'. *African Social Research* 36, 455–74.

Duncan, A.W. 2006. 'Religion and Secrecy: A Bibliographic Essay'. *Journal of the American Academy of Religion* 74, 469–82.

Ferme, M.C. 2001. *The Underneath of Things: Violence, History, and the Everyday in Sierra Leone*. Berkeley: University of California Press.

Fluehr-Lobban, C. (ed.) 2003. *Ethics and the Profession of Anthropology*. Walnut Creek, CA: AltaMira Press.

Fortune, R. 1932. *Omaha Secret Societies*. New York: Columbia University Press.

Gable, E. 1997. 'A Secret Shared: Fieldwork and the Sinister in a West African Village'. *Cultural Anthropology* 12, 213–33.

Gal, S. 2002. 'A Semiotics of the Public/Private Distinction'. *differences: A Journal of Feminist Cultural Studies* 13, 77–95.

———. 2005. 'Language Ideologies Compared: Metaphors of Public/Private'. *Journal of Linguistic Anthropology* 15, 23–37.

Geschiere, P. 1997. *The Modernity of Witchcraft: Politics and the Occult in Postcolonial Africa*. Charlottesville: University Press of Virginia.

Gusterson, H. 1996. *Nuclear Rites: A Weapons Laboratory at the End of the Cold War*. Berkeley: University of California Press.

Herdt, G. 2003. *Secrecy and Cultural Reality: Utopian Ideologies of the New Guinea Men's House*. Ann Arbor: University of Michigan Press.

Johnson, D.H. 1991. 'Criminal Secrecy: The Case of the Zande "Secret Societies"'. *Past and Present* 130, 170–200.

Johnson, P.C. 2002. *Secrecy, Gossip and Gods: The Transformation of Brazilian Candomblé*. New York: Oxford University Press.

———. 2006. 'Secretism and the Apotheosis of Duvalier'. *Journal of the American Academy of Religion* 74, 420–45.

Keen, I. 1998. *Knowledge and Secrecy in Aboriginal Religion*. Oxford: Oxford University Press.

Kelly, J.D., B. Jauregui and S.T. Mitchell (eds) 2010. *Anthropology and Global Counterinsurgency*. Chicago, IL: The University of Chicago Press.

Kirsch, T.G. 1998. *Lieder der Macht. Religiöse Autorität und Performance in einer afrikanisch-christlichen Kirche Zambias*. Münster: Lit-Verlag.

La Fontaine, J. 1986. *Initiation: Ritual Drama and Secret Knowledge across the World*. Manchester: Manchester University Press.

Lattas, A. 1998. *Cultures of Secrecy: Reinventing Race in Bush Kaliai Cargo Cults*. Madison: University of Wisconsin Press.

Lochrie, K. 1999. *Covert Operations: The Medieval Uses of Secrecy*. Philadelphia: The University of Pennsylvania Press.

Luhrmann, T.M. 1989. 'The Magic of Secrecy'. *Ethos* 17, 131–65.

Luig, U. 1997. *Conversion as a Social Process: A History of Missionary Christianity among the Valley Tonga, Zambia*. Münster: Lit-Verlag.

———. 2000. 'Der Kampf der Regenmacher: Geistbesessenheit, Macht und Magie in einer Tonga-Familie (Zambia)'. In *Subjekte und Systeme: soziologische und anthropologische Annäherungen*, ed. G. Best and R. Kößler. Frankfurt am Main: IKO, 13–34.

McKeon, M. 2006. *The Secret History of Domesticity: Public, Private, and the Division of Knowledge*. Baltimore: Johns Hopkins University Press.

Mahmud, L. 2012. 'In The Name of Transparency: Gender, Terrorism, and Masonic Conspiracies in Italy'. *Anthropological Quarterly* 85, 1177–208.

Masco, J. 2006. *The Nuclear Borderlands: The Manhattan Project in Post-Cold War New Mexico*. Princeton, NJ: Princeton University Press.

Meyer, B. and P. Pels (eds) 2003. *Magic and Modernity: Interfaces of Revelation and Concealment*. Stanford, CA: Stanford University Press.

Murphy, W.P. 1980. 'Secret Knowledge as Property and Power in Kpelle Society: Elders versus Youth'. *Africa* 50, 193–207.

Nippert-Eng, C. 2010. *Islands of Privacy*. Chicago, IL: The University of Chicago Press.

Nuijten, M. and G. Anders (eds) 2007. *Corruption and the Secret of Law: A Legal Anthropological Perspective*. Aldershot: Ashgate Publishing.

Paley, J. 2002. 'Toward an Anthropology of Democracy'. *Annual Review of Anthropology* 31, 469–96.

Piot, C.D. 1993. 'Secrecy, Ambiguity, and the Everyday in Kabre Culture'. *American Anthropologist* 95, 353–70.

Price, D.H. 2004. *Anthropological Intelligence: The Deployment and Neglect of American Anthropology in the Second World War*. Durham, NC: Duke University Press.

Scott, J. 1990. *Domination and the Arts of Resistance*. New Haven, CT: Yale University Press.

Scudder, T. 1962. *The Ecology of the Gwembe Tonga*. Manchester: Manchester University Press.

Simmel, G. 1906. 'The Sociology of Secrecy and of Secret Societies'. *The American Journal of Sociology* 11, 441–98.

Taussig, M. 1999. *Defacement: Public Secrecy and the Labour of the Negative*. Stanford, CA: Stanford University Press.

———. 2003. 'Viscerality, Faith, and Skepticism'. In *Magic and Modernity: Interfaces of Revelation and Concealment*, ed. B. Meyer and P. Pels. Stanford, CA: Stanford University Press, 272–306.

Tefft, S. 1980. 'Secrecy as a Social and Political Process'. In *Secrecy: A Cross-Cultural Perspective*, ed. S. Tefft. New York: Human Sciences Press, 319–45.

Warren, C. and B. Laslett 1980. 'Privacy and Secrecy: A Conceptual Comparison'. In *Secrecy: A Cross-Cultural Perspective*, ed. S. Tefft. New York: Human Sciences Press, 25–34.

Wax, D.M. 2008. *Anthropology at the Dawn of the Cold War: The Influence of Foundations, McCarthyism, and the CIA*. London: Pluto Press.

Weber, M. 1948. 'Bureaucracy'. In *From Max Weber: Essays in Sociology*, ed. H.H. Gerth and C.W. Mills. New York: Oxford University Press, 196–244.

———. 1978. *Economy and Society*. Berkeley: University of California Press.

Whitehead, N.L. and R. Wright (eds) 2004. *In Darkness and Secrecy: The Anthropology of Assault Sorcery and Witchcraft in Amazonia*. Durham, NC: Duke University Press.

Thomas G. Kirsch is Professor of Social and Cultural Anthropology at the University of Konstanz. He has published two books on African Christianity – one of them entitled *Spirits and Letters: Reading, Writing* *and Charisma in African Christianity* (2008) – and articles in some of the major refereed journals for anthropology and sociology in Germany. Other articles have been published in the journals *American Anthropologist*, *Visual Anthropology* and *American Ethnologist*. Since 2003, he has also conducted fieldwork on issues of violence, security and crime prevention in South Africa; he is co-editor of *Domesticating Vigilantism in Africa* (2010).

INDEX

Methodology and History in Anthropology

General Editors: David Parkin, Fellow of All Souls College, University of Oxford
David Gellner, Fellow of All Souls College, University of Oxford

www.ingramcontent.com/pod-product-compliance
Lightning Source LLC
Chambersburg PA
CBHW070924030426
42336CB00014BA/2531